COMMUNICATION IN EVERYDAY LIFE

A Social Interpretation

Communication: The Human Context

COMMUNICATION IN EVERYDAY LIFE

A Social Interpretation

Wendy Leeds-Hurwitz

University of Wisconsin-Parkside
Kenosha, Wisconsin

ABLEX PUBLISHING CORPORATION
NORWOOD, NEW JERSEY

Fifth Printing 1996

Copyright © 1989 by Ablex Publishing Corporation

Printed in the United States of America

Library of Congress Cataloging-in-Publication Data

Leeds-Hurwitz, Wendy.
  Communication in everyday life / Wendy Leeds-Hurwitz.
      p.   cm. — (Communication: The Human Context)
  "January 1988."
  Bibliography: p.
  Includes index.
  ISBN: 0-89391-812-1
  1. Communication.   I. Title.   II. Series.
P90.L377   1989
001.51—dc19   89-282
                                                                 CIP

Ablex Publishing Corporation
355 Chestnut Street
Norwood, New Jersey 07648

Table of Contents

Table of Contents for Research Sites

The descriptions of research provided in this book come from a series of contexts in several cities. Although I have drawn upon examples from all of the sites throughout the book, I can foresee the possibility of a reader wanting to locate all of the descriptions of data for a particular location and, for that reader, a guide to research sites may prove useful. As a background note, listings for each site are supplemented by the dates during which the research was originally conducted, the focus of the research, and the major research project of which my work was part, if that is relevant.

In the body of the text, descriptions of data taken from these various contexts are marked by the convention of putting a box around the material. This marking is intended to clearly indicate to the reader whether theoretical (or methodological) arguments are being made, or whether details from original research are being presented.

It will be immediately apparent that the research examples grow in length throughout the book. Chapter 1 sets the stage for the remainder, and so no data is included; in Chapter 2 descriptions of actual behavior begin to appear, a paragraph at a time; by Chapter 7 'the major portion of the chapter consists of detailed analysis of original research. This is a deliberate attempt to shift from the necessarily general statements made at the beginning of the book to extensive illustrations of the argument's implications in the final chapters. If the reader gets the feeling that descriptions of actual behavior gradually take priority over theoretical argument, that is exactly what I intended. In the end, it is only by demonstrating what a social interpretation of communication in everyday life can contribute to the field that my case will be made; logical force alone rarely convinces anyone to take up a new approach.

1. Washington, D.C., pp. 155-171
During parts of several years (1972-75), I worked in a large federal government office. At the time, I was fully a participant, rather than a participant observer: I was paid for my time, and did not prepare an analysis of what occurred until immediately after I left the job.

2. Philadelphia, pp. 133-134, 137-138, 140-147
In 1977 I studied stories told by young children in a day care center in Philadelphia. As background to that project, I recorded extensive details of interaction between the children throughout the day. In addition, I often specifically asked them to tell me stories that were taped and later transcribed.

3. East Baltimore, pp. 20, 23, 40, 55-56, 76, 119, 150
This research was conducted in 1979, as part of the larger East Baltimore Documentary Photography Project, funded by the Department of Housing and Urban Development and a large number of smaller grants from various agencies. I interviewed residents in order to provide text to accompany the images the photographers made; the focus of the project was on changes then occurring in the neighborhood.

4. South Milwaukee, pp. 18-19, 22, 25, 29-30, 35-36, 48-51, 66-68, 79, 82-83, 85-87, 90-93, 96-97, 104-106, 121, 124-126, 131, 134-135
In this case, the research dates from 1980-1981; the setting is a bilingual elementary school in South Milwaukee. My research was part of the Bilingual Education Community Study Research Project, conducted by Judy Guskin in Milwaukee, and Steven Arvizu and Eduardo Hernandez-Chavez in California, and funded by the National Institute of Education. The examples provided here are drawn from my notes taken while doing classroom ethnography for that project; the focus of the larger project was to describe how bilingual education programs mediate between school and community concerns.

5. Milwaukee, folk toys, pp. 53-55
This research from the summer of 1984 was funded by the Committee on Research and Creative Activity of the University of Wisconsin-Parkside. It was an initial investigation into the role of traditional forms of material culture (in this case, toys) in the acculturation process of recent immigrants to the US. I was interested in discovering the way objects served as symbols, either of acculturation or as ways of maintaining ethnicity.

Communication: The Human Context

INTRODUCTION TO THE SERIES

To be human is to live not in a world of things, but in a world of the meanings of things.

Every human must be born twice: once to a physical mother; and once to a social/cultural one. No infant becomes *human* except in *some* social/cultural context.

It is in that context—it is in the lap of our social/cultural mother—that we are in-formed, that we are made to be dealers in the *meanings* of things. Becoming human is not a matter of learning to see things as they are. It is a matter of slowly and imperceptibly learning how to see things and value things and explain things as those things are seen and valued and explained by those who thus in-form us.

To be human, we must each of us be made conscious of the meanings of things as given in the context in which we are made human. We must be made to "mind" ourselves and to "mind" the world through the meanings already ascribed to them. Thus everything that has been said of the world before we appear in it both enables and constrains our "minding" of it. And every way we have of recreating the world we know in our minding of it, or our speaking of it, constitutes the nature of our human existence in it.

That with which we "mind" the world is a child of the social/cultural mother of which it is born and in which it is nourished. We may improvise in some socially-acceptable way on the meanings and the themes and the scripts we have been made to express and to comprehend (to "understand"). But those improvisations validate our "membership" in the social-cultural context in which we have our human existances only if they are comprehensible to others. It is the *set* of minds that comprise a human society that collectively constitute the "reality" in which each must have one's own *human* existence.

The shape and the form of every human mind is given in how that mind is given to comprehend the world and to express itself in it. To be human means being a member of some human society. To be a member of some human society means being able to comprehend the world as others express it, and to express it as others will comprehend it. To be eligible to belong to any human society means being able to communicate "right."

So it is *in* communication that we create and maintain one another as human. And it is *in* communication that we create and maintain everything else that is human.

We literally "say" our worlds into existence, for the only existence they will ever have for us inheres in how we speak of them—in how we create and recreate the mental artifacts with which we must relate to them, to each other, and to ourselves. A way of talking about the world is a way of *being*.

The human habitat consists of what can be said of things. All humans everywhere make words. And with their words they make the worlds they inhabit. So all human consequences—of life or of mind—flow not from things, but from the ways we have been given to express and to comprehend those things. From how we name and explain things to each other and to ourselves.

In this series of books and monographs on Communication: The Human Context, we will explore the role of communication in human and social existence, and in the past, the present, and the future of humankind.

We will explore the human and the social consequences of how we comprehend and how we express the world. Every human activity emerges and has its life in that context of meanings that legitimates it. And those meanings are both the source and the consequence of human communication.

There is nothing we could explore that would have more relevance to the conditions of human and social life than human communication. Thus how we come to understand human communication is of more than mere intellectual interest. *How* we understand human communication bears upon the lives and the problems of every human and of every human society. The study of communication is the key to our understanding of ourselves and the social apparatuses within which we perpetuate ourselves. It is the key to our understanding of the nature of human nature itself.

So it will be our purpose in these volumes to bring to our readers the best, the most provocative, and the most useful thinking about human communication going on in the world today.

Lee Thayer
Series Editor

Foreword

In this book, Wendy Leeds-Hurwitz presents a remarkably concise and coherent introduction to the "social perspective" on the study of communication in which the traditional intrapsychic emphasis on what goes on inside the head is replaced by a relational emphasis that concentrates on interaction between people. There is a decisive difference between an intrapsychic and a relational perspective. An intrapsychic perspective assumes that what happens inside a person can be used to describe and/or explain what happens between people. A social perspective, on the other hand, assumes that the ways in which people relate to each other have little to do with internal processes that take place inside the head or under the skin of an individual. From the social perspective, what counts is the larger interactional environment referred to as the social, historical, and cultural context.

Consider some of the obstacles impeding progress in the science of human communication. People talk. Relationships change. Interpretations differ according to one's point of view. Language cannot be ignored or taken-for-granted. In order to describe language, one must use language. Paradox cannot be legislated out of existence. The reflexivity of our science is not just a methodological obstacle. It is an inherent, abundant, and undeniable aspect of inquiry concerning human communication. As communicating humans studying humans communicating, we fall inside what we are studying. Unlike our colleagues in the natural sciences, our object is a subject.

What is it safe to assume about such a "subject"—that is, a communicating person? Are the characteristics of a person "real"? Are they *in* the person? Or are the characteristics which seem so real actually embodied in interactions between one person and another person, between a person and an object, or between a person and a situation? The social perspective holds that terms such as *characteristics* or *properties* are only differences and they exist only in the context of relationship. As Bateson expressed it, "our own character is only real in relationship."

More than twenty-five years ago, Jay Haley made an initial attempt to describe relationships in terms of patterns of communication associated with a theory of circular systems. His book, *Strategies of Psychotherapy*, was only partially successful because no formal model existed that could be used as a framework for systematically developing a relational or social vocabulary. The book you are about to read shows how far we have come since then. The vocabulary employed by Leeds-Hurwitz directly addresses the need for terminology that is applicable to transactions between two or more persons who are participating in a social process. It is no longer necessary to apply terminology that describes an individual or a machine to transactions within relationships between people. Models that privilege such concepts as *transfer, transmit,* or *exchange,* are replaced by a perspective that focuses on *pattern, process, context,* and *multifunctionality.* The pendulum has swung away from behaviorists and cognitivists, making room for contextualists, structuralists, and conversationalists.

Readers should be forewarned that the shift to an interactional or social perspective, which is so well represented by this book, may be very challenging. A few simple propositions associated with the social or relational perspective that is set forth in this book may be helpful:

(1) *The message sent is not necessarily the message received.* The social perspective assumes that the distinction between sender and receiver is arbitrary. The distinction between a message and a receiver also is artificial, since the message may include the codification of the message by a receiver. We are left with the question of where a message begins and ends and whether such a "thing" as a message exists independent of its codifiers.

(2) *In a relationship between two people, both individuals share responsibility for the definition of the relationship.* What happens when communication fails? Who can be blamed if both share responsibility. Indeed, the concept of blame becomes unintelligible. No one can have linear control of a relationship that is by definition circular. How does one thing lead to another? Some understanding presumably can be gained by punctuating the sequence of events. But punctuation is usually arbitrary. Each individual may punctuate the sequence of events differently, and as Bob Dylan observed, "when they see things from a different point of view/They get tangled up in blue."

(3) *Wisdom is the knowledge of the larger interactional config-*

uration, a Batesonian maxim. How do we account for relationships between the victims and the victimizers, between the strong and the weak, between the powerful and the powerless? Are these stated "attributes" the traits of individuals or do they exist only in relationships between people? Can the relationship be changed if the individual in the "one-down" position refuses to follow the rules of the game? Weakness can be used as strength, powerlessness can be used to control, a victimizer cannot function without a victim. Power is in the rules of the game, not in the players. If the rules are changed, so are the "attributions" about who holds power, who is weak or strong, and how a victimizer can also be a victim. Is power the outcome of a relationship between people, or is it a "characteristic" of a person that exists independently of the person's relationship to other(s)?

(4) *What a person seems to be is not necessarily what he or she is.* A person may act as if he or she is shy. The question to ask is whether the performance we view is an adequate basis for making an attribution about the person's inherent qualities. Perhaps what we observe is only a function of the relationship or context. The person acts shy, but can we conclude that he or she *is* shy? Attributions have social consequences. An attribution can become a self-fulfilling prophecy. Once a person is labelled "shy," the person is likely to be responded to as a shy person and expected to act out the role shy people play. Almost any social action can be viewed as a move that is designed to perpetuate a well-organized game involving actions and reactions, manuevers and counter-maneuvers. We do not have to make the mistake of attributing *being* to *seeming.* We can simply try to figure out what game is being played by what rules for what purpose.

Communication in Everyday Life is a teachable book. Leeds-Hurwitz has successfully escaped the trappings of esoteric language and other excesses of a more scholarly style of writing. Difficult and complex ideas are presented in a lively manner. The book has a strong pedagogical orientation. Concepts are freely illustrated by numerous examples taken from research on classroom interaction, the use of toys, and a profound interpretive study of forms of address in a formal organization. The study of forms of address provides an explosive ending to the book. Another book could be written on this case alone. Leeds-Hurwitz strengthens the value of her case studies by resisting the temptation to "prove a point" and opting instead to "open a conversation." This pedagogical strategy may frustrate students who insist on being told what the author means. They simply will have to learn that in our science, meaning is "essentially contestable," to use Gallie's famous phrase. It is far more important to keep the conversation going than to counterfeit a single-minded interpretation.

Thomas Kuhn said that the function of a textbook is "to define the legitimate problems and methods of a research field for succeeding generations of practitioners." Measured by this yardstick, textbooks that introduce students to the study of communication usually fall far short of the mark. Most authors have erred on the side of simplicity and entertainment, showing little respect for the intellect of new students of communication and taking no pride in the achievements of communication research. *Communication in Everyday Life* is a striking exception to the norms of our field. I hope that it will be widely adopted and read so that succeeding generations of students will be wiser than we were about the larger configurations of interactional experience.

Arthur P. Bochner
University of South Florida

Preface

Social communication. Social interaction. Face-to-face interaction. Interaction in everyday life. All have to do with what happens when people are with other people. These are overlapping terms for either a particular field of study or for the subject under study. There is no one term currently accepted for this area, just as there is no one book which states, clearly and simply, the underlying assumptions of this approach.[1] My intention here is to take all the most useful concepts I know about social communication and put them into a single package. I have made a deliberate attempt to state the main points of this book plainly, and without jargon. No particular background knowledge is assumed; only an interest in the nature of social interaction is required for understanding. That is not to imply, however, that the ideas are either simple or obvious. They are not. In fact, many of the suggestions made may seem to oppose what is generally assumed to be common sense. Common sense turns out to be a not particularly good guide to understanding communication. Our everyday common sense is only one particular culture's way of viewing communication, and I believe we must develop a theoretical framework that is not limited in this way.[2]

At the same time, this is not "merely" a textbook intended for students. It is, more than anything else, for anyone who wants to

---

[1] This book was begun before Sigman (1987), which goes a long way toward fulfilling the need for a good discussion of social communication.

[2] Clifford Geertz says: "If common sense is as much an interpretation of the immediacies of experience, a gloss on them, as are myth, painting, espistemology, or whatever, then it is, like them, historically constructed and, like them, subjected to historically defined standards of judgment. It can be questioned, disputed, affirmed, developed, formalized, contemplated, even taught, and it can vary dramatically from one people to the next. It is, in short, a cultural system, though not usually a very tightly integrated one, and it rests on the same basis that any other such system rests; the conviction by those whose possession it is of its value and validity. Here, as elsewhere, things are what you make of them" (1983, p. 76). Elliot (1974) supplies further useful comments on common sense.

understand the basic ideas taken for granted by many of those who study social interaction; anyone who wants a single, coherent presentation of what the literature on social communication has produced so far. There has been much excellent work in social communication in the recent past. The views that communication is a process rather than a product, that it is a complex system created and maintained through the efforts of a social group, and that it should be studied in all its complexity even if this does not lead to neat, quantifiable results, are no longer uncommon in the field of communication. As with most new developments, however, insights have not appeared in a coordinated fashion, but in diverse places, over a span of many years, and in the writings of many authors. In addition, some generalizations have been hidden in arguments about relatively narrow or technical concerns, or stated in complex, difficult to comprehend ways. This book will bring together the most important conceptions of communication viewed as a social process in such a way as to be useful to non-specialists as well as communication students or professionals. There have been such books in related fields, (Lofland's (1971) *Analyzing Social Settings* is one) useful both as a concise synthesis of information for those who know the area, and as an introduction for those who do not. Hopper, Koch, and Mandelbaum describe an article of theirs as providing "guidance for beginners and bases for dialogue with colleagues" (1986, p. 169). This felicitous phrase could be applied equally well to my intent for the present work.

In a way, this book is intended as an answer to that rather plaintive question: "But what *is* communication?" Obviously, the book provides only one of the many possible answers to that question. There will continue to be many answers, depending on what part of the wide-ranging field of communication is studied. No one answer, no matter how good, can ever be complete. Here the focus is only on social communication. The word *social* is used in an attempt to stress that I will not be looking at what goes on inside one person's head (a focus better left to psychology) but rather at *interaction*, at what happens when people are together. My focus will be on observable behavior, i.e., on the behavior that constitutes communication as it occurs in situations of everyday life. It is important not to be taken in by the currently popular understanding of communication as only that which occurs when people reach an agreement. (As in, "what we need here is more *communication!*")[3]

---

[3] Katriel and Philipsen (1981) supply a nice analysis of the popular use of "communication" in American society.

This book develops a model of communication as a process in which people participate, rather than a message sent between them. In this view, "an individual does not communicate; he engages in or becomes part of communication" (Birdwhistell, 1959, p. 104). Communication is a process and event jointly created and continued through the efforts of the entire social group, it cannot be maintained by a lone individual. The actions of any one individual are closely linked to the actions of others, certainly those present, but to a surprising extent also those not present.[4]

The implied but missing word is *human*, for my concern is not with animal communication, although that can also be described as social. While recognizing that there is much to be learned from studies of animal behavior, I do not address that literature here. There is more than enough material to cover in looking solely at human interaction.

The above may be read as suggesting that what will follow is a definition of communication. But were my intent only to provide a definition, this would be a short article instead of a book. What will be provided is not so much a single definition as an overarching way of understanding and approaching communication. Definitions are easily memorized and quickly forgotten. A way of viewing a subject, a particular perspective, takes longer to understand and to remember, but it is more easily internalized and more difficult to forget. It is also more useful.

One of the basic tenets of this approach is that the traditional division of the field of communication into interpersonal, organizational, and mass communication may not always be the most appropriate way to divide up the world. The boundaries between these areas can be crossed by a researcher in search of regularities in human interaction, and it is my argument that they should be. Therefore, the examples provided in this book will be taken from a variety of settings, and will range from classrooms to offices to magazine advertisements. Despite this diversity, the majority of the examples could still be classified under the traditional rubric *interpersonal communication*. What I would argue is that it is time to update this part of the field, and bring it into line with the modern work done in several allied areas. Similarly, Pearce and Foss (1987) suggest that it is time for "a major renaissance in interpersonal communication" and that this is to be the result of the influence of

---

[4] This view is not all that different from the view proposed by Pearce and Cronen, who suggest that communication is "the process by which persons collectively create and manage social reality" (1980, p. 7).

"the so-called new paradigm in social theory" (1987, p. 99). They go on to examine seven major characteristics of this new paradigm, four of which are particularly helpful to consider here: they stress an expanded concept of communication, so that even small examples of social interaction are viewed as an appropriate site for study; and a more complex view of communication, seeing it as a process of doing something and of achieving coordination and coherence.[5] If this book helps others to understand the theoretical grounding of the new developments in the field, it will have met one of its major goals.

What I will present are not completely new and unique insights into communicative behavior. On the contrary, the majority of the theoretical concepts discussed have been accepted by at least by some researchers for some time now as a necessary part of understanding interaction. Three things are new: one, the particular combination of ideas, and the suggestion that, when taken together, they form a core of assumptions that permit us to understand and analyze human social communication. Two, the tie between these theoretical assumptions and their methodological implications as made explicit here. And three, the numerous and sometimes extensive examples presented are drawn from my own research in a variety of settings over a period of 10 years. This is hardly the standard form of reporting research, but the insertion of examples is designed to help readers make sense of the theoretical comments.

It is my contention that, although it is commonly done, separating theoretical statements and methodological texts can only get us into trouble. And separating methodological texts from reports of original research can only lead to more trouble. We need to remember, and our students need to learn, that theory, method, and research are all intertwined closely, and one cannot survive without the others. We traditionally separate them for practical purposes, but this can be misleading, and should not be done too often, and certainly not as a general rule. The particular theory a researcher subscribes to has implications for method; every method implies a foundation in theory. What I am trying to do, therefore, is fashion a book that returns theory, method, and research to one another, treating them as integrally related, considering each as but part of the story.

In this book, I am attempting to make the ordinary and hardly noticeable seem strange and noteworthy, because, until we are able to notice everyday interaction, we cannot study it. Details of

---

[5] Simons (1978), Fisher (1981), and Bochner (1981) set the tone for a good beginning in this revision of interpersonal communication.

method can be argued, but such details are a second step. The first step is learning to see the ordinary in a new way, to see it for the extraordinary accomplishment it is. Harvey Sacks suggested that, if his students learned nothing else, they should learn from him that "the world you live in is much more finely organized than you would imagine" (1984, p. 415).[6] I would have to agree: That single insight is the key to understanding what occurs in everyday interaction.

---

[6] See Douglas (1970b) for more elaborate discussions of this point of view, especially Zimmerman and Pollner (1970) in Douglas (1970a).

Acknowledgements

This book would not have been possible without the support of a great many people. Examples used in the text are taken from several of the research projects with which I have been involved, and so I must thank the East Baltimore Documentary Photography Project, and all of the residents of East Baltimore who were willing to be interviewed; Judy Guskin and her co-workers investigating bilingual education in Milwaukee; the teachers who let me observe them at their work both in Philadelphia and in Milwaukee, and all of the students in classrooms who have cooperated with the odd questions of an outsider. One of the projects described in these pages was supported by funds from the Committee on Research and Creative Activity of the University of Wisconsin-Parkside, for which I am grateful, and I want to thank the dozens of people who answered my questions about their use of toys, though they generally did think it an unworthy topic, of no interest to anyone outside the family. Régine Mahaux took the photographs that Susan Schuder turned into figures 5.4, 5.5 and 5.6. My thanks to both of them for their excellent work. A previous version of material in Chapter 7 was published in the *Working Papers in Sociolinguistics.*

This book is a distillation, synthesis, and expansion of the work of many others. My most significant intellectual debts are to Ray Birdwhistell, Dell Hymes, Gregory Bateson, and Erving Goffman, as will be apparent from the citations. Lee Thayer provided the initial challenge that led me to first try to set my thoughts down on paper. My students for the last 4 years have been faced with an incomplete draft as a textbook in their course "Communication in Everyday Life" at the University of Wisconsin-Parkside, and have given me extensive feedback on their reactions to it. My colleagues Stuart Sigman and Yves Winkin have been particularly supportive, and took the time to read through that early draft and provide extensive comments which I took into account in writing the final copy. My father Mort took the time to make editorial suggestions, and my husband Marc and son Aaron have put up with an absent wife and mother, busy writing when she might have been playing.

CHAPTER 1
Introduction

> The social order does swiftly clothe the actors born into it in the self-
> understandings they are, thereafter, reluctant to shed even for the
> rare privilege of a glimpse of themselves in their nothingness.
> —Philip Rieff (1964, p. xiii)

There is, without any question, a large degree of order to the social
world. Our behavior does not consist of newly invented actions or
words created for a unique situation, but of existing actions and
words, constantly revised in new ways. And each set of behaviors
is related to other sets, so that there is an underlying structure to
the whole. Thus we say there is order to interaction. Since communication is one of the primary ways we create and maintain the
social order, in studying communication we illuminate the ways in
which the social order operates. *Social order* is a concept used
widely in sociology, but rarely discussed in the field of communication. That is not to say that the term is not important in the field
of communication, however, only that its presence so far has generally been implicit rather than explicitly acknowledged. In this
chapter a discussion of social order, and the related concept *interaction order*, will be used to set the stage for the remainder of
the book. Taken together, they introduce some of the important
issues discussed in further detail later.

The concepts of social order and interaction order are two useful
theoretical constructs; they aid in the attempt to understand what
happens when people are together. Put very simply, social order
is the phrase used to cover *the unspoken organization or coordination between people which permits the social world to continue
to exist. Unspoken* because we do not, under normal circumstances,
begin our conversations with one another by discussing such details
as what we each expect from the interaction or what we mean by
the word *conversation. Organization or coordination* because what
we are discussing is essentially a template or pattern, just as a

tailor uses a pattern for what he cuts, rather than recreating the design each time anew. *Between people* because my focus will only be those interactions which occur between various individuals or groups of people. *Social world,* as opposed to *natural world,* which has its own "natural order" as an organizational force. The natural order is studied by biologists, zoologists, ethologists, etc., but rarely by those looking at human society. *Permits us to continue to exist* because, without social order, the world as we know it would vanish, and in its place we would have chaos and mayhem.

The early *Dictionary of Sociology* describes social order as a certain quality, permitting "the smooth, efficient, logical, aesthetic and ethical interactioning of individuals and groups" (Fairchild, 1944, p. 287). This is a graceful yet concise way of stating the matter. Social order is essential to the continued cooperation between humans; it is the unseen organization which underlies every smoothly functioning society; it is the unspoken pact which makes life with others feasible. But what supports the existence of social order? A natural identity of interests was the support suggested by Locke. We want to be left alone, and so we leave others alone, and it is in everyone's best interest to have it so. If you don't kill me, I won't kill you, if you don't steal my belongings, I won't steal yours, is the understanding referred to by the phrase *natural identity of interests.* Edgerton (1979) supplies one of the best of the current studies explicitly concerned with the creation and maintenance of social order in his analysis of an urban beach, looking at how so many people manage to be so close together (and in such a state of undress) with so little trouble resulting. He found that only the mutual agreement to leave one another alone, to pay little conscious attention to others on the beach, makes the entire event possible. This is not chance, but an agreement as to the appropriate ways to behave on the beach, an unstated contract as it were that beachgoers sign, agreeing to uphold the norms. Everyone must share a common definition of the beach situation, as well as a set of routine behaviors specific to that situation, in order for the entire situation to remain possible and relatively free of trouble (Edgerton, 1979, p. 209).

Social order is something which is created, it does not come into existence by spontaneous combustion. It suggests that, the majority of the time, the majority of people only rarely act spontaneously; instead, we act according to the pattern we know. That is, most of us act without thinking, and do what feels natural rather than spending time working out what might be an appropriate behavior, even if the extra thought might be called for at least some of the

we follow our parents' influences and examples

time. (Whatever my parents did is likely to be what feels natural to me, because it is what I expect. Doing what will shock my parents demonstrates their influence equally, of course.) Social order is the end product of generations of careful arranging; it is the result of many people agreeing, however tacitly, to follow the same rules of interaction in order to continue living together peacefully and uneventfully. It is the job of social order to make life fairly predictable and fairly uneventful, even boring at times. None of us can respond well to new stimuli all the time: we like a little of the new sprinkled on a lot of the old, as sugar is sprinkled over oatmeal. It makes the oatmeal palatable, but, aside from wishful thinking of children, none of us really wants to eat sugar all the time. So it is with the new and different: taken against a background of the old and trustworthy, we like it; as a steady diet, we cannot tolerate it.

Social order involves the study of what Lon Fuller (1981) termed *social architecture*, that is, the study of the (human-made) structures supporting and giving a frame to the social world. To carry his metaphor further, it is social order which provides the supporting walls to the building we call society. As such, social order is one of the central organizing concepts in sociology. This concept has very recently started appearing in a few articles in the communication literature. For example, Cronen, Pearce, and Harris say: "Today, we view ordinary communication as the locus of powerful forces through which persons cocreate, maintain, and alter social order, personal relationships, and individual identities" (1982, p. 64).

In their book *Communication, Action and Meaning*, Pearce and Cronen bring up the interesting related point that it is not only social order which needs to be studied, but also social disorder. "Where order exists, it is not necessarily logical or desirable, and more often the structure of social reality may be better described in patterns of disorder" (1980, p. 86). Their point is not that social order is not present or not viable, but rather that, when different social orders come into conflict, they can clash, thus leading to disorder. In the modern world, where peoples of different cultures (and, concurrently, different social orders) must often meet, they often clash, and there can be more occasion to view disorder than order. This does not, however, make social order any the less important as a subject for study within communication; if anything, it makes it a more central issue.

The theoretical question of interest here is how social order is maintained. Saying it exists is all very well and good, and we can argue forever about how it first came about; as none of us were present, we can never be absolutely certain of the answer. Since it is in existence today, the question we can more readily study is: "How does it actually *work?*" Once we have determined that the construction and maintenance of social order is our research topic, but also discovered that this is an abstraction which cannot be studied directly, we must decide which concrete phenomena are the appropriate focus for study. There have been several nominees which have a good argument in their favor, although it is more likely that a combination of all of them is the most appropriate.

The first nominee is *interactions.* This is the answer provided by sociologists such as Erving Goffman (1963, 1967, 1971, 1983) and Anthony Giddens (1984). In this view, social order is maintained through everyday interactions, through mundane and boring examples of people communicating with one another. One way of describing social order, therefore, is to suggest that it is the pattern which provides the structure underlying interaction. As such, it can be observed through interaction. By watching people as they communicate or interact with one another, we have a way to observe the theoretical construct social order, for it is through interactions that social order is instituted, upheld, and made visible. This provided Goffman, and it can equally provide us, the rationale for studying face-to-face interaction (Leeds-Hurwitz, 1986, 1987b).

In addition to Goffman and Giddens, Goldschmidt is another who has made the argument that we should focus on interactions in order to better understand how we create social order. In an article entitled "An Ethnography of Encounters," he argues that "social interaction is the very stuff of human life" (1972, p. 59). A similar position is taken by the ethnomethodologists: "Social order exists. But its existence always appears within interaction" (Mehan & Wood, 1975, p. 184).

The second nominee is *talk* (or, more formally, language), sometimes described as "the central communicative activity in organizing cultural life" (Speier, 1973, p. 60). In their classic book, *The Social Construction of Reality,* Berger and Luckmann put forth the view that "the most important vehicle of reality-maintenance is conversation" (1967, p. 152). Their concern is with how we establish and maintain social reality through our interactions with one another, and the answer they choose to stress is that it is through language. Thus they make the argument that we should not focus on interactions in their entirety, but on the language used within them, specifically on conversation over other varieties of discourse.[1]

---

[1] This is also the view maintained by ethnomethodologists such as Garfinkel, Sacks, and Cicourel. See the discussion by Bauman (1977, p. 42), Schegloff (1968), and Schegloff and Sacks (1973).

Michael Halliday supports the view that language is the critical phenomena to study with a wonderful analogy of text (a stretch of talk) as potlatch, assuming some knowledge of the Kwakiutl ritual in which someone gives away all his or her wealth and possessions to others, gaining honor and prestige in the process, and establishing debts which are paid by others in later potlatches.

> Text functions as it were as potlatch: it is perhaps the most highly coded form of the gift. . . . Such a gift has the property that, however great its symbolic value (and however much it may enrich the recipient), it does not in the slightest degree impoverish the giver. (1978, p. 140)

This is a superb image, conveying appropriately the uncommon attributes of speech. Though given, it does not lessen the speaker in any way; though frequently brief, it can convey much. Inasmuch as speech is but one aspect of interaction, we can say that this is not a separate topic so much as a narrowed focus. However, we must not be too quick to assume that what is an appropriate focus for linguists like Halliday is still appropriate when we are studying the entirety of social interaction. By definition, he is interested primarily in language; by definition, we are not.

The third nominee is *symbols*. Symbols are things that stand for other things. George Herbert Mead phrases what can be a difficult concept better than most: "Symbolization constitutes objects not constituted before, objects which would not exist except for the context of social relationships wherein symbolization occurs" (1974, p. 78). By definition, symbols are human creations that hold no life of their own but only exist after two or more people have agreed upon their use. Anything can be a symbol, so long as it stands for something else. Wearing an engagement ring or a boyfriend's fraternity pin have similar yet different meanings, but the meaning does not reside in the object, it resides in the minds of people. John Stewart provides an apt bridge from language to symbols when he says that "human language ability includes not only the capacity to craft and utilize signs and symbols but also the power to reveal or constitute the world in talk" (1986, p. 73). Language, of course, is composed of symbols (as will be discussed in more detail in Chapter 3), so, again, we are not faced with a wholly new focus of study but rather an emendation of one. Just as interaction is broader than language, so symbols are broader than language (though it would be a mistake to equate interaction with symbols).

George Gerbner is one who has pointed out that "The symbolic world, however, is totally invented. Nothing happens in it independently of man's will, although much that happens may again escape individual awareness or scrutiny" (1974, p. 97). It is this characteristic of having been totally a human invention that defines symbols, and it is this which marks them as a particularly important locus of study. Kenneth Burke begins his famous "Definition of Man" with the phrase "Man is the symbol-using (symbol-making, symbol-misusing) animal" (1968, p. 16; see the examples Berger provides demonstrating the proposition that "No sign is also a sign," 1984, p. 122). More recently, Cronkhite has suggested that we redefine the goal of the field of communication as the study of human symbolic behavior. He argues that, since symbols are a current focus of study in many fields, not just communication, it would serve us well to "declare ourselves unambiguously to be focused upon the study of human symbolic activity" (1986, p. 245). The suggestion that it may perhaps be useful to define the field of communication as the study of symbols appears in the work of others as well (Carey, 1975, p. 17; H. Duncan, 1962, p. 10).

Hawes has provided a twist in the argument, suggesting that "the basic term *social reality* refers to the larger system composed of particular arrangements of symbol systems" (1973, p. 17; his emphasis). Thus we do not so much look to symbols in our study of social reality, as redefine social reality as sets of symbols. In so doing, we accept symbols as our focus of study, arguing with Frank that "socially sanctioned symbols order and pattern human conduct and relationships and thereby contribute to the maintenance of social order" (1966, p. 11).

One way people use symbols is in the construction of *rituals*, and there are those who argue that not all symbols, but rituals particularly, aid in the creation and maintenance of social order, and that therefore these should be a special area of interest (see Rappaport, 1979, Turner, 1969, Babcock, 1978). Traditionally, what have been studied are sacred (religious) rituals, but as the collection of essays by Moore and Myerhoff (1977b) has illustrated, secular (non-religious) rituals can be an equally fruitful area of study. In their introduction to the volume, Moore and Myerhoff specifically speak to the link between ritual and social order, suggesting that any ritual "veils the ultimate disorder, the non-order, which is the un-conceptualized, unformed chaos underlying culture" (1977a, p. 17). This is similar to the previously mentioned comments by Pearce and Cronen (1980) about the disorder underlying the order: We create rituals (and other symbols and symbol systems) to hold disorder at bay.

What have been presented as four separate nominees for the concrete phenomena to be studied in our effort to learn about the social order are obviously closely connected. Turner tells us that "the symbol is the smallest unit of ritual" (1967, p. 19). Language and other symbol systems are used in interactions, as are rituals (Goffman titled one of his books *Interaction Ritual* for this reason). Clearly, all four are appropriate, and should better be thought of as a set of resources for our study of the elusive construction of the invisible social order.

Study of the normal and the everyday, whatever part of it we choose to examine, is not an easy task, though it is an important one. It has been argued that "The most difficult things to study scientifically are the familiar, the stuff out of which our everyday experiences are constituted" (Birenbaum & Sagarin, 1973, p. 3). The reason they are correct is that we find it hard to see the normal and the ordinary unless they are placed against a background of the abnormal and the unusual. Susan Philips titled her book *The Invisible Culture* as a way of calling attention to the fact that the communicative patterns which form the basis of her work "lack the tangible visible quality of houses, clothing, and tools" (1983, p. 12). The everyday forms the ground, not the figure, and by its nature we do not notice it. Yet, if we are to understand the highly structured behavior of others and ourselves, the not generally noteworthy is precisely what we must subject to study.

The study of everyday interactions has not developed de novo within communication. There is a long list of related inquiry in a variety of fields. This is hardly the place for a detailed history, but a brief summary may be helpful.[2] Of the many schools which have contributed to the study of social interaction, some of the major ones are the following:

To a large extent, research into everyday interactions is the outgrowth of the work of the ethnomethodologists and others within sociology who have taken as their subject the everyday. Schegloff, for example, suggests that

> The work in which my colleagues and I have been engaged is concerned with the organization of social interaction. We bring to the materials with which we work . . . an interest in detecting and describing the orderly phenomena of which conversation and inter-action are composed, and an interest in depicting the systematic

---

[2] Further information may be found in Murray (1983) and Winkin (1981), and the 1984 special issue of *Papers in Linguistics* devoted to an evaluation of the ethnography of communication.

Figure 1.1. Summary of Fields Related to the Study of Social Interaction.

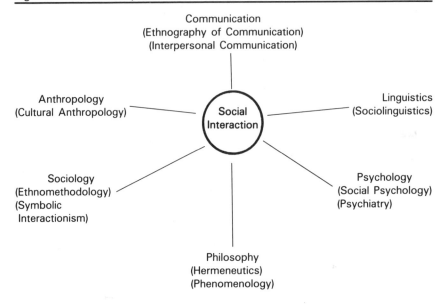

organizations by reference to which those phenomena are produced. (1979, p. 24)[3]

Staying within sociology, a similar interest in the accomplishment of everyday life is central to symbolic interactionism (see Blumer, 1969). Combs and Mansfield express this position as assuming that "we create and manipulate a 'symbolic environment' wherein [we] construct [our] interactions" (1976, p. xix). At times either of these approaches has been labelled *microsociology*, although this is a term more descriptive of methodological focus than theoretical assumptions.

Within psychology some of the research in social psychology, especially in nonverbal communication (such as Duncan & Fiske, 1977) and in psychiatry (particularly those involved with the Natural History of an Interview project, such as Brosin and Scheflen) is appropriate, although it has had less influence.[4] In philosophy, hermeneutics and phenomenology are the areas of concern, al-

---

[3] See Garfinkel (1967), Zimmerman (1978), West and Zimmerman (1982), Heritage and Watson (1980), Mehan and Wood (1975), and Douglas (1970b) for elaboration on ethnomethodology.

[4] See Leeds-Hurwitz (1987a) for further information on the *Natural History of an Interview* project, and the role played by the psychiatrists involved.

though these have been less influential than their reflections and adaptations in various social sciences (see Hawes, 1977).

In linguistics there was some small early concern with the mundane and everyday interactions that were usually overlooked in favor of the ritual and the ceremonial (see Sapir, 1949), as there was in cultural anthropology (Birdwhistell and Hall, after all, were trained as anthropologists). Yet it was probably the approach designed to fill the gap between the two, the ethnography of communication, developed by Dell Hymes in 1962 and now adopted by those in communication as their own, that has had the most continuous and profitable concern with the study of the details of social interaction.[5] One of the results of the influence of anthropology on the ethnography of communication is that much of the research has been in cultures other than American. While this is unusual in communication research, it is an advantage, for it adds a sense of perspective that would otherwise be missing. The ethnography of communication was originally labelled the ethnography of *speaking*, an important fact to know, for it explains why so much of the original research using this label focuses on speech rather than on other forms of communication.[6] In fact, much of the work to date is even more specifically focused on verbal art (traditional forms of discourse, such as jokes, stories, or political oratory).[7] But there is no reason it cannot be applied to everyday communication, and many reasons why it should be. The most important of these is the emphasis on ethnography, which means, among other things, that research centers on observed behavior in real settings. For, if communication is context-bound, it should be obvious that putting individuals into a laboratory setting results in the destruction of the very communicative behavior we are attempting to study. This is no longer a unique position within communication (see for example, McLaughlin's conclusion that the best data for studying conversations can be obtained from natural conversations in a natural setting—1984, p. 243).[8]

---

[5] For summaries of the development of this field, see Murray (1983), Bauman and Sherzer (1975). For the most current evaluations of the work, see Bauman, Irvine, and Philips (1987).

[6] See Leeds-Hurwitz (1984) for a more detailed discussion of the relationship between the two labels.

[7] Bauman and Sherzer (1974) and Gumperz and Hymes (1972) supply excellent examples of articles in the field; good examples of books in the field are Abrahams (1983), Bauman (1983), Sherzer (1983), and Katriel (1986). See Saville-Troike (1982) for an introductory text, and Philipsen and Carbaugh (1986) for a bibliography.

[8] Philipsen (1977) discusses some of the methodological issues concerned with doing the ethnography of communication, and Stewart and Philipsen (1984) give further comments on the approach.

Within communication, if studying the mundane and ordinary is not practiced as an elaboration of the ethnography of communication, it occasionally appears as an extension of interpersonal communication. By implication, interpersonal communication has always been concerned with what Goffman labelled *small behaviors* (1967, p. 1), although that concern has been expressed in a large variety of ways and is not always obvious in the published reports of research.

Social order is an important and complex idea, and sociologists have devoted much attention to its study during the last century.[9] Fewer researchers (in any field) have paid attention to what has been called the *interaction order*.[10] Erving Goffman is the sociologist best known for his publications on this subject, and he devoted much of his work to the study of the interaction order.[11] It can be described as one aspect of social order, one variety of it as it were. (Other varieties of social order would include the political order and the economic order.) For our purposes, the interaction order will be defined as *the set of understandings underlying everyday interactions among people*.

Social order, being an abstraction, is invisible, and as such it is impossible to study directly. Interaction order, being no less an abstraction, is also invisible, and also impossible to study directly. With interaction order as with social order, then, we must ask: What do we study? The answer for Goffman was daily interactions: specific, concrete examples of what happens when people communicate with other people.[12] It is through communication that we *create* the interaction order, and it is through communication that we *maintain* the interaction order. The interaction order is invisible; interactions, however, are visible. Thus we study interactions in order to learn eventually about the social order, as we observe the micro level (the small and mundane) in order to comprehend the macro (the large and meaningful). What intrigued Goffman were the implications of being able to observe social order only through individual examples of interaction; he took seriously the idea that

---

[9] What has so far been presented is hardly a thorough literature review of the subject, and one will not be included, but some particularly relevant comments may be found in Parsons (1951, p. 36), Mennel (1974, p. 116), Giddens (1976, p. 98; 1984, p. 69), and Douglas (1971, p. 3). Durkheim, Weber, and Schutz are the major sociologists known for their writings on the concept of social order.

[10] The discussion in Sigman (1987, pp. 42–56) is a welcome exception.

[11] In his last published paper (1983), Goffman was explicitly concerned with organizing his conclusions regarding the interaction order.

[12] See Leeds-Hurwitz (1987b) for details of Goffman's view.

we must study the small, unassuming behaviors of everyday life if we are to understand the larger underlying pattern of structure of society, and devoted his life to studying the ordinary. "The rules of conduct which bind the actor and the recipient together are the bindings of society. . . . The gestures which we sometimes call empty are perhaps the fullest things of all" (Goffman, 1967, pp. 90–91).[13] If we are to understand communication in everyday life, we must follow Goffman's lead, and study the "unpromising materials" which, it turns out, make up the major part of "gossamer reality" (Goffman 1963, p. 247). Given our new understanding of the connections between interactions, rituals, symbols, and language, gained from the analysis presented above, the clear implication is that interaction, as used here and as studied by Goffman, actually covers (at least) all four categories of communicative behavior.

What has been suggested so far, and what will be said later, fits within the research tradition Margaret Zabor (among others) labels the *social* approach to communication (as opposed to the *psychological* approach). In keeping with that perspective, "Communication is seen here not as expression of an individual's thoughts or feelings to another individual but rather as socially-regulated behavioral systems" (Zabor, 1978, p. 30).[14] If communication is viewed as a social phenomenon, and if we wish to study interactions as a way of learning how individuals create and maintain the social order, this has certain implications for the study of communicative behaviors. The specifics of a social view of communication will be expanded upon in the following chapters, but, for the moment, a slight detour into method may prove useful.

There are just as many names for the method used in studying interaction as there are names for the field: *qualitative, naturalistic, ethnographic, participant observation,* and *natural history* are the most common among the group. As with the names for the field of study, these names overlap but are not synonyms, even though they are sometimes used as such. My purpose here is not to define

---

[13] The works by Goffman which are the most useful in this connection are 1953, 1961, 1963, 1967, 1971, and 1983.

[14] An excellent summary of the differences between the psychological and social paradigms within communication (though others use different labels for them, they are the two major approaches often followed and cited) is provided on p. 136 of Zabor (1978) in a chart. Different but related discussions are available in Thomas (1980), which looks at the organic versus the mechanistic metaphors; Cowell (1972), where these two metaphors are extended to seven; and Lincoln and Guba (1985), where the catch-phrases *naturalistic* and *positivistic* serve as the center of the comparison.

these terms, but to provide a brief survey as an introduction to the qualities they all hold in common.

Qualitative research is most generally used to refer to any research that is not quantitative. In this usage, it would include any method or research technique that does not involve counting something. There have been many comments made about the differences between the two, few of them friendly. Weston La Barre has therefore overstated the case to good effect: "I firmly believe that, just as one is seemingly born a Platonist or an Aristotelian, a Parmenidean or a Heraclitean, so apparently one is born a quantifier or a qualifier" (1980, p. 13). Another who puts the matter strongly is Ray Birdwhistell, who states that "It requires very little training to count; a very intensive training is required to develop significant units for the counting" (1977, p. 107). This, of course, goes against the rarely stated but often assumed notion that quantitative research requires extensive training, whereas qualitative research is everything that can be done easily. Gregory Bateson continues the argument for qualitative research and against quantification by insisting that: "quantities are precisely not the stuff of complex communicating systems" (1978, p. 15). If the rest of Bateson's work is assumed to make sense, then this must be accepted as well, for it is one of the clear implications of his writings.

Naturalistic research is generally used as a slightly more specific term than qualitative research. It implies that the researcher uses only a natural setting or context for the research. For example, if conversation is the subject, then real conversations by real people in normal settings (not laboratories) are the appropriate source of data. Traditionally, communication has not used naturalistic observation as a method, yet it is becoming a more standard consideration and more acceptable as a method. For the most part, however, the theory necessary to support the use of naturalistic (qualitative, ethnographic) observation within communication has not yet been outlined. One of the purposes of this book is to provide the theory to support the method.

Susan Shimanoff (1980) draws a distinction between naturalistic observation and *participant observation*, such that the observer is a legitimate member of the group in the latter but not in the former. In other words, a woman studying hazing in fraternities could only ever be doing naturalistic observation, since by definition the usual participants are male. This draws a distinction that anthropologists have not normally made, but it is one that is becoming accepted in communication.

A *natural history* approach is very similar to a naturalistic one:

both focus on legitimate settings. Matthew Speier draws a parallel between ethnography within anthropology and natural history within sociology, and suggests that both begin "with the collection of data gathered from the natural habitats of humans who are doing things together in a shared environment" (1973, p. 6). Speier's distinction between natural history (research in the United States, as practiced by sociology), and ethnography (research in other countries, as practiced by anthropology), has not generally been maintained within communication, perhaps in part due to the increasing stress in anthropology on doing ethnography within the United States. In describing the Natural History of an Interview project, which used film records, Gregory Bateson says "Our primary data are the multitudinous details of vocal and bodily action recorded on this film. We call our treatment of such data a 'natural history' because a minimum of theory guided the collection of the data" (1971, p. 6). Use of this term most likely had been heavily influenced by Bateson's early training in biology.[15]

Ethnography is the traditional term used within anthropology for the study of naturally occurring behavior in natural settings by an observer who is as unobtrusive as possible.[16] It carries with it the implication of a long period of observation, traditionally a year. Most importantly, ethnographic work "involves the study of cultural patterning," but not patterns viewed alone, since that is virtually impossible; instead, patterns are viewed in comparative perspective, that is, behavior in one culture is always compared with behavior in another (Hymes 1977, p. 59). In addition, just to confuse the matter, ethnography is also the name for the product an anthropologist writes at the end of the period of research, the book describing a particular group of people. Geertz (1973) has named four characteristics of ethnographic description: (a) it is interpretive; (b) the subject of interpretation is social discourse; (c) one purpose of interpretation is to make the perishable more permanent; and (d) it is microscopic. We could do worse than to accept his statement.

Once we begin to use ethnographic (qualitative, naturalistic) research methods, it is important to stress the distinction between data and reality. Bateson pointed this out when he said: "data' are not events or objects but always records or descriptions or memories of events or objects. Always there is a transformation or recording of the raw event which intervenes between the scientist and his

---

[15] Scheflen (1973) provides a more detailed description of the methods of natural history.

[16] See Conklin (1968) for a classic statement of what constitutes ethnography.

object" (1972c, p. xviii). This is no different, of course, for quantitative research, though it is not often discussed in that connection.

One of the problems in doing ethnographic research is that it can be confusing and difficult for an observer faced with the entire stream of behavior to find something specific on which to focus. Explicit directions in terms of what to actually do are often necessary as a result, yet these same directions are, by the very nature of the work, not appropriate until the research is underway. Since the observer is unable to focus on everything at once, the best guidelines are to, first, seek to develop a set of general rules explaining what occurs; second, seek the general in the specific; and third, choose examples carefully, since they will convey much of the information to the audience.[17]

Another problem in ethnographic research is that providing transcriptions can bias the eye of the reader in a way that the researcher never intended. Ochs (1979) discusses this in detail, and she makes the argument that we should, as a result, devote considerable attention to the presentation of our data, rather than just taking for granted that there is a nonbiased way of presenting behavior. Others have devoted considerable efforts to the problems of transcribing social interaction in such a way that the transcription will retain much of the detail of the original behavior, without losing all usefulness as a shorthand summary.[18] In a recent, though posthumous, publication, Harvey Sacks has put the argument for the need of a study of everyday life perhaps better than anyone else. He clearly states the prevailing sociological assumption that certain parts of society are more important and revealing of the social order than the rest, but counters it with the still slightly heretical suggestion that there actually is "overwhelming order" and that "it would be extremely hard not to find it, no matter how or where we looked" (1984, p. 21). In other words, since all of social order is a human accomplishment, holding an analyst's candle up to any part of it, no matter how trivial, should be revealing. We achieve social order, we construct it in the process of interacting with one another, and the process can be observed in any interaction, regardless of larger significance.

It is for this reason that Goffman's writings are notorious for their

---

[17] There are a number of good textbooks available now that teach the specifics of ethnographic research. Spradley (1980) and Agar (1985) are two of the better ones.

[18] See McQuown (1971) and Leeds-Hurwitz (1987a). For further discussion of some of the more interesting aspects of data collection in ethnographic research, see Wilson (1986) and Dingwall (1980).

frequent examples of actual behavior, for these provide the evidence to back up theoretical postulates about what people do together. And it is for the same reason that this book utilizes examples from everyday life so extensively. Talking about face-to-face interaction at a theoretical level is all very well and good, but the proof of the theory is in what we are able to actually observe. Analysis proceeds either from theory to data (observation of behavior, in this case), or from data to theory. Either way, the two are inseparable. Thus, data and theory both hold their rightful place in the pages that follow. We see neither the social order nor the interaction order, yet our self-imposed task is to understand them. We can, however, see people as they interact, and so that which we can observe serves to illuminate that which we wish to study. Whether we choose to examine language, rituals, symbols, or daily interactions, in the process of studying the concrete we learn about the abstractions which we call social order and interaction order underlying all of these.

CHAPTER 2
Communication as Behavior with Pattern

We perceive in pattern, and we remember in pattern.
　　　　　　　　　　　　—Ray Birdwhistell (1970, p. 13)

Social interaction is patterned; it has a high degree of structure. This means that people interact in systematic rather than in random ways. "It is through culture patterns, ordered clusters of significant symbols, that man makes sense of the events through which he lives" (Geertz, 1966, p. 5). These clusters of symbols are what parents pass on to children, what distinguish one group of people from another, and even, at times, what wars are fought over. Since we all help to create these clusters and participate actively in them, the majority of others we spend our time with are not very often completely unpredictable to us, for they know the same patterns. Thus we understand what they do and say, and they understand us. There are unstated rules which govern interaction, and the majority of people are not only willing but adamant about following these rules.

The reason that our social life has become such a well-established pattern is in response to the fact that we live in a world made up of constant sensation. The use of patterns permits us to deal with the new, unknown, and potentially dangerous stimuli we constantly present to one another. Faced with a steady stream of information, our minds sort, and categorize, and label, to transform the new into the familiar. Human beings are not good at accepting the continuous stream of new stimuli as simply being composed of an infinite number of unique behaviors. We prefer, instead, to recognize the old in the new, and to view today's events in relation to the events of the past. Thus, we use our understanding of broad general patterns to help us make sense of the new by relating it to the old,

17

through noticing similarities and ignoring differences. We match reality against our expectations, and learn from the discrepancies.

As described in Chapter 1, people must come to terms with chaos, and this they do by supplying a structure otherwise lacking. Only in this way can anyone continue to deal with the impossible complexity of the world. The result is that, with James Fernandez, we as analysts need to study what it is that people do when they come to terms with "the inchoate—the dark at the bottom of the stairs—which lies at the center of human experience" (1986, p. xiii). That is, we must study the structure people impose on the world, which permits us to interact with and within it.

We make inferences based on that part of the world we are able to observe. We fill in any blank spaces with what we have found in the past to be the remainder of the situation. It would be impossible for us to observe everything which pertained to the situation at once; that would require omniscience. At best we complete our view of reality with knowledge of what has occurred in the past. We know the past in a way we can never know the future, and that is knowledge we can use to make sense of the incomplete view of the world we are generally shown.

In a South Milwaukee grade school, at lunchtime, in line at the cafeteria, I am standing near the third grade teacher, whom I have been observing that day. A student next to me in line, Ricky (not one I know), starts teasing and threatens to step on my foot. I answer that, if he does, I'll step on him in return.

Ricky: (said to the teacher) "Would she step on me if I step on her?"

Teacher: (looks me up and down, then looks at him) "She's just like me—of course she would."

Ricky: "Oh no, Miss S_____, you'd *kill* me!"

Ricky is given a category in which to put me, to help him know how I might react through a comparison with how his former teacher would react in a similar situation. This is only possible because he knows how to predict her reactions to events from past knowledge of her. In this example, however, he rejects the classification she provides, and puts me in an intermediate category instead. In so doing, he verifies that he does in fact remember what the teacher's reaction would be.

> At the same time he extends the teasing to her, by claiming that she has understated her probable response.

Communication is a system through which human beings establish and experience a predictable continuity in life. We know what the past held for us, and we assume the future will be a continuation of that. If life becomes somewhat predictable as a result, this is not necessarily a bad thing. Saying that behavior is not random is _not at all_ the same thing as saying there is no free will, or saying that there is no room for individuality in the world. "This rage for order, for the comprehensibility of phenomena, is often dismissed as an unfortunate limitation. It is, instead, prerequisite for any action, routine or revolutionary" (Barnlund, 1981, p. 117). We traditionally think of structure as something which limits creativity, and therefore bad. But my suggestion is not that there is no creativity in the social world, only that there is far less than we usually assume. We do not often invent new forms of communication, but we can and do frequently recombine and use the old forms in new ways. In addition to this, structure is an enabling force, in that it provides us with the tools (behaviors) and patterns for behaving in a way that is meaningful for ourselves as well as for others. We are constrained in what we create by what has been created before (Kersten, 1986). Perhaps this is to say no more than that a social group is an organized entity, not a mere collection of individuals (Scheflen, 1980, p. 11). At the same time, as Benedict told us over 50 years ago, "Society . . . is never an entity separable from the individuals who compose it" (1959, p. 253). We cannot grant all the power to society, saving none for the individuals who make it up.

Barnlund suggests that "humans appear to be at constant risk, poised between the threat posed by too much order and by too little order" (1981, p. 118). This is a nice point, one which helps us see the role of order in maintaining a stable society. We need some structure, but not too much; we need some freedom, but, again, not too much. We want to know what will happen so that we will not be startled; but we would die of boredom if we always could predict correctly what would occur. It is critical to remember, however, that no single compromise between order and disorder is ever possible; rather, new balances which work for a given context are continually achieved. The main problem of communication is how to correctly code the extensive array of communicative stimuli which we face (Rawlins, 1987, p. 65). The resolution is to have a general pattern or template for interaction to screen all of the stimuli which present themselves to us, and, in this way, make sense of the world.

Our choice of how to interpret any given situation is highly structured. We see what we expect to see, even when that is not what occurred, because that is what we have always seen in the past. And when we see something new, we interpret it in accordance with what is familiar. Thus, in Lewis Carroll's *Through the Looking Glass*, the pig in the carriage comes to be defined as a particularly ugly baby, but rarely as the pig it is. We assume that carriages have babies in them, despite evidence to the contrary, because they always have held babies in the past.

We must subject interaction to deliberate study if we are to discover the underlying pattern, for, although we participate in that pattern, we do not *consciously* know and therefore cannot often verbalize the pattern we follow. This may sound like a contradiction, but is not, for "it is unnecessary to know the abstract nature of a pattern in order to behave in a patterned manner" (Birdwhistell, 1970, p. 77).[1] We can remain unconscious of a structure though we be capable of following it faithfully. We immediately recognize, however, when someone does not follow that pattern, and we identify his or her behavior as unusual or inappropriate. If it is inappropriate, we frequently censor him or her for not doing the expected thing.

John Gumperz is one of those who has demonstrated that the choice between available alternatives, in this case languages or dialects, is automatic, not something we can consciously recall. People who know two dialects fluently and state clearly the rules for using each in particular circumstances presumably do what they say they do, but, even after he supplied a tape-recording of the speech of individuals showing their actual behavior to be different from the stated rule, the individuals concerned could still not make their behavior conform to the rules they thought they were following (Blom & Gumperz, 1972). What this and other examples show us is that rules of communication operate below the level of consciousness; they may not always be subject to conscious intent.

> Moving out of a neighborhood often involves more than moving away from a particular place. It can entail moving into a particular set of places as well. Residents of East Baltimore told me that there were a specific set of neighborhoods

---

[1] Mead put it similarly: "Awareness or consciousness is not necessary to the presence of meaning in the process of social experience" (1974, p. 77). Goffman applies this insight in his distinction between "expressions given" and "expressions given-off" (1959).

that were each one step up on the social ladder, and as a result were considered appropriate places to which to move. The result was that someone moving left one group of friends only to join another group, those who had previously left.

One of the local residents told me: "See, one of the things you did, years ago, was you kind of aspired to move up and out. Now if you moved up and out, that meant you moved to Dundalk or you moved to Essex, or you moved to Blair Road. And then you got yourself a nine by twelve lawn in front of your house that you got to mow every Saturday. And that was moving up and out. And your house cost maybe $5000 more than a house here. But people couldn't afford more than that. But that's how they moved up."

A few years later, when I did field work in Milwaukee, I found a similar hierarchy of neighborhoods. If you lived in South Milwaukee, you hoped to move one day into Greenfield; but if you lived in the Lower East Side, you aspired to Shorewood or Whitefish Bay. It would never have occurred to me, and no one had ever explained to me previously, that there was a system governing where you lived, and where you moved. Since then I have found that very few people spend much time discussing their own hierarchy of neighborhoods within a given city, but most people can verbalize it if you ask them to try. What we find surprising is that everyone else does not want to live where we live, aspire to a house in the neighborhood we value.

Anthony Giddens labels the information about communication that we know and use, but do not normally verbalize, *practical consciousness* and suggests that it "consists of all the things which actors know tacitly about how to 'go on' in the contexts of social life without being able to give them direct discursive expression" (1984, p. xxiii). He distinguishes between this practical consciousness and what he calls *discursive consciousness*, that is, everything we know and are readily able to discuss verbally. Both are important.

Communication is not only patterned behavior, it is *socially* patterned behavior. The order that exists is provided by an entity (society) rather than by individuals. The group creating order can be as large as a country, or as small as a couple. It can have obviously visible boundaries (race, sex, age) or not (religion, birthplace, friendship). It can have many markers of group membership (constraining the majority of activities and behaviors) or a few (constraining a single behavior).

No behavior in and of itself conveys meaning; rather, behaviors fit into the larger societal pattern and take their meaning from that pattern. And that larger pattern (or, rather, set of patterns, for it is not a single structure but a set of coordinated structures) is rarely overtly discussed, since it is so completely taken for granted by the members of a given society (Hymes, 1980). Each social group creates symbols which are then used in "transforming the world around them into a symbolic cultural world of meanings and of patterned conduct for group living" (Frank, 1966, p. 5). We learn to recognize others as members of our own group by the fact that they demonstrate knowledge of the patterns we follow, and learn equally to separate out those who demonstrate a lack of such knowledge. Order results from a group of people being sufficiently predictable to one another that they can get on with the business of living, and rely on the knowledge of a body of symbols in common to get them through the basic communication needs.

> We become so accustomed to belonging to a particular group, and to having our behavior sanctioned by the group members, that someone who makes the attempt to mediate between groups is sometimes viewed as engaging in difficult and extreme efforts. When doing fieldwork in the South Milwaukee school, I was told: "You must be a saint. I wouldn't do your job." The rest of the conversation made it clear that the reason I was a "saint" was because I was gaining a reputation for being able to talk with both sides in a political dispute. At one and the same time, the speaker was impressed with what I was doing, because she thought it was difficult, but did not want to do it herself, because of the lack of group support. In addition, it was regularly assumed that I viewed one or the other side as having the better case, and people often asked, "Which side are you *really* on?" They were surprised if I managed to remain (or appear) neutral; perhaps even a bit insulted. They must not have made their case sufficiently clear if I did not "really" side with them.

Patterns of communication do not hold for everyone in a country or even in a large culture. There are many smaller subcultural or other groupings today that frequently interact, but which maintain different patterns for interaction. The particular set of rules any one participant follows in particular interactions is what Scheflen labelled a "program," and what he found to vary according to ethnicity, social class, institutional membership, geographic locale (1967, p.

9). As Gumperz and Cook-Gumperz have stressed, in the modern world, "Perhaps the most important characteristic of the social environments in which we live is their unprecedented cultural and ethnic diversity" (1982, p. 2). This diversity must be recognized and taken into account in any study of interaction. It has served as the impetus for the research Gumperz and his colleagues have conducted over the past decade or more (Gumperz, 1982b). It is a factor that others not occasionally overlook.

Often, cities have been described as "urban villages." This is meant to imply that they are collections of people who have frequent and intense interactions with one another, but only within a particular boundary line. The limits marked off by boundary lines can be surprisingly small, and the view that only members of the group belong surprisingly vehement. Sometimes the feeling is strong enough that even those outside the group recognize it as a distinct entity. A newspaper publisher in Baltimore told me: "The geography of Baltimore is not very broken up, it's all pretty much one unit, but if any section can be said to stand out it has to be East Baltimore. That is the only one where, when you write it for a newspaper, putting it in print, you capitalize the direction of the geography. East is uppercased, capital letters. If somebody lives in south Baltimore, or in west Baltimore, or above North Avenue, the letters there are all lowercased."

The work Gumperz has done on prosodic conventions, the cultural variations that exist, and the problems that this can cause, is one example of how we can apply an understanding of culturally learned patterns of communication to the particular social meanings attributed to behavior. By demonstrating that West Indian pronunciation of English in Britain is different in systematic ways that cause great trouble for the speakers as well as listeners, Gumperz shows us how we use language conventions as group markers, how little it matters what the words are, and how much it matters how they are said and understood (1982a). It is in this way that we establish our social identity, and mark our ethnicity, heavily relying on language and other communicative behaviors to signify group membership.

Gumperz and Cook-Gumperz (1982) suggest that there are three major aspects of interaction between members of different groups to take into account:

1. different cultural assumptions about the situation,
2. different ways of structuring information, and
3. different ways of speaking.

These are discussed in detail in their work, yet it is rare to find researchers attempting to account for more than one of them.

Language (the abstract phenomenon) has long been recognized as patterned. Linguistics, the study of language, is based on the assumption that languages are highly structured and that analysts can study that structure. Speech (the more concrete phenomenon: actual utterances) has only more recently been recognized as having an equal degree of patterning (Hymes, 1962). We normally assume that, as we speak, we are creating new combinations of words, but an enormous amount of speech is in fact formulaic, and can be therefore automatic rather than newly generated for the occasion. Examples that readily come to mind include proverbs or riddles, which often depend upon a particular word order and word choice for their effect. Everyday interaction is full of less rigid but no less structured phrases that we all know and use to keep from having constantly to invent new word combinations. That takes extra effort and thought, and we would never finish speaking if we had to create new combinations of words for each and every utterance. Such phrases as "How are you?" or "Have a nice day" readily come to mind as examples, but there are others less trite that are still common: "What are you doing after class?" or "Care to join me for lunch?" These depend equally upon easy recognition for their effect. If conversations are to be coherent at all, we must use talk in "ordered, patterned, nonrandom ways" (Ragan, 1983, p. 157). Conversation analysis has taken as its primary task the study of the nature of that pattern (Craig & Tracy, 1983; Heritage & Atkinson, 1984).

It has been only very recently that other aspects of communication (such as nonverbal behavior) have been recognized as having pattern (Birdwhistell, 1970). Only a limited number of sitting positions are expected of a woman in a skirt, and putting her feet up on the desk in front of her is not usually one. It has by now been clearly demonstrated that we use various aspects of communicative behavior as markers of belonging to one group or another (whether age, or gender, or ethnic group). This is one of the main functions of the pattern: it identifies those who are "one of us."

But we cannot take all aspects of even one group, over any geographic space or period of time, and consider all as part of the same pattern. It is Anthony Giddens who has been the most vehement about the need to consider the elements of time (and change over time) in our understanding of patterns of interaction. He points out that *"any patterns of interaction that exist are situated in time;* only when examined over time do they form 'patterns' at all" (1979, p. 202; his emphasis). It is too easy to assume that the large patterns underlying society remain the same over long periods of time, and he encourages us to remember that this is not the case. Societal patterns of communication, as with all other aspects of society, change swiftly, and anyone who would study them must include the element of time in the analysis. Perhaps we should, as Leonard Hawes suggested, recognize communication as being "patterned space-time behavior" (1973, p. 13).

Different vocabulary words are used depending on age. This seems a simple fact to learn, but actually knowing what words are appropriate at what chronological or social stage can be difficult, and sometimes requires explicit instruction.

In the third grade classroom in South Milwaukee, in doing math problems students sometimes used the words they had been taught in first or second grade, only to be corrected by their teacher.

Teacher: Did anybody realize what you were really doing yesterday?
Class: Times.
Teacher: That's a baby word. What do we call it?
Class: Multiplication.
Teacher: That's right.

A similar discussion had occurred a few days earlier, when a student said the operation she had to perform was to "plus" the numbers, and the teacher reminded her to use the word "add" instead. Learning vocabulary can thus be seen to be a lifelong task: parents who use the slang of their youth when it is no longer in vogue run the risk of their children's laughter, just as much as children in third grade risk ridicule for using first grade vocabulary words.

Gregory Bateson puts this bluntly in his article "The Pattern Which Connects." He argues that "we have been trained to think of patterns, with the exception of music, as fixed affairs. It's easier and lazier that way, but, of course, all nonsense" (1979, p. 13, see also 1975a). Instead, he wants us to begin to think of patterns, first, as "a dance of interacting parts," and only second as influenced by physical limits. He encourages us to remember that communication does not just happen, it is "artfully accomplished" (to use the phrase proposed by Stewart & Philipsen, 1984, p. 211). This is intended to remind us that communication requires a great deal of effort on the part of a large number of people, not all of them obvious participants in any given interaction.

Patterns, then, exist in a constant state of change. Group members must not learn the pattern only once, but must keep current with the changes. This is easier than it sounds, for it is those same group members who themselves are involved in bringing about the changes, and changes occur slowly and in a connected fashion. It is not the case that you can make periodic adjustments to your vocabulary, spending 1 week a year catching up on the latest changes. Rather, you make constant and minor shifts and revisions on a daily basis, as they occur, and so they are both easier to manage and less noticeable. In their research on Israeli school children, Katriel and Nesher demonstrate this when they conclude that it is through the active participation of the children in the creation of *gibush*, or group cohesion, that they learn "that the form and quality of group life are a product of an ongoing social dynamic rather than a preestablished pattern" (1986, p. 229).

The fact that social communication is patterned leads to a series of related statements: It is rule-governed, it is predictable, and, perhaps most important of all, it is analyzable. Each of these concepts will be expanded upon in the following pages as a way of further describing what is intended by the use of the word *pattern*.

RULE-GOVERNED

Rules are social devices people use to coordinate their actions (Donahue, Cushman, & Nofsinger, 1980). They are implicit agreements about what will *generally* occur, although they do not always describe what, in a specific case, *does* occur. By saying communication is rule-governed, I mean simply that, for any given group, there is a set of rules held more or less in common that govern interaction among the members.[2] Without these, there can be no

---

[2] There has been much discussion of rules in the literature; Shimanoff (1980), Sigman (1980), McLaughlin (1984), and Morris and Hopper (1987) are the sources most relevant to this discussion. Cushman and Whiting (1972) and Cushman and Sanders (1982) have been particularly influential on the investigation of social rules within the field of communication.

communication, since communication assumes shared understandings (rules) for symbols and their use. "If every symbol user manipulated symbols at random, the result would be chaos rather than communication" (Shimanoff, 1980, p. 32). We use rules to help us make sense of the stream of behavior which the world presents to us everyday. They are "guides for action," as Goffman puts it (1967, p. 48).

Using the phrase *rule-governed* to describe communication is a common practice, but one with inherent problems. To many people the phrase implies rules that cannot be broken, that are consciously known and followed, that are always true. For Shimanoff, who has devoted a great deal of time to the study of communication rules, the best definition of a *rule* is: "a followable prescription that indicates what behavior is obligated, preferred, or prohibited in certain contexts" (1980, p. 57). This is not inconsistent with the approach followed in this chapter, and, if a specific definition is wanted, hers will serve. But my goal is less to define rules than to describe their function, their role in social interaction.

One way to elucidate the functions of rules is to clearly separate *social rules* from *laws*. Rules govern our social interaction implicitly; laws govern explicitly. Laws are conscious and deliberate, and passed by a legislative body of some sort. Rules are unconscious, and established by general consensus, because "it has always been that way."[3] Laws are rigid and applied even at times when the specific details of the case may suggest it would have been better if had the law been broken. Rules are flexible and permitting a greater range of choice (this is one of the reasons they are, under normal conditions, never written down). Rules are also generally put forth as a hypothesis by a researcher, rather than being made definite by the general population. This is not to imply that they are solely a creation of the researcher, for it is apparent that "interpersonal actors act as if they know these rules" (Sigman, 1980, p. 38). Let me summarize this information in a more direct comparison (see figure 2.1).

It may help to explain a few examples in some detail, so the relation between rules and laws is clear. Laws are easy to describe; everyone has extensive prior experience with them. Laws which govern social interaction include those which require us to stop at

---

[3] Wiemann and Knapp make a related point, although they do not use the same terms: "Unlike other societal rules (e.g., criminal laws), interaction rules are seldom specified, and consequently the actions they govern are usually carried out unthinkingly" (1975, p. 77).

Figure 2.1. The Relationship between Social Rules and Laws

Social Rule	Law
implicit	explicit
unconscious	conscious
may choose not to follow	must follow
flexible to context	rigid
researcher codifies	general population codifies
hypothetical	definite

traffic lights, or forbid murder. In both of these cases, at least one function is to make people predictable in their interactions with strangers.

Rules are more difficult, because most people have little experience attempting to verbalize them. A set of related rules put forth a few years ago by Susan Ervin-Tripp (1972) supplies a good example; they are general enough that, once understood, they apply to many different behaviors. She labels them the *rule of alternation* and the *rule of co-occurrence*. The rule of alternation suggests that, for every piece of behavior exhibited, there is a range of behavior possible, and that, by choosing one member of the class, the others are by necessity eliminated. For example, I can either move to Milwaukee or New York, but not to both. In other words, the rule of alternation states that you can't do two different (contradictory) things at one time. The rule of co-occurrence suggests that, when once you have chosen the first piece of behavior out of the first range of possibilities, this limits the available choices for future behavior. For example, if I move to Milwaukee, I am unlikely to attend Broadway shows every week.

There are several problems involved when an analyst tries to state social rules. They can be stated too rigidly, on too little evidence, or can be based on the wrong evidence. Beginning observers of behavior often work out rules and then truly expect the world to conform with those rules forever. Or rules can be established based on only one or two cases, ignoring contradictory information. (This is not usually a deliberate tactic, but an unconscious one. It is easy to think you have been thorough, when in fact all you have done is to search your own experience, checking behavior for the types of situations you recognize.) Or rules can be chosen which are intuitively appropriate without bothering to use actual examples of behavior as a check on intuitions. Since we do not normally have the rules we follow outlined in our heads in a clear, verbal form, when we attempt to put a rule into such a form, there is a good chance that it will be stated incompletely or incorrectly. This is not to say that people do not know the rules; they are good at following them, they are just not very good at stating them (Snyder, 1971).

There is an important distinction among three kinds of data relevant to this discussion:

1. what people think should be done (or said),
2. what people say they do (or say),
3. what people can be observed doing (or saying).

These three are not always the same. I may tell you that faculty advisers should spend a minimum of 30 minutes with their student advisees, and may admit to only spending 20 with mine, but, if you observe me, you may discover that in fact I spend between 10 and 60 minutes with each student, depending on a variety of factors. Because of this, what people state as the rules they think they follow—when they are able to verbalize something—needs to be considered as only one part of the data to be taken into account. As Clifford Geertz writes, "what we call our data are really our own constructions of other people's constructions of what they and their compatriots are up to" (1973, p. 9). Data should not be confused with analysis. Analysis is a separate step which cannot be completed until all of the data have been collected, although it can be started earlier.

In the South Milwaukee school, the fourth grade teacher assigns students to particular tasks on a regular basis. Once she puts their name up on the chart for a particular job, it is their job for the rest of the year, or until she changes the list. When I arrived in the room in February, the lists had been posted since September. I asked what the lists were for, and she explained that each student in the room had a particular task to complete, as a way of gaining a sense of responsibility to others. The primary list looked like this:

Attendance	Michelle
Lunch order	Eric
Supplies	Anna
Waste basket	Jesse
Shades	Doug
Pencil sharpener	Deanna
Language arts center	Todd

Lunch tickets	Shirley
Erasers	Michelle
Windows	Eric
Erase board	Michelle and Anna
Calendar	Todd
Check desks	teacher
Messengers	Michelle and Brad
Fish	Linda
Count scissors	Todd
Paste	Melissa
Chairs down	Edwin
Carpenters	Sylvia and Tony
Library	Hector
Science center	Deanna
TV	Deanna
Social studies center	Gloria
Get milk	Kandi
Pass out milk	Justin
Return cartons	Edwin
Check secretary names	Linda
Names on lunch tickets	Rachel

On a separate list two additional tasks had been added:

Sharpen pencils	Raymundo, Jackie, Deanna, Tony, Linda, Rachel, Carmen, Edward
Doors	Raymundo, Tony, Michelle, Carmen, Jackie

What is interesting about these lists, for present purposes, is that the teacher explained to me carefully how important it was for each child to have his or her own particular task, yet seven children in the room actually had no tasks assigned. When I questioned her, she responded that I must have made a mistake, for she made a point of giving each child a job; otherwise, they would not learn to be responsible. When I showed her a list of those left out, she was astonished, and equally astonished to discover that some children had more than one task. She changed the lists the next day so they would be in keeping with her perceptions of them.

One problem in constructing rules is that it is very easy to state them at the wrong level. There is no point in having a rule which in final form has a dozen hedges (qualifiers) necessary before the rule can be recognized as true. It makes more sense to state the rule in abstract terms, sufficiently general to apply to a large number of situations without the use of extensive qualifiers. This is called *moving up* a level of abstraction. For example, if I say a social rule is: "If you live in Milwaukee, you can't go to Broadway plays often" (referring to the earlier example), this would have little relevance to behavior observed in a large number of interactions. But a general rule, such as Ervin-Tripp's rule of alternation, accounts for this situation and many others in a way which needs no qualifiers. The rules of alteration and co-occurence are quite abstract, which means they accurately account for behavior in a large number of cases. Rules which are stated in a very general way will be appropriate for a large number of contexts, and are therefore most useful to the analyst.

Returning to the viewpoint of the actor, we follow rules most of the time because it does not occur to us that we have any alternative. In some cases a specific consequence is applied when a rule is broken, but for the remainder we follow rules regardless of the lack of consequences. Using the work of Bateson and his colleagues as a starting point, Frederick Ford (1983) provides a neat summary of what he calls the family of rules. He introduces the following five members of his "family":

1. the rule;
2. the counter rule;
3. the rule about qualifications and exceptions;
4. the rule about consequences of breaking the rule; and
5. the rule that tells how the rule is to be implemented.

An example he provides to help make the theory concrete is a rule which he suggests is common in family communication, Be nice. Other rules he mentions that are common in American families are Look good, Say the right thing, Do the right thing, Don't say what you think, and Don't say what you feel.

If you have any doubt of the social force lurking behind the rules of social interaction, try breaking one. You do not need to choose a major taboo with a mandatory and explicit consequence when broken. Something minor will make the point just as well. Try saying "goodbye" instead of "hello" when answering the telephone, or don't extend your hand when someone else extends his or hers for a

Figure 2.2. Family of Rules

Rule	Be nice
Counter rule	Be bad
Qualification	Except to people who are unkind to you
Consequence	We punish people who go around making trouble
Implementation	Speak softly

NOTE: Obviously there would be other qualifications, consequences, and implementations; these are indicative, not exclusive.
(Adapted from Ford, F.R. (1983). Rules: The invisible family. *Family Process, 22*(3), pp. 135–145).

handshake. When I have given as an assignment "Break one social rule and report the consequences to the class," there are always a few students who are so uncomfortable with the exercise that they "forget" to do it. They would rather break the rule that says "Do what the teacher says to do," and be penalized in class, than be perceived as performing ineptly in the social world, and be penalized by peers.

Following minor social rules of this sort is actually one way of demonstrating that we are willing to follow larger, more significant social rules. Thus, being polite is one way of showing others that we can be depended upon not to deliberately cause disorder. In fact, of course, we can lie in this as in other matters, since following rules of politeness is no guarantee that we will not shortly commit murder, even though it is generally understood to have that implication.

Goffman saw social rules as an intermediate abstraction bridging the gap between what is observable (interactions) and what is implied (the interaction order). It is rules of conduct, arrived at through the observation of interactions, that serve to introduce us to the underlying structure of society. In his discussion of social rules, Goffman introduces an important elaboration: the notion that the fabric of social life can be easily torn. Despite their apparent inconsequentiality, rules of interaction help to create our sense of reality; however, in knowing that social rules are easily broken, we learn how easily our sense of reality can be shattered. "To be awkward or unkempt, to talk or move wrongly, is to be a dangerous giant, a destroyer of worlds. As every psychotic and comic ought to know, any accurately improper move can poke through the thin sleeve of immediate reality" (Goffman, 1961, p. 81). In order to sustain joint activity, people share a set of rules for interaction. Otherwise, interactants will not know when to speak, when to be silent, what to say, how to say it. Those who refuse to follow the social rules can make interaction virtually impossible for others.

Note Goffman's use of the phrase *accurately improper*. It is similar in implication to Ford's counter rule. Both refer to the reverse of the expected being still a part of the system, as opposed to the truly unexpected, which would have to be developed out of another system. This is one reason why cultural misunderstandings are so frequent. We expect people to follow the rules we have internalized, and we are prepared to cope with the deliberate breaking of our rules, but we have trouble responding to those who do not even acknowledge our system of social rules.

Giddens provides an elaboration of the idea: "Let us regard the rules of social life, then, as techniques or generalizable procedures applied in the enactment/reproduction of social practices" (1984, p. 21). It is the rules we follow in common that enable us to jointly create, and in the process to jointly continue to reproduce, the social world. Therefore, though they rarely are stated explicitly by participants in an interaction, rules are crucial to study.

It may be necessary to again qualify this discussion of rules before moving on, lest any reader assume that either (a) rules are absolutes that *should* be followed, or (b) rules hold for large groups of people. First, rules are frequently broken; they simply are expressions of regularity within at least one particular group. It is better to think of them as resources which can be manipulated by participants to accomplish particular goals than as rigid guidelines always followed (Craig & Tracy, 1983, p. 15). And second, it is possible that rules can exist for only two people, though they usually are described for larger groups. But it would be incorrect to assume that rules hold for an entire country, since there are so many smaller groups within political boundaries that have their own sets of rules (Gumperz, 1982a, p. 26). Pierre Bourdieu provides a clear warning of the dangers of taking social rules too seriously or too literally in speaking of them as a "refuge for ignorance" (1982, p. 22). They are useful constructions for a variety of purposes, but, as he cautions, they can be misused as well (especially when the analyst reifies them).

PREDICTABLE

The fact that communication is rule-governed leads to a very nice result; it is also predictable. If everyone follows the same rules, they should be able to predict one another's behavior with a high degree of accuracy. Having rules does imply that people will act in accordance with them, and thus that they will be predictable. Since rules tell us how to act, they also "provide the basis for the prediction, interpretation, and evaluation of behavior" (McLaughlin, 1984, p. 21). For society to function, a majority of its members must be predictable a majority of the time, so as to establish a "shared and sensible frame for the interpretation of daily practice" and permit us to understand one another (Rosaldo, 1980, p. 223). It is difficult to interact with unpredictable others, for they always require a unique response to unique behavior, which requires more effort than responding in traditional ways to expected behavior. In comparing the structure of culture to a grammar of a language, Clyde Kluckhohn concludes that the grammar of a culture makes for orderliness in interaction, just as the grammar of a language makes for orderliness in discourse (1959, p. 273).

Obviously, communication as a system must facilitate the transmission of new information, but, as Birdwhistell pointed out 25 years ago, "we have every indication that its central function is that of giving continuity and predictability to the social system" (1963, p. 136). Research since then has only validated this claim. There is a limited amount of new information to convey, but an unlimited amount of consistency to maintain. We must reaffirm our intention to remain predictable to others often.

If this is taken too literally, it is possible to make the incorrect assumption that we do not ever display new or unpredictable behavior. That is, of course, ridiculous. But we do normally act within a range of predictable behavior. The key concept here is *range of behavior.* We may not know if a particular greeting is likely to begin with a kiss or a handshake or a wave, but we know what types of behaviors generally are included in the category of *greetings.* A headstand is not, under typical circumstances, a member of that category, and therefore can be ruled out as expected behavior. Any fully socialized member of the group can generally predict the majority of what makes up the range of expected behaviors for a particular category. Usually what happens is that we do not invent original instruments of communication, but instead make use of the available ones in new ways (Perinbanayagam, 1985).

As Leonard Hawes puts it, rules "state what sequences of actions *may* occur not what sequences *will* occur. Consequently, knowledge of the communication rules alone is insufficient to explain, in a deterministic sense, human action in symbol systems" (1973, p. 17; his emphasis). This is why we cannot view rules as providing an absolute guideline for behavior and why we cannot use them to predict future behavior. Instead, we should view rules as merely providing a map of possible paths to take; which path we take is still left to individual choice.

We need a certain amount of predictability to help us know where the interaction is going, what will occur next. Even something so simple as a conversation has basic system requirements that must be met (participants must agree on beginning and end points, if nothing else), and these constraints can be difficult to meet if ways of notifying others of our intent to begin or end discourse are not held in common. Gumperz, Aulakh, and Kaltman refer to the "necessary predictions" for understanding where a given example of discourse is headed (1982, p. 30); the same level of predictability is needed for all interaction, nonverbal as well as verbal.

What about people who act unpredictably? "Society depends upon predictability and regularity. Every human society finds it necessary to kill, specially define, rehabilitate, or isolate unreliable or unpredictable symbolizers" (Birdwhistell, 1968a, p. 25). In other words, those who insist upon being unpredictable are not tolerated by the group as a whole. They cannot be accepted, if the group is to continue to function smoothly. "For Western societies, at least, being noticeable and being deviant seem intimately related" (Sacks, 1972, p. 280), so we strive to fit in, to not stand out from the crowd, lest our doing so draw negative sanctions.

During a discussion of Mexico and Puerto Rico in the third grade class in South Milwaukee, one of the Puerto Rican students, Dawn, calls out an answer in response to the teacher's question.

Teacher: Dawn, first of all, what is the rule in this classroom? What is the rule? Raise your hand.

A few minutes later she calls out again.

Teacher: You yelled out again, Dawn. Three times and you're out.

Dawn puts her hand up for several implied questions, gives much visual feedback (nodding, looking directly at the teacher), and raises her hand for questions successfully for an hour. But then she, Sean, and Nicole all call out an answer to a question.

Teacher: Dawn, that was three, and you're out.

Dawn does not move.

Teacher: Get out and stay out until I can find some tape wide enough.

Dawn leaves the room, sits in the hallway for 10 minutes.

Teacher: Would somebody please go and get Dawn and tell her I want to speak to her.

Another student fetches her, she returns to the room, talks with the teacher for a few minutes.

Teacher: Boys and girls, Dawn has something to tell you.
Dawn: I'm sorry.
Teacher: For what?
Dawn: For being rude.
Teacher: Thank you.

The teacher tells me later she is working on Dawn's appreciation of others, and that it was difficult for her to apologize.
   Examples such as this one are common in school settings, where teachers are explicit about the need to teach their students the consequences of behavior inappropriate to the smooth functioning of the group.

If we do nothing else in response, we generally at least label those who will not conform as belonging to a category of *predictably unpredictable.* That way, we remember to expect unusual behavior from them, and it is not so difficult to respond to their actions. That way, we also have to spend less time searching for the meaning of their behavior. There are a series of such labels available to every group. One is *insane,* and another is *young children* (Birdwhistell 1970). Because communication is learned after birth, children do not arrive already prepared to be predictable. But they do need to learn the necessary information fairly quickly (certainly within the first few years), if the society at large is not to take action against them. Such action can vary widely.

In some societies the nonassimilator will be allowed to die; in others he may be given a special institutional position. This special treatment can range from deification to incarceration. But ultimately the goal is the same: to make his behavior sufficiently predictable that the society can go about the rest of its business. (Birdwhistell, 1959, p. 111)

It is interesting to study a society's response to anomalous behavior: When there are two clear categories, what happens when something falls between them, instead of neatly into one or the other? Mary Douglas has studied this extensively (1966), and suggests that "Some social structures can tolerate anomaly and deal with it constructively, while others are rigid in their classifications. This difference is probably the most important subject on which sociological research can focus" (1975, p. 227). I am uncertain that it is the single most important topic, but at least it is one fruitful topic for study.

There are two very important things every child born into a group must learn:

1. what society expects of him or her, and
2. how to demonstrate his or her new knowledge in appropriate ways.

Knowing what should be done (passive knowledge, sometimes referred to as *competence*) is of little use if it is not accompanied by the ability to do what is required at the appropriate time (active knowledge, referred to as *performance*). Having theoretical knowledge of what must be done in response to a fire in the house is not the same as being able to do everything necessary the day there actually is a fire.

There has been much written on the nature of competence and its relationship to performance.[4] One of the more interesting proposals is that of Linda Harris, who suggests that there are a series of levels within a social system:

1. minimal competence (few mutually coherent episodes)
2. satisfactory competence
   (a) normal satisfactory competence (works well within a group)
   (b) clever satisfactory competence (moves with unusual effectiveness within the system)

---

[4] See Hymes (1971, 1976) for seminal statements. Diez (1984) and Van Hoeven (1985) summarize the work from within the field of communication.

3. optimal competence (able to control own enmeshment within a system)

   (a) alienated optimal competence (the act of control alienates the participant)

   (b) transcending optimal competence (able to wander in and out of various systems at will).[5]

This suggests that the simple notion of competence can usefully be expanded to include a variety of stages of competence. Harris suggests that people can have differing levels of competence in different areas requiring expertise; but I would argue that there should be significant overlap, since learning in one area can be beneficial in other areas. (It would be unlikely to find someone who had achieved what she labels transcending optimal competence in one area, but who was minimally competent in all others.) Bateson's notion of learning to learn should come into play, so that some of what was learned in old skills should transfer to each new skill. Knowing how to fix a car does not tell me much about how to write a book, but it does teach me something of how to learn new skills.

One of the ways in which we maintain pattern is through social roles; these are first a product and then a further cause of predictability. Each of us can be classified as at least one type of person (a dentist, a mother, a poet, etc.). Certain behaviors are expected of people who fit each label. A role can be defined as that set of activities expected of a person who fills a given position in a group. In fact, we each carry out more than one role, at different times in the day (moving from student to gang member), or in our lives (from child to parent). We learn a repertoire of role relationships as we become socialized (Schutz & Luckmann, 1973, p. 70–73). What Schutz and Luckmann point out is that we learn far more than roles; we learn role relationships. This distinction means that we learn, not only how a role works from one side, but how to understand both sides of a given relationship. (By learning how to play the role of a child, we observe the role of father, and so learn how to play that as well.) We must understand both sides in a relationship in order to act appropriately, and to continue interacting appropriately as we move from one role to another. We often display only one role at a time, but we may be called upon to comprehend and correctly interpret the roles a large number of others display in their actions with us. To do so correctly demon-

---

[5] Harris (1979) is an unpublished dissertation, but it is outlined in some detail in Pearce and Cronen (1980).

strates tacit knowledge of more roles than we have ever actually filled ourselves.

Tracing the combination of roles a given individual comes in contact with is one way of learning more about a person, and establishes a network of social relationships. No two people have exactly the same network, but many people have a large number of elements in common (most of us meet secretaries, and grocery clerks, and grandparents, but whether we usually interact with chief executives of large companies, or a large supporting group of cousins, may vary). The roles available in a given group are part of what can be described as the *communicative economy* for that group. Other parts of the communicative economy are the languages or dialects available for use, and the major ritual events. It sometimes helps to use the metaphor of economy in describing communication, especially when trying to remember that there is a choice involved in every interaction, since economy lends itself well to the notion that specific choices must be made every time an interaction occurs (Hymes, 1972; see McLaughlin, 1984, p. 92, for a variation on this theme: a conversation as an economic system).

We have many roles based on attributes of age, sex, occupation, family position, etc., and we are able to shift easily from one to another. At the same time, these are distinct; we will not address someone as "waiter" even if we see someone we recognize as having that role, if they are out of context. Also, roles can be extremely brief: many of us play the role of "pedestrian," or "spectator," but these are often short-term roles that we relinquish easily. Our assumptions as to roles can seem obvious but be nonetheless incorrect (as when a "grandmother" turns out to actually be the mother of the young child she holds by the hand). We frequently have misunderstandings that are due to shifts in role. Moving from father to husband to tennis player calls for fast thinking on the part of various participants in an interaction, and a newcomer to the scene can easily become confused if he or she misses the shift cues. A point worth mentioning is that not all roles have equal status and prestige; thus we employ a variety of symbols to designate the different roles (such as a jacket known to members to indicate group membership). If a role we can play has status associated with it, we may insist that others recognize the symbols we use to mark it (for example, knowing who is the judge in a courtroom depends upon correctly interpreting a combination of clothing, spacing, and forms of address). In short, roles are valuable because they help us sustain ongoing communication with a minimum of effort. They help us "locate" others socially, and permit us to "handle" them appropriately (Berger & Luckmann, 1967, p. 42).

Among the traditional landmarks in cities are bars. There are significant distinctions between neighborhood bars, and those that are not only open to outsiders, but that usually cater to people who do not know each other. Neighborhood bars have a consistent clientele, and once you become a part of the group (a process that can take years) you are a member forever. If you move away, you are simply a member who has moved away, not a nonmember. In East Baltimore I was told: "Every neighborhood, every block or so, you had a tavern. Still do. See? I mean each one had its own clientele. You never had no strangers coming in there."

This contrasts with the singles bars now found in most cities, where the entire purpose is to meet new strangers who are potential friends or lovers.

Related to the existence of roles is the fact that we wear "uniforms" to permit others to identify our social roles more easily. Some of these are more formal than others. A police officer wears a rigidly prescribed uniform, while in the 1960s blue jeans became the informal student uniform. In both cases the function is the same. The uniform allows others to classify us more easily, and permits others to have some advance warning of the types of behavior we are likely to exhibit. Clothing is but one part of such uniforms: Haircuts (think of any of the punk hairstyles), jewelry (from a wedding band to a fraternity pin), or cars (think of the difference implied by driving a new Mercedes versus an old Volkswagon) are all part of the way in which we convey information about ourselves, the roles we fill, and the behaviors which we are likely to exhibit. This is not to suggest that, when we are with other people, we intentionally convey our role to them. We simply behave appropriately to the then-relevant role—in fact, we know no other way of behaving—and this behavior provides role information.

One final point: I do not mean to be saying that roles *cause* particular behavior, or adherence to particular rules. Rather, it makes more sense to say that we construct role identities through the behavior we perform. Role is the abstract, person-centered label assigned to particular patterns or sets of rules of behavior. This returns us to the idea that behavioral roles are socially patterned, rather than idiosyncratically created.

Roles are not the only labels attributed to behavior rules. Communication events are similarly *constructed* out of behavior (Berger & Luckmann, 1967). The event does not exist in and of itself; instead, we agree that it exists based on the behavior we see demonstrated. In Dell Hymes's conception of the ethnography of communication, the notion of communicative event is central. At one time he summarized the approach as asking four questions:

1. What are the communicative events, and their components, in a community?
2. What are the relationships among them?
3. What capabilities and states do they have, in general, and in particular events?
4. How do they work? (1967, p. 25; see also 1972).

There are a few contexts for which the known rules no longer hold, and these are especially valuable research sites. Monica Heller has studied Montreal, a city which must cope with two languages, whereas most are limited to one. She found an extreme awareness of language and suggests that every interaction now involves a preliminary negotiation of language choice (1982, p. 109). Through examples of explicit negotiation of language use which sometimes stop all interaction until they can be completed, she demonstrates that shared norms of language use must be present for interaction to take place. When it is not possible to assume shared norms, these become the initial topic of discussion. Heller concludes that, "in the absence of norms, we work at creating new ones" (1982, p. 118). In Montreal this has resulted in conventionalizing the negotiation strategies, in order to minimize the amount of time and energy devoted to discussing language choice and move on to the interaction itself.

The balance between the old and the new, between the existing pattern and the creation of new patterns, is the important characteristic. "The life-history of the individual is first and foremost an accommodation to the patterns and standards traditionally handed down in his community. . . . By the time he can talk, he is the little creature of his culture" (Benedict, 1959, pp. 2–3). As "the little creature of his culture," he has learned to demonstrate culture-appropriate behavior the majority of the time, and to take it for granted all of the time. Steier, Stanley, and Todd point out that "social systems, in general, seek to maintain a balance between flexibility and stability" (1982, p. 148; see also Eisenberg, 1984, p. 230), and it is this effort to achieve balance that we must study. It is a precarious balance, but all the more interesting for its fragility. Society and the individual may not be antagonists, as Benedict asserts (1959, p. 253), but since their goals and needs are not always identical, the struggle for stability by the society and flexibility by the individual is a pretty fight to watch and an important one to study.

ANALYZABLE

If communication is patterned behavior then it is also analyzable. From the participant's viewpoint, we use what we know of behavior through social rules, first, to predict what will occur, and second, to analyze what actually does occur. As McLaughlin has put it: "We locate ourselves in social episodes by comparing the action as it develops to the constitutive rules of social practice" (1984, p. 21). At least in theory, anyone can learn, not only how to observe social interaction, deliberately and carefully, but how to discover the underlying patterns. If behavior were random and unique rather than rule-governed and predictable, it would not be possible to analyze it, for there would be no consistency to what we observe. Once something is characterized as having structure, it must be possible for that structure to be analyzed and understood. This entire book is based on the assumption that communicative behavior is analyzable. If it were not, we could not spend time talking about it, or reading about it, or writing about it.

Margaret Mead suggested that "anthropological field work is based on the assumption that human behavior is systematic, that it is one of the properties of the human organism to systematize experience in ways that can be learned and taught and used in human relationships" (1951, p. 189). In her words, the principal tool used by anthropologists (and by extension, the principal tool used by anyone who would study social interaction) is consciousness of pattern, and training in how to do this sort of research is primarily training in the recognition of pattern. Ethnographers of communication, as with ethnographers studying other aspects of culture, must learn to recognize patterns when they come across them. "A culture, like an individual, is a more or less consistent pattern of thought and action" (Benedict, 1959, p. 46).

Those who see communication as analyzable can be understood to suggest that it is a text, and that, as analysts, our job is to read this text. We could not decipher the text if it were not inherently readable, and so, by our own actions, we imply that it is.[6] Geertz has suggested that:

---

[6] See Geertz (1980) for elaboration of three related analogies as they are used in current social scientific research: life as game, life as stage, life as text.

Doing ethnography is like trying to read (in the sense of 'construct a reading of') a manuscript—foreign, faded, full of ellipses, incoherences, suspicious emendations, and tendentious commentaries, but written not in conventional graphs of sound but in transient examples of shaped behavior. (1973, p. 10)

Like children learning to read the alphabet, we must be trained to read and analyze our social text, but the point remains that this lies in the realm of the possible. "Seeing is not a unique God-given talent, but a discipline. It can be learned" (Nelson, 1977, p. 7). As Stewart & Philipsen have phrased it, "Wherever people participate in social life, they exploit communicative resources in a systematic way, and thus the observers and the creators of social life can discern it as patterned" (1984, p. 211).

Once we know it is possible to analyze communication, the question arises of whether or not we should bother to do so. I would answer with Bateson's statement: "any study which throws light on the nature of 'order' or 'pattern' in the universe is surely nontrivial" (1972c, p. xvi). The discovery of communication patterns or orders sheds light on the human condition; they are what make us socially human. Giddens tells us that: "All social actors . . . are social theorists, who alter their theories in light of their experiences" (1984, p. 335). Assuming that Giddens is correct, and that we invent theories as participants in interaction anyway, the question really becomes only how much deliberate effort to devote to the doing of it, not whether it is worth doing.

CHAPTER 3
Communication as Behavior We Learn

Our communication system is not something we invent but rather something which we internalized in the process of becoming human.
—Ray Birdwhistell (1970, p. 15)

We are not born knowing how to communicate; it is something we learn just as we learn to tie our shoes (or wear them). Clearly, if we do not come with the knowledge "built in," it is knowledge we must "pick up" somewhere. We can speak of children being "inducted" into the use of appropriate symbols for our culture, much as we speak of adults being inducted into an army (Frank, 1966, p. 7). Since children learn communication, this implies that it should be possible to observe children as they learn what is involved in communication, as in fact social scientists can and do. Only through learning how to communicate appropriate do we join other humans and become a society. "Communicative competence is not just another useful skill, like shoemaking; it is one's ticket of admission to human and social life" (Thayer, 1982, p. x). Our primary job as children is to learn to understand and display the appropriate communicative system for the group of people into which we are born. Thus:

a child must learn to transform the world of actual things and events, of signals and signs, into a symbolic world of meanings and purposive striving in accordance with the symbolic patterns which have been devised to make human living more orderly and goal-seeking. (Frank, 1966, p. 7)

Only when we learn to communicate appropriately are we accepted into adult society. Hawes puts this idea in terms of a child needing to learn to engage in rather than disrupt the systems of communication used by the available adults (1973, p. 16). A child who only disrupts and refuses to more constructively participate in the system causes major repercussions and as a result calls for some response from the surrounding adults.

Even the most ordinary of conversations cannot take place until the participants in the interaction have agreed upon certain basic assumptions. They need to be able to assume that those they talk with will know, not only the generalizations (such as the rules for turn-taking within conversations), but also the subtleties (such as the rule that those with greater social rank and power can take longer turns if they so desire). There is a wealth of cultural knowledge that must be imparted to children before they are capable of becoming reasonable conversation partners, as there is a wealth of knowledge presumed in all social interaction, verbal or not. Bourdieu shows us the central role of schools in reproducing the culture (1973).[1]

Jokes are made about children being grown up when they can play golf properly, but every family has its own internal markers for adult status within the group. In my parents' house, the major distinguishing marker between children and adults was that, long after the children went to bed, the adults sat in the kitchen, having tea and cake, talking about the day's events. As the years went by, I gradually took over the responsibility of putting my two younger sisters to bed, which was certainly one marker of growing up. It meant that we no longer needed a babysitter: I performed that role. But the day I was permitted to join my parents for tea and pound cake in the kitchen at 10:00 p.m. (much later than my previous bedtime) was without question the day that marked their acceptance of me as more an adult to be reasoned with than a child to be handled.

Conversational style is just one of the aspects of interaction that must be learned, but it is a critical one with influence on other behavior.[2] Deborah Tannen's research demonstrates that conversational style is learned and strongly influenced by family factors,

---

[1] There has been much research on classroom settings for this reason: Mehan (1979), Corsaro (1985), Green and Wallat (1981) are among the many excellent studies. See Philips (1983) for a description of what can happen when the community and the classroom cultures are in conflict, in this case Indian as opposed to mainstream American.

[2] There has been much research on this topic in linguistics. For the methodological problems of faithfully reproducing oral style in written publications, see Tedlock (1972). One of the few publications in communication is Sanders (1984).

among them ethnicity (1980, 1982). She makes the further suggestion that conversational style seems more resistant to change than more obvious indicators of ethnicity (her example is retention of the language of parents and grandparents, 1982, p. 230). This supports David Efron's (1941) finding that gestures learned within a family setting last until the third generation; thus, even when the language of the grandparents is no longer in use, the gestural system which had originally accompanied it remains.

The phrase used so far is that "we must learn communication," and not that "we must be taught communication." The notion of teaching gives the impression of deliberate, conscious efforts to teach something; we rarely learn to communicate in either deliberate or conscious ways. But just because the processes by which we communicate are not easily articulated does not mean they cannot be learned. What is necessary is to shift the focus from teaching (something done on purpose) to learning (something which can occur without either deliberate or conscious effort). Weinstein (1969) phrases this same issue as the difference between *direct training* and *incidental learning*. (At times others have called this the difference between *formal* and *informal* learning.)

George Gerbner uses the phrase *hidden curriculum* for all of the information about the culture that children need to learn. (It has come to have other definitions in later usage.) He defines it specifically as "a lesson plan that no one teaches but everyone learns" (1974, p. 476). He takes the analogy of a lesson plan even further when he argues that:

> Every culture, as any school, will organize knowledge into patterns that cultivate a social order. The fundamental lessons of the curriculum are not just what pupils learn in mathematics, history, physics, etc., but also the fact that *those* are its commonly required subjects and not basketweaving, harmony, or Marxism-Leninism (except where *that* is required). (Gerbner, 1974, p. 476)

What he is describing are patterns that create one particular social order, and no other, which children must acquire if they are to be considered socialized.

Another way to conceive of the difference between teaching and learning is to describe teaching as something generally performed with full awareness, and learning as something which can be performed out-of-awareness. We do it, but we can't always describe exactly what it is we are doing.

> George Ray asked an informant questions about her non-verbal communication; she replied: "I don't know how to think about that" (1987, p. 174). Though few others have put it so bluntly, the general problem is common. We do not normally learn words to describe what we do nonverbally, and we do not learn even that it is a subject one can discuss: for all intents and purposes, then, it is a "nonsubject" even more than our traditionally taboo subjects (such as death).

In their research, Charles and Marjorie Goodwin have made the point that it is unlikely adults could deliberately construct a method of teaching children to manipulate their language which would function better than those children have devised for themselves. (One they have studied in detail is argumentation.) They go on to point out, however, that, rather than notice the value of arguments and be pleased with the resulting control over language, most parents and teachers try to regulate and, if possible, eliminate them (1987, p. 227).

In order to examine communication, it is necessary to shift the focus from the individuals who are doing the teaching or learning to the process itself. Instead of asking about the motivation of a particular individual to pass on or to acquire a particular bit of behavior, it is more appropriate to ask about the learning situation as a whole. This is because we are less interested in individual motives (why someone tells us something is being passed on) than in results (what is passed on). Among other questions, this leads us to ask who learns what within a culture, for everyone does not learn everything. I may know a lot about climbing mountains, but little about how to repair a car, may be good at maintaining friendships, but not be comfortable in front of a camera. Such differing learning contexts and experiences are not individually created, but consistent within a group.

> Particular teachers in a school develop reputations for teaching particular things. Within the South Milwaukee school, the first grade teacher I observed had the reputation for teaching children to read; no student got out of her classroom without that ability. The third grade teacher taught them how to work on their own, at their own pace, with little explicit instruction, and focused on reading and math. The fourth grade teacher taught them how to be flexible and creative, to set their own goals rather than simply meeting hers, did very little reading but a lot of science and art. It seemed as if the school as a

whole had reached agreement on what students needed to learn, and only after did individual teachers become specialists in achieving these various goals, though it is rare for this sort of overt decision to occur. A student with access to all the teachers in the school would eventually reach all of the goals that the school set, over the course of 6 years. The problem with this solution, however, is that schools cannot coordinate their grades: the teacher who is good at teaching individual effort will not always be the third grade teacher. The result is that a student who changes schools has a good chance of missing out on one or more of the skills that schools later assume.

Some of the best research clarifying the concept of communication as something we learn has been conducted by sociologist Hugh Mehan. After a year's observation of a primary school classroom, he concluded that "competent membership in the classroom community, then, involves weaving academic knowledge and interactional skills together like strands of a rope, providing factually correct academic content in the interactionally appropriate form" (1979, p. 170). Others before him had suggested that students have not only to provide technically correct information in response to teacher questions, but also to provide it in the interactionally correct form; it was Mehan who demonstrated this in great detail, and beyond all question. He outlined the structure of a classroom lesson in detail, finding that the students learned not only academic content but the appropriate interactional structure as the academic year progressed (1979, p. 186).

Examples of teachers in early grades rejecting correct content in order to stress that both content and form of response must be appropriate are easy to find. In the first grade classroom in South Milwaukee, students were always answering the teacher's questions without raising their hands to be called upon. Within a single hour, I heard the following statements made by the teacher:
"Don't tell an answer, raise your hand if you know."
"You didn't raise your hand—you had a nice answer."
"Let's raise our hands."
"Raise your hands."
"Carmen, I wish you wouldn't answer out loud all the time. Give someone else a turn."
Teachers in later grades assume (correctly) that their stu-

dents have been sufficiently socialized in this area, and, as a result, such comments are rare.

Examples taken from the education system might be understood to imply that we learn a system of communication once, as children, then never need to learn anything more about communication. This is hardly the case. Each new context has new rules to be internalized; children are not exposed to all contexts, and so cannot learn all the rules they will have to acquire as adults. Certainly we learn the majority of what we know about social interaction as children, but it must be stressed that learning to communicate is a continuous process; it begins with birth, but continues until death.

One of the things we must learn is when to break the rules. Every parent and teacher can tell stories of children who have not yet learned that the rule governing interrupting adult conversations is to be broken if something important occurs. Perhaps the problem is that adult and child versions of what constitutes "something important" vary so greatly.

In the third grade classroom in South Milwaukee, students were used to getting permission for things like leaving the room and did not always understand when emergencies could take priority over the standard procedures (or what constituted an emergency). One day a student, Porfirio, got a nosebleed, and waited for permission before leaving to go to the bathroom to take care of the blood. This entailed calmly raising his hand, getting the teacher's attention, and requesting and receiving permission to leave the room. He then walked quietly out, alone. When he returned, the teacher told him, "After this, don't wait, just leave the room." (She then sent him to the office, so someone could check him over, before permitting him to rejoin the class activities.)

This incident can be contrasted with a nosebleed in a different setting that I observed. The main events of a 12-year-old's birthday party were completely upstaged by one child with a nosebleed, and that child became the center of attention for close to an hour. Everyone panicked, from the child involved to the mother of the birthday girl, and everyone took it very seriously indeed. The girl with the nosebleed was told to lie down on the living room couch, until the bleeding stopped, regardless of possible damage to the fabric (one of the major signs of concern on the part of the hostess). This was a far different response than that of Porfirio, who knew that *no one* could leave the room without permission, but did not know when to appropriately break the rule. Here, personal discomfort (nosebleeds are not particularly painful, though they are messy and sometimes scare young children for that reason) took a back seat to following the social rule governing appropriate class behavior.

The fact that communication is learned has many implications. Three of the most important of these will be discussed here. It implies, first, that communication is socially based; second, that it stands in a particular relation to culture; and third, that it is arbitrary. Each of these ideas will be considered below. Explaining them may be the easiest way to explain what is intended by the suggestion that communication is behavior we learn.

SOCIALLY BASED

If, as biological entities, we all came into the world knowing how to communicate, we would presumably all communicate in the same ways. In that case, no matter where in the world we were born, we would be able to interact with people from all other parts of the world and immediately understand each other. We all know that this is not the case. What is true instead is that every culture or social group has patterns of communication unique to that group. A new member of the group, such as a baby, must learn to display appropriate knowledge of communicative behavior at some point in his or her life in order to be accepted. This is generally referred to as becoming *socialized*. Adults, children, or older babies are also said to be socialized into any new group they may later join. Our concern here, however, is mainly with what may be referred to as the *primary* socialization process, learning to adapt to the first group we encounter, and the one we have the least choice about joining. As Ruesch says, "Man is born into a communication system that he did not choose and a social system that tells him how to behave without asking him for his consent" (1974, p. 74). The extreme point of view suggests that newborn babies only have the potential for becoming human; they are not fully human until they have internalized appropriate modes of communication, and can demonstrate what they have learned.

All communicative behavior is based on membership in a particular group. This implies that little of social interaction is universal; it is not "built in" to the physical body. What newborn babies have to do is to figure out what constitutes appropriate behavior in the group in which they find themselves, and then exhibit that. In fact, they probably must first learn that there is such an abstract concept as *appropriate,* and that all behavior is not accepted by all others in all situations. This is not to suggest that they do these things consciously or on purpose. They don't. But they do them nonetheless. Birdwhistell suggests: "The human infant is an amoral mass of wrigglings and vocalizing; it lives in a milieu of moral speakers and movers" (1959, p. 114). As used here, *moral* behavior is that which is appropriate, expected, and condoned by the society at large. (*Moral order* is, in this respect, a near synonym for social order.) *Amoral* behavior is that which is inappropriate, unexpected, and not condoned, sometimes even shocking or forbidden to a particular society at large. Babies are not *immoral,* which would imply a deliberate contradiction of the norms, but amoral, implying a lack of knowledge or consideration of the rules. That is, society's norms are simply not taken into account by very young children; they cannot be, since they do not as yet understand them.

None of us invents his or her own ways of communicating out of nothingness. If we did, our behavior would be completely incomprehensible to others. There would be no way for anyone to correctly interpret our actions, since they would have no prior knowledge of what we were likely to be doing. Luckily, it is neither possible nor necessary for each of us to invent communication anew each time we want to interact. We are exposed to a fully developed, complex system from the moment we are born. "The child begins life as a social being within an already defined social network and, through the growth of communication and language, the child, in interaction with others, constructs a social world" (Corsaro, 1985, p. 73).[3] The ways in which we begin to communicate are common to the group in which we find ourselves, and understood by other members of that group. The assumption here is that there is no behavior which can carry meaning outside of some reference group. In fact, it is often the case that behavior which is appropriate—moral—in one particular group will be viewed as being inappropriate—immoral—in another.

Generally the first group within which we learn communicative behavior is the family. Both deliberately and inadvertently, parents teach children much of what they know about appropriate and

---

[3] Birdwhistell has made the same point: "The child is born into a society already keyed for his coming. A system exists into which he must be assimilated if the society is to sustain itself" (1959, p. 111).

inappropriate behavior. Like grade school teachers, parents are among the few who traditionally explicitly state the rules of interaction they expect their children to follow. Perhaps some of the more interesting examples of how parents socialize their children are those which are implicit and rarely deliberate or well thought out.

Folk toys are traditional toys made within a particular ethnic group, and they are one of the ways parents can help their children maintain ties to a country or culture in which they no longer actively live or actively participate. Several years ago, I found a series of steps that appear to be fairly consistently followed by families from a wide variety of backgrounds in their use of traditional toys as an expression of their feelings about maintaining ethnic traditions. I was looking specifically at recent immigrant groups in the greater Milwaukee area. The steps that seem to exist are the following:

1. When a family immigrates to the United States, the children initially play with toys brought from the home country. When the family returns to the home country to visit, the parents either buy or are given toys for their children, which they bring back to the United States with them. If they do not return for visits, friends and relatives bring or send traditional toys for the children. I found a specific example of a family with three children under the age of 6 from North India, who had just returned from a visit there, who had been given toys for their children by friends.

2. As the children get older, and return visits to the home country become less frequent, the traditional toys are outgrown and not replaced. They are put on a shelf and treasured as one part of the family's traditions, but no longer actively played with. For example, a family from South India with a 10-year-old boy and a 14-year-old girl has put away the toys the children formerly played with, but keeps them where they are daily a visible reminder of the past.

3. As the children grow up in this country, their parents can buy traditional toys for them at import stores, which, although they are not made specifically for their children (as such toys often would have been at home), are at least of the appropriate tradition. The owner of a Greek import store said that the customers who buy dolls from him are

most often recent immigrants buying the dolls for their own children.

4. At the same time, the children are learning about American toys from their friends, television, and stores, and they are beginning to ask for these toys. Several parents said that, in the beginning, they would not permit their children to have mass-produced American toys, but that, as time went on (the exact period varied), they gave in and bought what other children had. Also at the same time, the children are learning to make some American folk toys from their friends, such as paper airplanes and cootie catchers.

5. *Syncretism* (a combination of the old and the new) occurs within a few years, as the children learn to consider all toys a part of the same continuum and not separate them out by place of origin. I found, for example, Hmong quilted doll clothes being put on Barbie dolls.

6. When these children grow up and become the second generation, they frequently decide they have missed something. At this point they may become interested in learning how to make the toys of their childhood. I discovered a Swiss doll-maker who saw traditional dolls on a visit to Switzerland and learned how to make them from someone in this country once she returned home. Or the example of a Croation woman who moved away from her parents, then decided to make traditionally designed clothes for her daughter's doll; she found the patterns in a book.

7. Eventually, at the last stage, traditional toys become objects without a context. They are sold in art galleries and shown in museums. An art gallery contacted me while I was doing my research, to see if I could help them find folk toys to put on display.

When I started the research on traditional toys, my assumption was that I would find parents using the toys to help their children maintain ethnic traditions. Instead, through a series of steps, the children were gradually moving away from folk toys, and accepting mainstream, mass-produced American toys. This occurred even though other ethnic traditions, such as cooking, were rigidly maintained in the home. My conclusion was that the parents saw their children as being oriented to the future. If the children are to be successful in the new country, they must learn to accept as much of the culture as possible, and become assimilated as quickly as possible. So, although the parents maintain various forms of material culture they have learned to take for granted (whether food or ritual objects), when it comes to the children's possessions, such as toys, they more quickly switch to mainstream American objects. It is only once the children have grown up and become assimilated that they themselves may feel they have missed something, and try to reconstruct the past for the next generation.

Brown and Ragan (1987) provide an excellent example of how communication is learned within a particular group, and, therefore, how it is socially based. They describe blessings before the meal within a particular family and show how family members manipulate the use of these blessings, playing with the form as they demonstrate knowledge of it. We begin by learning our communication within a family setting, and examples such as this one demonstrate how this happens.

The group exists before the individual. A person does not create his or her own social group; rather, in an important sense, the group creates the individual. The individual is but a moment in the history of a particular society, shaped in important ways by the society into which he or she has been born. Society lasts longer than any single individual; it contains the patterns of behavior that individuals learn and display. Sharing patterns of behavior and symbols that are mutually comprehensible, we maintain the boundaries of our groups. If you understand me, we must be members of some group in common; if you do not, the line of membership is drawn between us. The solidarity of the group is strengthened by the fact that we have, if nothing else, symbols and patterns of interaction held in common (Warner, 1962, pp. 61–62). Children must learn the social patterns to which they are exposed if social order is to be maintained (Cicourel, 1970, p. 166).

After the family, one of the most basic membership groups is the neighborhood. Many of us who live in large cities today have never participated in a neighborhood in the sense in which it has traditionally existed: a group of people who live together, know each other, look out for each other's welfare, and have frequent and regular contact.

Many traditional examples of neighborhoods are around still today: East Baltimore is one. Several of the comments residents made to me explained that the neighborhood feeling was so great that even the act of selling a house, one traditional way for a newcomer to join the group, is limited to those already ratified as group members. One person told me: "As the older people die out, well, the younger people are moving in. . . . And it's sort of a family affair. They never have to put a sign out, for sale sign, because from one ear to the other and the home is sold. You've never seen a for sale sign in this block." Another, in a separate interview, added: "My grandmother sold her house—she sold it to my brother. You don't sell things to strangers—you keep things in your family. Everybody lives close together. You can walk to everybody's house."

One of the results of this sort of close feeling in a neighborhood is that residents are more concerned with where the house they buy is located than with what it looks like inside. I was told a story by a woman who had bought a house without even looking inside, because she had always wanted to live on that block, and when a house came up for sale, she bought it immediately, sight unseen. "I walked in this house, I started crying, because it was one piece of junk. It was terrible. It was a door here and a door here and everything was blocked in—you know—boxed in, everything, all the rooms were separate—everything was boxed in. So I start crying and my husband says, 'Well, Estelle, don't cry,' he said. 'You like the street—we bought the street, you didn't buy the house. Let me fix it up and see what happens and then if you don't like it we can sell it.' I says, 'Well, that way, all right.' So I never forget it, Froni comes in: 'Oh, what junk you bought. What's the matter? Where was your eyes?' I says, 'Where were my eyes? In my head. But I didn't see the house. I bought the street. Don't you understand?' " It was this story which clarified the idea of neighborhood for me.

The traditional term used within sociolinguistics to describe "a bunch of people who can understand each other when they talk" is *speech community*.[4] Traditionally, the definition of speech community incorporates several different ideas: (a) the group of people must have at least one language in common, (b) they must have particular norms for use of the language in common, and (c) they must spend time together so that they continue to have the same language and norms for use of the language, instead of growing apart. Historically, linguists idealized the speech community and

[4] For further discussion of speech community see Bloomfield (1926), Gumperz (1968), Hymes (1972), Saville-Troike (1982), and Irvine (1987).

assumed that its boundaries were the same as obvious geographic or political boundaries. In addition, they assumed that speech communities remained stable over time, so that individuals were born into a particular speech community, spent their lives within it, and eventually died within a single speech community. In today's world, this is no longer an appropriate assumption, and the concept of speech community has become more of an ideal conception than a practical one.

The phrase *interaction community* has no parallel history, but it could be used to express the expanded notion of a group of people holding the same ways of interacting in common. Hymes (1972) expanded Noam Chomsky's notion of *linguistic competence* (knowing the language) to a more complete notion of *communicative competence* (knowing how to appropriately use the language). Just as speech community involves the group having a language in common, an interaction community can be described as the group having the same rules for the use not only of the language but of other communicative systems as well.

An interaction community can be posited as the next larger analytic level after neighborhood (parallel to the speech community). As with speech community, we would assume there are a variety of interaction communities, depending upon similar variables such as age, gender, race, geography.[5] After family, neighborhood, and interaction community, there is really no relevant larger analytic level to be studied. Instead, what comes next is the comparison and analysis of interaction between groups with different interaction norms, whatever their size. In this way, the ethnography of communication leads directly to the study of intercultural communication.

> It is a natural extension from ethnographic study of systems of communication within a group to study of systems of communication between groups, and to study of the problems of interference and misperception to which differences between the indigenous systems of communication of two groups may give rise. (Hymes, 1967, p. 31)

(Thus, it would make sense to view intercultural communication as an expansion of social communication rather than as a separate field of study.)

As described in Chapter 2, one of the first things we learn when

---

[5] See Treichler and Kramarae (1983) for an analysis of differences between interaction communities based on gender, and Kochman (1981) for differences based on race. Although these authors do not use this term, I do not think they would object to the concept being applied to their work in this way.

we learn about communication is that there is at all times a range of behavior rather than a single behavior which is appropriate in a given situation. We normally have a series of choices to make from slightly different behaviors, each of which conveys a slightly different meaning. Thus we do not rigidly learn a single behavior for all occasions and display it expecting, and receiving, a particular behavior in response. We learn behaviors (or a behavioral "repertoire"), and learn to fit our choice of behaviors to the particular contexts we encounter, and to understand the implications of each behavior in context. At the same time we learn that only a very narrow range of behaviors is acceptable in any context; we have choices to make, but not as many or as significant choices as we usually assume. The group in which we hold membership has made some of the choices already, and we must stay within predetermined limits if we are to be understood by others with whom we interact. Ray Birdwhistell has put this very clearly:

A human being does not invent his system of communication. He may make additions to it, and he may vary the direction of its formulations. However, as a system, it has been in existence for generations. He must learn it in order to be a member of his society. (1963, p. 128)

That is why, if anything, the system of communication "invents" the individual, rather than any individual inventing a new and unique system of communication. Giddens provides an elaboration of this idea when he suggests: "Human social activities, like some self-reproducing items in nature, are recursive. That is to say, they are not brought into being by social actors but continually recreated by them via the very means whereby they express themselves *as* actors" (1984, p. 2; his emphasis).

Basil Bernstein pointed out that language is a process where actors select their form of speech from a limited range of alternates (in other words, from a repertoire) made available to them through socialization (1961, 1971). This is now generally accepted for language, but it holds equally true for all forms of communication. We have, at all times, choices to make from a limited repertoire of possibilities, and we learn the limits of what is possible from observing what those around us choose to do.

Any one individual only learns particular sets of behaviors within a society. I will learn to display either male or female gender appropriately, but it would be rare for me to learn exactly what constitutes the gender display I do not need to demonstrate. I gradually learn to display age through a variety of behaviors, and in this case do learn more than one set, as I grow older. If I change jobs, I will learn particular sets of behaviors to go with different job categories: what types of clothes a waitress will wear as opposed to a student, what forms of address to use for my customers as opposed to my professors. No one person ever learns all of the repertories possible for his or her society; instead, we each learn those appropriate to our public or private selves as we have need of them.

This is part of the explanation for why it can be said that people do not communicate, but rather *they contribute behavior to the larger, ongoing process of communication within their society*. Communication is not an act performed by one or two people, but a performance to which all the members of a society contribute equally. If we wish to understand behavior, we must explore the cultural constructions that underlie it.

Toy advertisements are one of many places to look for information about how we as a culture view gender roles today. In a study of the toy advertisements found in six of the traditional "women's magazines" *(Better Homes and Gardens, Ladies' Home Journal, McCalls, Family Circle, Women's Day,* and *Good Housekeeping)* for the year 1984, I compared the verbal and visual components of the advertisements. Briefly, what I found is that, although the words of the ads generally *were not* marked as to sex (words such as *children* and *kids* occurred most often as opposed to *boys* and *girls*), the pictures *were* marked as to sex. That is, girls play with dolls and boys play with trucks in the photos accompanying the text, even when in the text itself there is no indication of any gender role stereotype for the users of the toys. Less obvious would be an ad for a Crayola designer kit, where the text encourages the reader to imagine designing "fabulous trend-setting homes for famous clients" or "the ion powered intergalactic spaceship that will put the first astronaut in another solar system." The photo accompanying the text shows a boy holding up a picture of a spaceship and a girl holding up a picture of a living room. In addition, there are photos of the covers of the kits—the cover of the one for designing vehicles has a photo of a boy on it, while the cover of the one for designing interiors has a photo of a girl on it. In ads of this sort (and there were many), only rarely did any of the words chosen suggest that there might be a target sex for the toy. My conclusion is that, although

> at the verbal level the advertisements recognize (and make use of) the current relaxing of gender role stereotypes in many part of American society, at the visual level these same stereotypes are in fact utilized to sell toys.

The ability to stand back from what we are learning and learn about a range of behaviors rather than a single behavior at a time, is part of what Gregory Bateson has called "deutero-learning" or "learning to learn" (1972a). It is a critical ability, for, without it, the theoretical newborn baby we have been discussing would not be able to get very far. There are too many possible behaviors fitting into each analytical slot for any of us to go out and deliberately learn them all, as well as learn the rules governing when to use all of them. If you try to work out the structure of even a very simple example, say, all the greetings you know, matched to a list of all the people you might ever greet, and the different situations in which you might ever meet them, you will begin to see the complexity involved. Then, for the sake of reality, add to the list of greetings every kind of speaking you might do in a day: job interviews, idle chit-chat, telling jokes, etc. Remember to include all the different people you might talk to, and the different contexts where you might run into them and need to engage in talk. Recognize that this list only includes a small amount of language so far, and has not yet addressed any nonverbal behaviors. Imagine that we worked out all of these lists of possibilities and put them together into a *Handbook of Communication.* That *Handbook* would then serve as the beginning of a representation of what each child learns when learning communication.

But there are several problems with our *Handbook of Communication.* First of all, how would we teach each new generation what they need to know? It is unrealistic to assume that we could simply give this book to each newborn infant, the way owners of a computer are given a user's manual. We can't say, "Everything you need to know is written down here," and leave the child to his or her own devices. What would the child do for the time from birth until able to read? And how would he or she learn to read the book in the first place? Obviously this is an absurd notion, but perhaps visualizing the rules of communication as a user's manual will help to convey something of the vast amount of information a child needs to learn in order to become an accepted member of the group.

A second major problem is that the hypothetical *Handbook* has no flexibility whatsoever. It cannot account for new situations, which we bump into all the time in the real world. What am I supposed to do when I want to look up a particular context, let's take "meeting a former spouse at a friend's party" as an example, and the book does not include such an event as a possibility? It will not tell me how to act towards him, or what subjects are appropriate to discuss. Even if the *Handbook* were so comprehensive that it included every possible contingency, there is no guarantee it would continue to be correct for more than a few months (days? hours?) after it had been compiled, for the rules governing behavior change constantly. And if the *Handbook* were really so comprehensive, it would have to be as large as a library to contain all the necessary information, and would never be on hand when it was needed anyway. Perhaps this exercise shows something of the difficulty involved when we talk about the need of the group to pass down the rules governing (and permitting) social interaction from one generation to the next, and the need of the individual to acquire those rules, and for this to be done in some practical way.

Many behaviors which we have traditionally assumed are individual and not social in nature can be questioned. There is, for example, the matter of coughing. We each cough when we have to, and this has nothing to do with what other people around us are doing, right? But then how can we account for the following description of coughing as a response to boredom?

> One cougher begins his horrid work in an audience, and the cough spreads until the house is in bedlam, the actors in rage, and the playwright in retreat to the nearest saloon. Yet let the action take a turn for the better, let the play tighten up, and that same audience will sit in a silence unpunctuated by a single tortured throat. (Ardrey, 1969, p. 85)

Sari Thomas has just published an analysis of what she terms *nonlexical soundmaking* which includes coughs, throat clearings, sniffs, and sneezes produced by audiences in a lecture setting. She demonstrates that such behaviors are subject to social regulation, that they are in fact communicative rather than just meaningless physical actions (Thomas, 1987).

Once you begin looking for behaviors which may be under some sort of social control, rather than individual control, it is surprising how many examples suddenly seem to fit. Even supposedly biological behavior—such as smiling—may involve social conditions of usage.[6] Birdwhistell points out that "In one part of the country,

---

[6] See Ekman and Friesen (1972) for further comments on nonverbal communication in this connection.

an unsmiling individual might be queried as to whether he was 'angry about something,' while in another, the smiling individual might be asked 'What's funny?' " (1970, p. 31). If the smile "means" something different in different parts of the country, it should not be counted as the same act of communication, but as a different one.

RELATION OF COMMUNICATION TO CULTURE

So far, the word *culture* has been used only briefly, although it is probably obvious it is an important concept, and one related to the matters being discussed here. This is not the place to review the many possible definitions of culture existing in the anthropological literature. For our purposes, it will be sufficient to assume that *culture is all of the knowledge that we do not have in our heads when we are born, but which we learn in order to become members of a given society.* Culture is everything a group of people needs to be able to pass down from one generation to another. This includes a wide range of knowledge, from ideas about appropriate shapes for houses to appropriate gender role behaviors, from what constitutes appropriate meals to our conceptions of the natural and supernatural worlds.This view of culture obviously has been selected for a particular reason. What I want to suggest is that *communication is the process through which a society passes down culture from one generation to another.* This is not the most common understanding of the relation between the terms, but it is one I have found useful. In this view, culture is the passive form and communication is the active form of the same thing. To put it very simply, it is possible to view culture as the noun form, and communication as the verb form, of the same concept. We have culture, and we do communication; we do culture, and we have communication.

Dell Hymes has suggested that "it is revealing and essentially true to regard a culture as systems of codes and rules for their use" (1967, p. 18). While this is neither the standard definition of a culture nor the one that I have given above, it is an appropriate elaboration on the concept of communication as rule-governed presented in Chapter 1, and as such may help bring the material in these two chapters together. Note that he is not proposing this as an alternative definition of culture, but as a revealing way of looking at what comprises culture. In this conception, language would be one code;

other aspects of communication (such as nonverbal communication systems) would be others.

A related view of the concepts of culture and communication has been suggested as being the view of Gregory Bateson and Kenneth Burke, but always by others. It is never stated directly in their own work (although I do not mean to suggest that it is any the less correct for that). Weston La Barre has said that "Gregory Bateson has taught us that *all culture is communication*" (1980, p. 289; his emphasis). And Fred Davis has suggested that, to Kenneth Burke, "human cultures are 'rough drafts' for action realized in and through communication" (1985, p. xi).

Ray Birdwhistell is one of the few authors to directly address the relation of communication to culture in his own work. In an early publication, he suggests that "communication provides the means of sustaining the patterned interpersonal relationships without which culture would be impossible" (1963, p. 129). In a later work, he warns about the dangers inherent in taking too simplistic a position, and, since his point is complex, the entire passage will be quoted here.

> culture and communication are terms which represent two different viewpoints or methods of representation of patterned and structured human interconnectedness. As "culture," the focus is upon structure; as "communication," it is upon process. Yet, again such a formulation can be misleading for it may seem to imply that process is without structure and that structure is inert. Perhaps a more illuminating way of stating the case would be to say that I believe that the studies of those who look at patterned human interconnectedness, as it were, from above and derive *cultural* generalizations from their observations will produce data which will be coextant ultimately with data derived by those who study it from below and who derive *communicational* generalizations. (1968b, p. 157; his emphasis)

Given this extensive warning about collapsing the two terms, it should be clear that my intention is not to suggest collapsing the two terms culture and communication into one. If that were done, we would lose much of value. My point is rather that, since the terms are generally used by different people in different fields of study, it is not often even recognized that they are in fact closely related. (This is parallel to the way in which the concept of social order has been overlooked in the communication literature, because it is a term largely confined to the field of sociology.) Both culture and communication can be described by the adjectives patterned, learned, context-bound, multichannel, and multifunctional (Leach, 1976).

Virtually all definitions of culture stress the concepts of pattern (or structure, or underlying support) and the fact that we must learn the pattern (it does not come built into the physical system). The significance of context has been less often overtly mentioned, although anyone reading the anthropological literature with this in mind will easily find it. Functionalism has been an influential approach within anthropology; despite the fact that, as generally conceived, it implies a single function at a time, there is no reason why the more complex view of multiple functions co-existing should cause theoretical problems. Multiple channels are less often explicitly noted as characteristics of culture, but they are nonetheless applicable to culture as to communication. All the anthropologists who have studied material culture have assumed this.

There are a few places where further comments on the links between culture and communication can be found, most of them in the work of anthropologists (Mary Douglas, for example, writes "If we ask of any form of communication the simple question, What is being communicated?, the answer is: information from the social system. The exchanges which are being communicated constitute the social system", 1975, p. 87.) Within the communication literature, Sari Thomas suggests that we can separate "the organization of any one 'moment' in the past or present (culture)" from "the process which brought forth the moment and delivers it to the future (communication)" (1982, p. x). James Carey has used the concept of communication creatively in his presentation of cultural studies of mass communication, though this has had little influence as yet on research looking at interaction (1975, 1983; see also White, 1983). Other authors have simply stressed the significance of culture for research into communication without defining how they view the relationship between the two (such as Rosengren, 1983, p. 193). Pearce, Stanback, and Kang have put the matter very forcibly when they recommend that the goal of communication research should be "to illumine the relationship between culture and the communication process," although, again, they do little to directly address the relationship between the two (1982, p. 3).

The Italian semiotician Umberto Eco is less reluctant than his American colleagues to collapse the concepts of communication and culture. He affirms that "communication encompasses the whole of culture" (1973, p. 59). At the same time, he must be understood to say this for rhetorical purposes more than as a literal suggestion that we collapse the two concepts theoretically. He is trying to enlarge the scope of semiotic inquiry beyond language, and into other aspects of culture. His argument essentially is that the whole of social life can be viewed as a system of semiotic systems, that is, as a set of human-made meaning systems, which are arbitrary, and which we learn from other humans and which we use in order to interact with them. For Eco, "to communicate is to use the entire world as a semiotic apparatus" (1973, p. 57). Eco is referring, among other things, to the fact that we give meaning and thus reality to the world we see, and we do so through the use of symbols we create and which have only such meaning as we bestow upon them.

Edward Sapir was one of the first to suggest that society "is being reanimated or creatively affirmed from day-to-day by particular acts of a communicative nature which obtain among individuals participating in it," and, further, that "every cultural pattern and every single act of social behavior involve(s) communication in either an explicit or an implicit sense" (1949, pp. 15–16). By their very nature, cultural patterns convey meaning only to those who participate in them; as with other uses of symbols, the meaning we attribute is learned and socially agreed upon, rather than somehow inherent in the behavior. But patterns do not continue to exist by themselves once they are created: they must continually be given new life by passing the meanings down to a new generation. We do this through various sorts of communication.

This has more recently been elaborated upon by Anthony Giddens in his theory of structuration (1984). Giddens forces us to look at change in the social system, where we might otherwise simply assume stability. He stresses the active side of social patterns, rather than the passive side, through his use of the concept *structuration* rather than the more traditional but also less active *structure*. In this, at least, his ideas are compatible with those proposed here.

An important extension to the culture/communication pair is that we must remember there is cultural variability in the ways in which we communicate, verbally as well as nonverbally (Philips, 1976, p. 94). This means that there are no universals of which we can be sure in the study of interaction, and we must continue to pursue all suggested universals of interaction into a variety of cultural settings, in order to determine the extent to which they are culturally bound.

Recognizing the ways in which the concepts of culture and communication are related is more useful than pretending that they have nothing to do with one another. This way the concepts illuminate one another instead of being considered singly, by researchers in separate disciplines.

ARBITRARY

To say that behavior is arbitrary is to suggest that the meaning of a particular behavior is not inherently tied to that behavior. That is, the meaning of each action or word does not have a direct and obvious link to that which it refers or implies. If the connections between the communicative behaviors and the ideas for which they stand were not arbitrary, every action would have a single and obvious meaning built into it and there would be only one interpretation for any interaction. Every language would use the same sounds to describe the noises animals make; every culture would use the same gestures to mean the same things; every gesture would mean the same thing in all contexts. We would immediately understand all of the behavior we observed, without knowledge of the context, or participants, or special concerns of that event. In fact, this is patently false.

The phrase *I don't got no gray* does not immediately convey a single meaning; we must rely on context to provide clues as to what meaning is intended. It could refer to people in their forties saying they had no gray hair, a sales clerk stating that there was no gray cloth available, etc. In fact, this sentence comes from my field notes of a first grade classroom in South Milwaukee, where students were coloring worksheets handed out by the teacher.

Carmen: I don't got no gray
Wendy: What do you do when you don't have a color?
Carmen: Ask
Wendy: Go ask someone
Carmen: I don't know who
Wendy: Go ask Monserrate

She walks over to Monserrate, and stands, without speaking, three feet away from her desk. Monserrate looks up after several minutes go by.

Carmen: Can I borrow gray?
Monserrate: Gimme that gray
Donald: Where?
Monserrate: Right there

Donald hands her the gray crayon near him, Monserrate passes it to Carmen, who uses it right away and returns it to her.

Aside from the fact that the sentence in context now can be understood, there are several other interesting things to notice about this interaction:

1. Carmen stands three feet away from Monserrate when she wants to speak with her, whereas an adult or older child would stand much closer;
2. Carmen doesn't speak, but waits for Monserrate to notice her presence, whereas an adult or older child would generally speak or at least do something to attract attention;
3. The entire conversation is brief, with few explanations: Carmen doesn't explain that she needs a color of crayon that her table doesn't have, Monserrate doesn't explain to Donald the reason she needs the crayon, no one says thanks at any point, or even verbally acknowledges the responses.

It is not only the *use* of particular behaviors which requires some discussion of context before they make sense. Words themselves are arbitrary, although this may at first be difficult to recognize since we take them so much for granted. But if words were not arbitrary, then all languages would have to use the same words for the same objects. Far from this being the case, the word *cat* bears no necessary relation to the animal which it names (to use a famous example). We should never forget that the word *cat* has no whiskers (Bateson, 1972b). In other words, we must remember that there is no *intrinsic* relation between the word we use to designate an object, and the object so designated. Since we are accustomed to having our words accepted generally as supplying meaning this can be a difficult point to grasp, but it is nonetheless an important one. This is the case, not only for words, but for the entire communicative system. It is a social construction, not a natural one, and so there are few natural links between behaviors which can be observed in interaction and the meaning we take from them.

At one point during research in South Milwaukee, I was told that "Spanish has more of a *mean* sound than English. It sounds meaner when they say it." We do not generally recognize that we interpret meaning, not only from words, but from the way in which those words are said. Here, not only one person's way of speaking, but the inflection of an entire

> language, is credited with carrying a particular "meaning." Consider the implications, since the speaker was working in a bilingual school, where the majority of the children, and many of the teachers, spoke Spanish the majority of the time.

The main reason it is important to understand this business of arbitrariness is that what holds true for language, holds true also for other aspects of communication. There is nothing intrinsic about a wink that links it to a conspiracy, although that is one of the meanings we can give it (see Geertz, 1973, pp. 6–7 for a lengthy description of winks and the difference between a wink and a twitch: the movements are identical, but the meanings are not). As Goffman suggests, "an act can, of course, be proper or improper only according to the judgment of a specific social group" (1963, p. 5). An act of behavior has no meaning built into it; the people who use and interpret the act must supply the meaning themselves. This becomes most readily apparent when moving from one culture to another, for then what we normally take for granted is made obvious, by our being confronted by different meanings and behaviors. Thus, the same American who is accused of being pushy in England (for standing too close, among other problems) will be accused of being uninvolved in Argentina (for standing too far away). It is not the distance he is standing from others which conveys the message: it is the relation between the distance he stands and the distance local residents in that context would normally be expected to stand (Hall, 1959).

In fact, it is not only particular discrete behaviors which are arbitrary, but the entire social order. We need social order of some sort but the forms we choose are various. As Goffman argues, "That our form of social organization has any *necessary* features is, I take it, rather questionable" (1977, p. 302; emphasis added). In other words, the shape our interactions take is created by us (or rather, by the group in which we claim membership). Since that shape is significantly different for people of different cultures, it becomes obvious that it does not have to take any one particular form, but changes as people wish it to change.

What our society teaches us is in large part what we use to separate ourselves as a group from other groups. This occurs through a large number of rather small and individually unimportant behaviors. Few of these are critical in and of themselves, but the whole is what helps us to maintain our "group-ness." For example, consider the use of time. We learn that particular activities occur at particular times and begin to think that they must occur at these times, just because we are accustomed to them. If I am accustomed to eating supper at 6:00 p.m., as many Americans are, it is difficult for me to perceive the reasonableness of eating dinner at 8:00 p.m., as many in France think more appropriate. Or, to give another example, we would be much astonished if someone tried to sell Christmas trees in August, or set up a lemonade stand on the sidewalk in December.[7] It is for this reason that Zerubavel suggests:

> a temporal order that is commonly shared by a social group and is unique to it to the extent that it distinguishes and separates group members from "outsiders" contributes to the establishment of intergroup boundaries and constitutes a powerful basis for mechanical solidarity within the group. (1981, p. 67)

The problem of behavior being arbitrarily linked to our interpretations of it is sometimes a difficult concept to understand, but it is nonetheless a critical one. Among other things, it points us toward situations of intercultural interaction as one of the more interesting settings in which to study communication. When we see the misunderstandings that can arise, we are able to recognize more easily the difficulty involved in the understandings we normally take for granted. From the society in which we live come our understandings of how to behave and how to communicate. From other societies come our understandings of how culture-bound and idiosyncratic our behavior and communication really are.

---

[7] Bourdieu (1982, pp. 89–91) makes a similar argument for physical space.

CHAPTER 4
Communication as Behavior in Context

Nothing has meaning except it be contextualized.
—Gregory Bateson (1978, p. 12)

As indicated in Chapter 3, no behavior exists in a vacuum. There is always further behavior surrounding the piece which is of current interest, and, in order for it to be interpreted, all of that surround must be taken into account as well. It would certainly be convenient if we could remove the piece of behavior we wanted to study and analyze it at leisure, especially if this could be done in a laboratory or other setting where there would be no external influences to confuse the matter, but such comfort is not possible. The slice of behavior considered by itself is different than when it is part of a larger whole, and we learn something different as a result if we assume that we can separate a single interaction out from the stream of behavior.

In addition, by moving from the natural context of whatever interaction we are studying into a laboratory, we run into the "fish out of water" problem: it is all very well to study a fish out of water, so long as we remember it does not behave in the same way on land as in the water. If what we are interested in studying is fish *behavior*, the fish out of water problem becomes virtually insurmountable. We can learn fish physiology when the fish is out of water, but not fish behavior. By ignoring the context, and extracting a single act from its normal setting, we destroy the interaction we seek to study. The only solution to studying fish behavior is to study the fish in its proper place, in the water with others of its kind.

This has implications for the choice of research methodologies and research sites. If we want to study social interaction, we must observe people in as close to their normal setting for the behavior under study as possible. Moving strangers into a laboratory, where a camera can be conveniently set up, and requesting that they begin conversations, will generate good data if, and only if, the question we wish to answer is "How do strangers in a research laboratory begin an interaction?" If we wish to know how strangers begin interactions in bars, or on buses, we must seek them out in those contexts. And if we have little interest in strangers, but wish to study intimates, we must observe them, and no substitutes will suffice.

In order to behave acceptably, people need to know, among other things, what is appropriate behavior in what context. Therefore, we all must learn to recognize a given context and to recognize when shifts in context occur. We are expected to display context-appropriate behavior at all times, once we pass the age of reason (for other purposes this has often been defined as traditionally around 7 years of age, but younger children display some context-appropriate behavior, and older children display some context-inappropriate behavior, so this is hardly a figure to be safely assumed). The capacity for monitoring contexts is an essential feature of social competence. William Wentworth has proposed that "context considered as a sociological place is the basic unit of the social order" (1980, p. 103). As such, it is one of the first aspects of communication children begin to learn. From toilet training to school versus home differences, we encourage our children to display an adult sensitivity to context as soon as possible; we are pleased with them when they do and impatient with them when they do not.

> Parents traditionally exchange stories of times when their children unexpectedly display a working knowledge of the influence of a particular context. A friend recently reported to me that her son was labelled a "perfect Montessori child" by his (Montessori) teacher, because he loves to sort and categorize objects, just as they are taught to do in that school. She was quite delighted with the comment, and pleased to pass it on. Parents tell at least as many stories of when their children flaunt the expected contextual influences on behavior, especially behavior that is particularly embarrassing at the time but accepted as funny later. A child who asks questions about sex in grocery stores, or one who gives detailed descriptions of what is occurring while in a public bathroom with others than parents present, are common examples.

Beattie suggests that "If possession of a language is the most essentially human of all attributes, then the *use* of language in its appropriate social context must be the most essentially human of all activities" (1983, p. 1; my emphasis). There has been much research into how children acquire language, and a little into how they learn to use it in its appropriate context. But research on how children learn to communicate differently in a variety of contexts, and how they make the transitions from one to another, is still needed. Since, as Bateson tells us, "contexts are but categories of the mind" (1975, p. 147), children do not come preprogrammed with the knowledge of contextual boundaries, any more than they come having knowledge of a particular language or set of body movements.[1]

Context is not simply a matter of physical setting or particular combinations of individuals. It is more involved than that. Context ultimately is formed of a combination of *what* people generally do and *where* and *when* they do it. Frederick Erickson and Jeffrey Schultz, who have devoted much time to the study of the creation of contexts in educational settings, have suggested that "ultimately, social contexts consist of mutually shared and ratified definitions of situation *and* in the social actions persons take on the basis of those definitions" (1977, p. 6; their emphasis). Their work supports a view combining *place* and *action* as the foundations of context. Geertz argues that "culture is not a power, something to which social events, behaviors, institutions, or processes can be causally attributed; it is a context, something within which they can be intelligibly—that is, thickly—described" (1973, p. 14). This harks back to the discussion in Chapter 3 of the relationship between culture and communication, but here the emphasis is slightly shifted, to permit the relationship between context and communication to come to the fore.

Because communication is context-bound, we must recognize that there is nothing inherently normal, appropriate, or sane in any particular example of behavior. Judgment of normalcy, appropriateness, or sanity can only be made when looking at the wider context. Whether my calling you names is understood as the beginning of a friendly exchange of insults or as the first move in a fight depends upon far more than the choice of words. The ways we know to interpret it are: first, to look at what behavior co-occurs with it (such as tone of voice, movements, synchrony or lack of it); second, to look at what has gone on before, both in words and actions; and third, to look at what occurs after (again, both in words and deeds). As Sherri Cavan points out, "Not infrequently, what would pass for civil inattention in other settings is taken as an invitation for interaction in the bar" (1973, p. 144). It is the context

---

[1] See Bateson and Mead (1942) for an example of visual juxtaposition of images from a variety of contexts for research purposes.

of the behavior that determines how it will be interpreted, not the behavior itself. This cannot be said often enough.

No individual communicative behavior can stand alone; each is only part of what Birdwhistell labels larger *cross-referencing* contexts (1963, p. 136). That is, only when the larger contexts (*patterns* could easily substitute here) are understood with regard to one another do they make sense. Sense comes from understanding how a number of contexts and their behaviors fit together, not from any one behavior, nor even from any one context. The implications for research here are many. Among other things, this implies that extensive knowledge of the group under study is required before any (correct) analysis of behavior can occur. James Fernandez is making this point when he calls the significance of an event "the fruit of participation over the long term in a culture" (1986, p. xi). Traditional methods of documenting small items of behavior from large numbers of people generally will be ineffective if the behavior under study is communication. If use of touch is heavily influenced by context, for example, simply noting how many touches a given person experiences in a given day in order to compare the final number with others, tells us very little.

As Stewart and Philipsen summarize this view, "communication is a process which is situated and situating, is contextualized by and constitutive of society" (1984, p. 178). This helps to bring together ideas from the last several chapters with ideas presented in this one. Through the process of providing a context for interaction, communication creates the group or society in which that interaction can take place. The group is created and maintained in part by having norms of interaction in common, and some of these norms are ideas about what constitutes a context. In a similar vein, Cronen, Pearce, and Harris tell us "An adequate theory of communication must do *more* than acknowledge that the nature of communication depends on the context in which it occurs. An adequate theory must account for the creation of contexts through communication" (1982, p. 64; their emphasis). As a result, when we study context, we must always be willing to reverse the process; it is appropriate to use context to help us understand communication, but we must also use communication to help us understand contexts.

What may be overlooked here is the fact that no one context by itself creates anything; it is the combination of holding a set of possible contexts in common that has the potential for creating a sense of group. Geertz (1973) has referred to the interplay of "an ensemble of texts" which the researcher must study not in their individuality, but in relation to one another. In their research, Cook-

Gumperz and Corsaro found that "specific properties of social context are part of the information children *make note of and utilize* in combination with shared background knowledge (conventional expectations) to create cultural and normative sense throughout the course of interactive episodes" (1976, p. 39; their emphasis). As with children, so with adults.

The obvious question at this point should be: "How do we decide what is sufficient context?" In other words, where do we draw the line? If we no longer assume that crossed arms invariably mean a defensive posture and discouragement of further interaction, as some recent and very popular books have suggested (Nierenberg & Calero, 1981; Fast, 1971), we must first add an understanding of who is crossing the arms and who else is present at the interaction. Then we add the location, the time, and the larger event of which this is but a small part. Then we add the words, other body movements, and positions of the participants, how close they are to one another, whether there is any touch, and who is looking where. We must also add the lighting, the style and relative locations of the furniture, whether there is any music playing, what clothes each is wearing, and what objects they are handling. And the past history: what prior events these people have attended that resemble this one, what they know of the general nature of this sort of event for people like themselves, their prior conversations and knowledge of one another. And the future history: What would be the logical progression of events after this one? What alternatives do they see as open to them? At this point we are coming closer to an approximation of what is necessary to understand what a particular behavior means. This is, after all, exactly what each of us does in real life, when encountering others and needing to interpret their behavior, and thus must be one part of what we do in interpreting what we observe. Unfortunately, it does not lead to the sort of facile interpretation of behavior that the buyers of these popular books are seeking. But it does lead to more nearly correct interpretations.

One particularly critical aspect of context is time. Zerubavel concludes that "the meaning of social acts and situations is largely dependent on their temporal context" (1981, p. 100). He outlines four major dimensions of the temporal profile of any event, that is, four things related to issues of time that need to be taken into account. First is the sequential structure of an event, or the order in which things happen. Second is the duration of an event, how long it lasts, especially when compared to norms for that event (is this example longer than might reasonably have been expected? shorter?). Third is the temporal location, or when an event takes place (on what day, week, or year?). Fourth is the rate of recurrence, or how often events of this sort generally occur (Zerubavel, 1981, p. 1). By taking all of these facts into account, we learn an important part of what we need to know about the context of any particular behavior.[2]

In describing "the good old days," an informant in East Baltimore told me about the relative influence of two different contexts on the same participants. The same people who dance together in one context, the pavilion, fight together in another, the street. The context made all the difference as to appropriate behavior. This was sufficiently well understood by all concerned that the adults did not interfere unless they had reason to believe that there was an unusually large fight coming. There is no absolute connection between ownership of brass knuckles and fighting, since the context determined when and whether the owners of the brass knuckles began to fight. My informant said:

The pavilion, which was a large sort of open air thing with windows all around it, and a stage, and a place for music, was a dance center. And we used to check the kids in, as they came in, and we used to check their brass knuckles quite—I mean this was automatic. You took their coat, their hat, and their brass knuckles as they came in, and when they left you gave them their coat, their hat, and their brass knuckles and they went out and beat each other up out on the brick pavement on the way outside. And if you had taken in a great many brass knuckles in the course of an evening, you tried to get a call in to the Park Police before you gave them back out at the end of the evening.

What is amazing in this story is that the same participants were able so clearly to separate their actions by a combination of time and location: dance in the pavilion early in the evening, but fight in the street later in the evening. It would have been as unlikely to see a fight *before* the dance as *in* the pavilion.

One question which might be asked is whether there is anything that does not fit into a larger context. Williams tells us that "Nothing, except the universe, perhaps, lacks relationships to larger, comprising structures" (1981, p. 42). I especially like the qualification

---

[2] See Hall (1984) and Bruneau (1979) for other discussions of the role of time in organizing social life.

perhaps when even the universe is the topic. I suspect that Williams is right, for, once the notion of context is understood, it becomes second nature to look for the wider context of every situation. Nothing can be viewed as separate and complete any more; there is *always* more information that is a necessary prerequisite to understanding any particular example of interaction. The philosopher Alfred North Whitehead has often been quoted for saying "There is no [independent] mode of existence. Every entity is only to be understood in terms of the way in which it is interwoven with the rest of the universe" (as cited in Powers, 1985, p. 257). The problem becomes not whether to draw the line, but at what point.

Thus, the definition of *context* evolves from simply "the immediate situation in which a particular piece of behavior occurs," to the more elaborate *anything and everything which needs to be taken into account in order to understand a particular piece of behavior.* Context is thus everything related to a given behavior, except the behavior itself. The problem is to consciously *not* limit the boundaries too quickly or too arbitrarily. That is, we cannot decide beforehand that every behavior will be understood if exactly 2 minutes of the preceding interaction are taken into account. This sort of context-dependent definition of how much context to take into account does not make the researcher's life any easier, certainly, but it can only make the resulting conclusions more adequate. In the end, only familiarity with the context in question will tell a researcher what needs to be taken into account.

This is one reason why a stimulus–response model of communication is inadequate. Rather than being two separate events, stimulus and response "define each other, create each other, and indeed are part of the same process" (Perinbanayagam, 1958, p. 18). No one participant in an interaction creates the meaning of the event; that is a joint creation of all of the participants, quite possibly including even some who are not physically present. Interaction patterns established with parents may be represented through interactions with spouses years later, and the physical presence of the parents is very nearly irrelevant (so current understandings of alcohol- or spouse-abuse tell us, although there are obviously many other significant influences as well).

One whose work has stressed the central importance of context is Aaron Cicourel. He points out that "Social settings create informational resources necessary for logical and practical inferences" (1978, p. 34; see also Cicourel, 1981). Participants need to make use of tacit knowledge about settings and their prior experience with them in order to make sense of interaction. This knowledge is likely to be nonverbal as well as verbal, and therefore it is difficult for us to tell others even a small part of the information about context that we know and take for granted.

In conversation, much of what is spoken is fragmentary, yet we understand it as coherent. This is because we impose sense on those fragments we hear. As novelist Richard Powers so clearly puts it:

> When I mention Nijinsky, you know exactly who I mean, smoothing out the snags between the dexterous faun and the aging, confined lunatic. In cementing a familiar name to an adjective phrase, I am simply the amiable volunteer from the audience, pouring one colorless liquid into another. My conversant is the magician, causing the resultant fluid to shine with the colors of the rainbow. (1985, p. 40)

More than half the work in a conversation must be done by the listener if the result is to be comprehension of what a speaker says; in the end both must work hard to ensure that comprehension will occur.

For Beattie, as for others, "Conversation is without doubt the foundation stone of the social world—human beings learn to talk *in* it, find a mate *with* it, are socialized *through* it, rise in the social hierarchy as a result *of* it, and, it is suggested, may even develop mental illness *because* of it" (1983, p. 2; his emphasis). Conversation, in this view, is far more powerful than we generally assume. The only surprise is the extent to which we ignore its capabilities, presumably due to our familiarity with them. (The central importance of language to the construction of social reality has been stressed in Chapter 1, and the idea should not require much more than invocation here.)

Communication can be viewed as an uninterrupted sequence of contexts, each of which helps to form and inform the others, just as each helps to shape the behavior occurring within it. "To act or be one end of a pattern of interaction is to propose the other end. A *context* is set for a certain class of response" (Bateson, 1972c, p. 275; his emphasis). In other words, the context helps to shape the event, and then the event helps to shape our understanding of the context. Beth Haslett follows Bateson in her conclusion that "contextual influences are bi-directional: the context shapes the interaction that occurs within it, yet may itself be transformed by that interaction" (1987, p. 109).

At one point, Bateson suggested that context be understood as a term for "all those events which tell the organism among what *set* of alternatives he must make his next choice" (1972c, p. 289; his emphasis). That is, no context restricts behavior completely, permitting only a single behavior. Rather, different contexts carry with them a set of choices, participants choosing their behaviors from that set. Of course, each choice both limits future choices and introduces new possibilities. Notice the close connection here between Bateson's discussion of context and Ervin-Tripp's discussion of rules of alternation and co-occurrence (explained in Chapter 2). It is also possible to draw a clear connection between the idea of pattern and that of context. Bateson did so when he suggested that one definition of context is "pattern through time" (1978a, p. 11). In other words, *the consistencies we come to label as a particular context are a pattern.*

Although one of the steps in learning to communicate is learning to identify contexts, so that we will be able to display context-appropriate behavior, no two contexts are ever quite the same. Therefore we need to learn to recognize the critical, identifying factors across contexts. At the same time, contexts are not rigid, but flexible, available for participants to manipulate as they wish. This means that if the participants in a classroom so desire, they can move outside and have class under a tree. So long as all members of the group are in agreement that what is occurring is still a class, and one of a set of classes within a particular larger set, it will be so. But it is much easier to break frame and destroy the context if all the factors are not what might be expected; thus, it is easy to lose the attention of a class when outside on a warm spring day.

In the fourth grade classroom in South Milwaukee, the students are preparing an art project.

Michael: Miss R____, can we start?
Teacher: Don't ask me when you should start. I don't know when you're ready. When you're ready, you should start.

Here one of the participants is reluctant to assume responsibility for changing the definition of context from "preparation for art project" to "art project in process." Some teachers reserve for themselves the right to make such determinations, but in this example the teacher returns the responsibility back to the student.

Understanding that communication is context-bound leads to three important conclusions: the first is that meaning does not reside in bits of behavior, but rather in the entire interaction; the second is that there is a hierarchy or series of levels of contexts, each fitted within the others, that aid in the study of interaction; and the third is that communication often is punctuated (or divided up) by different participants in very different ways.

MEANING

No piece of behavior has meaning in and of itself. The phrase *piece of behavior* is used on purpose here, to indicate that each example of behavior should be viewed as a fragment, as but one part of a larger whole, as a puzzle piece is but part of the whole puzzle, having little meaning in itself but conveying much once it is viewed in its proper place in the completed puzzle. If we want to discuss the social meaning, the appropriateness, or the consequences of a particular behavior, then we must know the social context in which that behavior has occurred. Meaning does not reside in the symbols, words, or actions of which we make use, but rather in what happens when particular pieces of behavior are exhibited. What do other people do in response, and what do they stop doing? Understanding social meaning requires that we know much more than just whether or not a particular piece of behavior has been exhibited, although that is a good starting point.

Any communicative act can be interpreted in more than one way. Not even dictionaries are so rigid as to assign only a single meaning to a given symbol. As with dictionaries, so even more in everyday interactional life. There always is a set of meanings, and the choice of which is correct depends upon what other behaviors are displayed at the same time. In addition, understanding any one piece of behavior requires that participants know what else has occurred, not just concurrent with it, but immediately before and after as well. This is why we say of a joke that falls flat when retold, "I guess you just had to be there." The same participants do not act in exactly the same ways in different situations, and different participants do not respond in the same way to the same "stimulus." A joke taken out of a sequence of jokes does not have the laughter from previous jokes to support it.

Ragnar Rommetveit provides an excellent analysis of the various twists and turns meaning can take, once all possibilities are considered. His example of possible interpretations of a man mowing his lawn includes such assumptions as: He was doing it to make the lawn neat, to get away from his wife, to annoy his neighbors. These differing assumptions are shown to lead to disparate conclusions. On the one hand, mowing the lawn becomes a demonstration of leading the good life; on the other, it becomes a demonstration of leading a bad life (1981, p 155).

There is no behavior which is appropriate in all situations. Consider the difference between undressing to a bathing suit on the beach, a perfectly appropriate and common action, and undressing to a bathing suit on the street, a bizarre and unusual occurrence which would require substantial response from onlookers (Ruesch & Kees, 1972, p. 72). Consider further the difference between the American method of having a bathing suit on underneath regular clothing, and undressing to it, as opposed to the French method of holding a towel up as an impromptu dressing room on the beach while changing into a bathing suit inside it. Doing either in the wrong country will alarm observers.

We are taught that there are environments and objects, or contexts and behaviors. But when we separate the two, we lose the meaning, for any communicative act taken out of its wider context or environment is senseless. It may help to think of meaning as the contribution of a piece of behavior to the context. Meaning derives from a variety of elements in a scene. At the very least, this must include participants, setting, and type of event. What else needs to be taken into account will vary. Mead tells us that "the nature of meaning is thus found to be implicit in the structure of the social act" and implies that we must look to the social process of experience to discuss meaning (1974, pp. 81–82).

It is impossible to stress sufficiently that meaning does not lie in the item itself but in the interdependent system in which it occurs. The phenomena we study "take their meaning as much from their contexts as they do from themselves" (Lincoln & Guba, 1985, p. 189). The meanings we seek lie not in the item itself (whether a word, object or act) but rather "in connections that can only gradually be discerned" (Hymes, 1980, p. 94). The complexity of interaction resides in implicit meanings that must be discovered, rather than in explicit meanings that lie on the surface for anyone to pick up.

Meaning comes from a variety of factors in the environment; gender, age, ethnicity, and social class are part of what supplies meaning to behavior. We take for granted our knowledge of the ways in which gender, age, ethnicity, and class are usually marked, but that does not mean we can ignore them in our analysis of interaction. We must first make them part of our conscious knowledge, and second, systematically analyze them to see how they function in interaction.

> There is a widely publicized photograph of then-president Jimmy Carter talking with Anwar Sadat during the Egypt-Israeli negotiations, and holding hands with him. This was likely to shock many American newspaper readers, who would be expected to interpret it the way it would be understood if two American adult males were holding hands. Many of the newspapers that printed the photograph, however, also printed a comment stating that holding hands is a sign of mutual respect and friendship in Arab cultures, and that it was a sign the peace talks were going well. Presumably, this aided those readers who looked past the image to the explanation to understand what they were observing in a new way. Obviously, the State Department had done its work in training Carter so that he would understand the gesture's meaning in a new context, and respond appropriately.

One of the problems in accepting the fact that meaning lies, not just in the behavior, but in the context in which it occurs, is that context is actually different for every one of the participants present. They can only use the knowledge of the world that they individually possess in the attempt to make sense of what the world presents to them; they do not share all of their knowledge of the world with each other, and so it cannot be assumed that they share all of their understandings about interaction.[3] Only to whatever extent participants share a joint history, will they share interpretations of a particular communicative act or event. The more they correctly assume they have in common, the more readily they will interpret each other's actions in a similar manner. Even when information is shared, however, each participant in an interaction has a particular viewpoint: his or hers is the center of the universe, and it is the remainder that is background, never one's own self.[4]

> One of the first things I did in each classroom in South

---

[3] See Grimshaw (1980) for detailed discussion of misunderstandings.
[4] See Bourdieu's comments on point of view (1982, p. 96; 1987).

Milwaukee was to draw a diagram of the students' desks, labelled with their names, as an aid to recognizing the cast of players. At lunch in the first grade classroom the first day I was present, a group of students came over, saw the diagram, and began finding their names on my picture. One said, "Where's your name?" and was not satisfied until I included a sketch of the chair by the bookcase where I was sitting, labelled with my name. It had not occurred to me that I needed to be included: after all, I knew where I was sitting, and knew my name. But to her, my presence in the classroom was the newest, most noteworthy thing that had occurred that day, and it was logical to include me. Her point of view was different from mine, and resulted in a different diagram of the classroom.

One way of visualizing meaning is to think in terms of a set of concentric circles surrounding the piece of behavior in question. First, there is a small circle of intimates who know exactly what is intended with very little in the way of cues, because extensive shared knowledge can be drawn upon for contextualization. Then, there is a larger circle of friends and acquaintances who share enough past history that they will know enough to make partial sense of behavior, but who need more information supplied before they can make sense of what occurs as intimates would. Thirdly, there is the general public, those who have enough of the larger culture in common to understand if sufficient cues are supplied, but who need more cues than friends would. And lastly, there are people from other cultures, who need an astonishing amount of material supplied before they can make sense of any interaction.

Edward Hall has suggested that we can describe all cultures as being high or low context cultures. By this he means the extent to which interpreting the meanings of a message depends on the overt explanations given (*transmitted information*) which would imply a low context culture, versus explanations assumed (*stored information*) which would imply a high context culture (1984, p. 61). He is careful to stress that no value judgments should be applied; rather, these are simply the different ways of sharing meaning available for use by different groups of people around the world. Basil Bernstein (1961, 1971) was interested in similar distinctions in his studies of elaborated (low context) versus restricted (high context) linguistic codes in England.

When Mary Douglas says, "In the end, all meanings are social meanings" (1975, p. 8), this has profound implications for the study of communication. We must be willing to discover the meanings other people have for their behavior, rather than imposing upon them the meanings their behavior has for us. This is important for us as members of a culture, but it is critical for us as researchers.

In a class on semiotics, I used a necklace I happened to have on that day for the example of how meanings were not inherent in the object, but placed there by the people who used them. I explained the meanings the necklace had for me and my family, meanings that my students could not possibly know (there was a long story about exchanging the necklace for another my sister had, along with the fact that both had been given to us by our grandmother). They then joined the group of those who understood some of the meanings I drew on when looking at the necklace.

One of the students in the class then took this a step further. When creating a poster for a department picnic at the end of the semester, she included caricatures of each of the students, and of me as well, since our class was sponsoring it. In the picture, I am wearing the necklace discussed in class that day. Only the students in the class knew why that was appropriate. It had come to represent their new knowledge of symbols, in addition to the meanings it initially held for me.

Meaning is not just taken from the combination of behavior and its context; it is also taken from the combination of all the behavior manifested within a particular context. We combine everything we see and hear, and take sense from the whole rather than from the sum of the parts (Sanders, 1983, p. 75). We do this automatically and forget that we do it even as it occurs, but we notice what we miss if we for some reason are presented only part of the information we usually possess. (Talking on the telephone is one example of a context in which we notice that we are missing movements, and often will misunderstand people who we understand if we can we see them. Exchanging mail is even more difficult, since not only is sight lacking, but hearing as well. Correspondence can thus lead to greater misunderstandings than other forms of communication, because so much is missing from the usual stream of behavior; only the words are present, with neither intonation nor movements to qualify them.)

One of the interesting facts about meaning is that it changes often and easily. Participants jointly construct meaning; therefore they can *reconstruct* it as well. They can change the meaning they started out with during the course of an interaction, or even at a later time, if they so desire. It is surprisingly easy for any member of an interaction to change or destroy the cultural meaning of any event, since "all *social* forms of communication require a shared or coordinate cultural logic" (Harris, 1982, p. 21; her emphasis).

> In the first grade South Milwaukee classroom, Michael's crayons fall out of his cubby and spill over the floor. He says "Who did that?" and does not pick them up. Esmerelda comes over and picks them up for him. He has redefined the event, and by so doing changed it from an event he caused to an event someone else caused. By picking up the crayons, Esmerelda has not only permitted him to redefine the event for himself, but has ratified that redefinition. What remains unclear to me is whether or not she had observed him knock the crayons out of the desk.

Researchers have spent much time studying the influence of context on language behavior specifically. There are distinct varieties of a language used in different contexts, called *registers*. Registers are particular combinations of vocabulary, syntax, semantics, and paralanguage which are linked to specific contexts, holding specific meaning for participants (Montgomery, 1986; Halliday, 1978). Frow (1980) has recommended classifying registers into three types: those where the text itself is the most significant (examples would be all the languages of science or technical analysis, political discourse, sports commentary); those where status and role have the greatest importance (gossip, prayer, conversation); and those where the choice of symbolic mode and rhetorical channel adopted have a significant function (sacred or scriptural discourse, impersonation, jokes). Children must learn to distinguish between registers at an early age, but we give them plenty of practice through the use of a register all their own, baby talk (Ferguson, 1964).

> The third grade teacher in a bilingual South Milwaukee school, but a monolingual classroom, said in an interview: "I just won't use Spanish. If I have to go down to teach in Mexico, then I will speak the language. But this is my own country and I speak English." In fact, she occasionally used some Spanish words in joking fashion on several occasions. One time, the text her students were using included a story with the word *serape* in it. The teacher started a class discussion about the use of a serape, in the course of which one student

(Dawn, who is Puerto Rican) says it is on the *burro* in the picture (using Spanish pronunciation). Immediately following this discussion, the teacher told Michelle not to miss any more school, using the phrase *it is impossible* (said with her version of a Spanish pronunciation). Dawn corrected her pronunciation softly, smiled to herself, looked up, caught my eye on her, and grinned. Several days later, a former student, now in the fifth grade, came to the door to get the attendance folder in the morning. The teacher told him to wait *un momento* and went to get it for him. Conclusion: the only questions that get answered are those we ask. I had asked whether the teacher used Spanish, and she assumed I meant whole sentences for extended periods of time. What I had really intended to ask was whether or not she used *any* Spanish in her classroom, since it was a monolingual room within a bilingual setting. In this context, the use of even a few words of Spanish counted.

Conversation analysts have shown that, although the discourse *tasks* are universal (participants in a conversation need to do the same sort of work: decide how to identify the person who will speak, so that only one person is speaking at a time, how to start the conversation, and how to end it, etc.), their *realization* in any given case is specific to the culture or smaller group involved (Gumperz, 1982b, p. 208). This means that they use conventions that have been previously established in order to achieve the necessary tasks; it also means that, although the tasks are universal, there is no reason for the particular methods chosen to achieve those tasks to be universal, and in fact they are not.

John Gumperz uses the phrase *contextualization cues* to refer to what is being described here: information supplied during interaction which helps the participants understand both the unspoken assumptions and appropriate interpretations of what is said (1982b, pp. 130–152). As with other parts of communication patterns described in Chapter 2, contextualization cues are normally used and understood out-of-awareness. It is rare for anyone except those training young children to have to spend time describing what is intended by such cues. It is not only uncommon, but often actually difficult, to spend time talking about the contextualization cues we have used, because we generally devote so little conscious thought to their use.

Sometimes, contextualization cues are related to prior joint experience of the participants, but other times they draw on knowledge of the culture in general. In the South Milwaukee first grade classroom, the first day I was present, 6-year-old Mark and I had the following conversation:

Mark: Can I ask you something?
Wendy: (nod)
Mark: Wendy's from a cartoon too?
Wendy: Yes
Mark: Bye (walks away)

Understanding this exchange depends upon knowledge of a particular cartoon show that children watch, "Casper the Friendly Ghost," in which one of the characters is named Wendy. There is little in the explicit conversation that would tell me what Mark was talking about, if I had not been familiar with the cartoon from prior experience.

When contextualization cues are understood properly, there is little need to discuss them. In fact, their value lies in the fact that they permit interaction to occur with a minimum of interruption devoted to clarifying methods of communication. It is when contextualization cues are misunderstood or ignored that they become a topic for discussion. It is the genius of Gumperz' work, and the work of his students and colleagues, that he and they have been able to point to particular contextualization cues which cause critical misunderstandings between participants in an interaction who have differing backgrounds and assumptions, and who therefore would normally use different cues. Participants can only interpret the cues they are presented with as they would intend them if they had used them, and, since contextualization cues are not normally discussed openly, it is often difficult to bring the misunderstanding out into the open until a major problem has already developed.

As Gumperz has pointed out, knowledge of conventional forms of communication, such as contextualization cues, is necessary for effective participation in a variety of contexts of interaction. However, this sort of knowledge is not what is normally taught in language classes, and it can be difficult for speakers of a second language to acquire. Long term personal relationships depend upon holding similar knowledge of communicational patterns in common, but someone who has not yet learned those patterns will have trouble establishing the very relationships that would permit their acquisition. This is the dilemma all second-language learners face; few people other than mothers or grade school teachers will permit

continued mistakes, despite the fact that it is impossible to learn the appropriate use of a language without someone willing to stand in that role. "The ability to get things done in face to face public settings is often a matter of shared background" (Gumperz, 1982a, p. 210), and this can be understood to mean that even the most basic tasks cannot be completed if the background is not shared.[5]

Conversation analysis has gone to great lengths to demonstrate that meanings are not absolute, created by either a single participant in an interaction or existing in an already frozen form all must follow. Rather, they are a topic for negotiation between participants. We can at any point in a conversation change the meaning of what has occurred, so long as we all agree to do so. All it takes is further negotiation. There is no meaning to a single utterance until the complete interaction is known, for it is only created through that interaction. For this reason, Linde (1981) argues for taking the complete discourse as our unit of study rather than the more common unit of a single sentence or utterance.[6]

Even something which we "know" has its own built-in meaning, such as a photograph, should be viewed as only one part of a larger event. Paul Byers, who has spent much time using photographs, suggests that we consider photographs as containing information but not meaning. That is, they record objects and minimal context, but meaning is something attributed by the participants, and, as such, it cannot be recorded on film. Instead, we impose the meaning on the photograph, based on a combination of the information it gives us and our past experience and expectations (Byers, 1966). John Berger is in agreement with this conception of photography when he suggests: "photographs are not, as is often assumed, a mechanical record. Every time we look at a photograph, we are aware, however slightly, of the photographer selecting that sight from an infinity of other possible sights" (1973, p. 10). It can thus be easy to "prove" that an accident was "caused" by either of two parties, depending on careful choice of photographs taken by the same photographer present at the event (as demonstrated by novelist Jerzi Kosinski, who has one of the characters in a novel take photographs of a car crash and distribute them unevenly to the different parties involved, giving each sufficient material for a court case against the other, 1975, p. 207). We are able to influence

---

[5] What Gumperz calls *contextualization cues*, Erickson and Schultz (1982, p. 71) describe as *telling the context.*

[6] See Hopper, Koch, and Mandelbaum (1986), or Sigman, Sullivan, and Wendell (1987), for discussion of methods in conversation analysis.

the interpretations others take away from an event, since meaning is negotiated, and not a given, in social interaction.

HIERARCHY

Communication does not occur at just one level; there is a hierarchy of levels through which it can be approached. "Human acts are imbedded in a hierarchy of contexts such that each frames and thereby influences the meanings that arise within it" (Barnlund, 1981, p. 108). That is, it is inappropriate to conceive of a single behavior and its immediate context as complete, any more than we could view the behavior in and of itself as complete. We need to recognize that contexts can be set one into the next, like the Russian dolls each of which opens to reveal a smaller doll inside. A single level, then, is a moment of organization in a hierarchical arrangement.

There is no one division of the world which is appropriate to all situations. There are, instead, various systems available for dividing up the world of experience into manageable pieces. One of the most useful is that proposed by Dell Hymes (1972), who suggested a series of four levels: domain, situation, event, and act. A *domain* is the general context in which communication occurs, most often limited to a single physical setting. It might include such examples as school, church, the doctor's office, or a grocery store. A *situation* is an activity which occurs within a particular domain, and there are many situations which can occur in each domain. A situation has a single purpose, topic, group of participants, and lasts a specific amount of time. Examples would include show and tell at school, community announcements in church, a physical exam in the doctor's office, or buying the week's groceries at the store. An *event* is a single interaction within a situation, and there are a series of events in most situations. Examples would include Johnny's turtle as one part of show and tell, an announcement of next Wednesday night's bingo game in church, being given a shot as part of a physical exam, or deciding whether or not to buy candy at the store. And an *act* is the minimal unit within an event, a single utterance or movement. When Johnny holds up the turtle for all to see, and one of the children screams because it moves and is alive, those are two acts within the larger event.

It is helpful to think of acts as nested within events, and events as nested within situations. That is to say, a number of acts constitute an event, a number of events constitute a situation, and a number

Figure 4.1. Levels of Context

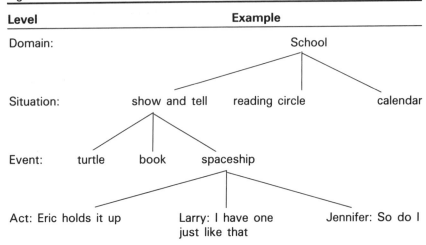

Level	Example

of situations occur within a single domain. The examples presented above can easily be drawn to help make the point of nesting more obvious (see Figure 4.1).

One of the important points to note is that, in a hierarchy, different levels do not "cause" each other; they are relaed to each other as constituents or as superordinate categories. Thus, the levels cannot exist without each other. An act takes on meaning in relation to the event of which it is part, as well as sequentially in relation to the other acts that precede or follow it.

> When one of the South Milwaukee first grade students was in the hospital having her appendix taken out, the teacher had the other students make cards for her. Out of the scraps left over from the card she had just completed, Monserrate made a crown for Michael and gave it to him. When Monserrate made a card, that was a specific communication act. When Michael made a card, that was another act. Both of these acts occurred as part of the larger communication event of "making cards for an absent student." As well, both were part of the larger situation of "first grade classroom," and the domain, "school." When Monserrate made the crown, that was a separate activity from the one the teacher instigated, making cards. In this case both occurred as part of the same event, "making cards for an absent student," and, as such, her deviation from instructions was just the sort of behavior the teacher is likely

to stop (in this case, the teacher was busy and did not seem to notice, but, in other examples, similar crossing of boundaries was not permitted). One of the rules teachers explicitly state to their students is that only certain acts are permitted to occur within certain events. (The only question is which teachers permit which acts.) When students have been told to work on math problems, they are not allowed to draw pictures; when they have been told to make cards they are not to make crowns. Among the most important of the rules children have to learn is to "Be Appropriate"; their problem is to learn what constitutes appropriate behavior in the contexts they will encounter.

As with the rules of alternation and co-occurrence, these levels are intended to be extremely abstract concepts readily applied to a large number of different examples of behavior. Acts and events especially, but also situations, may be defined in different ways by different participants, and, once established, the boundaries between them are not permanent but must be reestablished each time. (Domains are usually less subject to individual differences.) Only the fact that there will still be a series of related contexts progressing in size remains constant, not the exact boundaries between specific acts or events. Participants generally have an idea of what acts make up an event and what events occur in what situations, but it is the analyst who is most concerned with these categories.

Behavior contributes to each level simultaneously. That is, the act (holding up the turtle), is one part of an event (Johnny bringing in a turtle to show and tell), which is one part of the entire situation (show and tell) as well as one possible occurrence in this domain (school). The fact that a given act contributes to the event in no way prevents it from being an act in and of itself, nor from contributing as well to the entire situation, and to our understanding of that domain. What we tend to remember are particular events, but, if questioned, we can usually describe the larger situation of which they were part, and the smaller acts which occurred. We do not normally discuss the larger domain, but only because we take it so much for granted. At the same time, it is our experience with past events and situations, along with the particular acts occurring this time, that together make up our understanding of what the situation or domain is. They are more abstract than the individual acts, but they are no less important.

Sometimes the transitions between acts or between events is clearly marked, and sometimes there is considerable overlap. Part of this is that all of the participants may not make the transition at the same moment. Some people are more rigid than others about everyone crossing an act or event boundary at the same time. To a large extent, grade school teachers have the responsibility of training children to recognize the importance of respecting such boundaries.

In the South Milwaukee third grade classroom, the teacher was quite specific about crossing boundaries, especially about crossing the boundary between domains (home and school, in this example, where students use a specific ritual to mark the beginning of their day together as a class).

Teacher: Good morning, everybody.
Class   Good Morning, Miss S_____.

Students say pledge of allegiance, and the teacher takes attendance.

But in the fourth grade classroom, there was often no beginning marker at all for events, and sometimes there was no marker at even such major boundaries as the beginning of the school day. For example, the teacher started class one day with a discussion of the *Field Guide to Birds*, then asked someone to turn on the lights, then students stood and sang the pledge of allegiance. On other days different acts occurred, in different orders.

What follows is a typical example of overlapping events in the fourth grade room. The teacher began giving dictation. In the middle, she stopped to ask if Michelle had taken attendance, Kandi left to get milk, Eric called for those who were staying for lunch to pay him for it, and some discussion of the content of one of the dictation sentences occurred.

Teacher: Yesterday morning we had our Valentine's day party.
Lisa: Yesterday morning?
Teacher: Yes.

After four sentences were given, they were checked and various exercises were completed (underline all the words that begin with capital letters, etc.), before the remainder of the sentences were given. Some students were permitted to take dictation at a different time, if their alternate activities interfered sufficiently.

Teacher: Linda, are you taking the test later?

[she had been cleaning up an art project she started]

Linda: Yes.
Teacher: Oh, so the secretary will give the test later to Eric and Linda.

This method works within a particular context, where all the participants have the opportunity to become accustomed to what overlaps are permitted. But the day after this example, the teacher was absent, and there was a substitute teacher. As she reviewed the schedule for the day, prepared by the regular teacher, Eric was taking lunch money, which led to a heated discussion.

Teacher: Eric, are you supposed to be taking lunch money while I'm explaining, or am I supposed to wait for you?
Eric: Both at once.

[The teacher was dubious, and expressed her disbelief. Other students confirmed that Eric was telling the truth.]

Teacher: Let Eric do his job and let's see if we can listen to Mrs. B____ (herself).

Other students were walking around, doing the things they usually were responsible for, and would not stop when she asked them to sit down. She grew increasingly anxious about their behavior, and kept requesting them to sit still and be silent. She specifically requested that the "class secretary," sitting next to the teacher's desk at the front of the room (assigned to run interference for the teacher), take her own seat. The class called out that she was to stay there. The teacher told her not to help other students, nor talk to them while she was talking, but again the class called out that she was to do so. The teacher said: "It's not polite for two people to talk at once" and required her to take her seat. This sort of extended discussion of what constituted appropriate overlapping behaviors rarely occurred when the regular teacher was present.

There are other methods for dividing up experience.[7] One that is significantly different, yet which meshes nicely with Hymes' model, has been proposed by Erving Goffman, who suggests a division between two types of situations: social gatherings and social occasions. A *social gathering* is "any set of two or more individuals whose members include all and only those who are at the moment in one another's immediate presence" (1963, p. 18). Notice that this definition includes what occurs when two or more people are in one another's immediate presence, *even if they are not necessarily doing anything to indicate that they are aware of each other.* People waiting in line together at a bank, or everyone on a particular plane, generally have not arranged to all be in that place at the same time, although they are all there for the same basic purpose. A movie such as *Murder on the Orient Express* relies successfully upon our assumption that the people on the train would not have arranged to all be on that train at that time, when in fact they have. Gatherings are unfocused, or diffuse, meaning they have no single center of action, no main protagonist to watch. They are "loose" arrangements of individuals, each with his or her own trajectory to consider.

A *social occasion,* on the other hand, is best described as focused. It is more organized, in the sense that it involves participants who are deliberately present in the location to interact with one another. These participants share a common focus, and contribute their behavior vis-a-vis each other with this focus in mind. In an occasion there are still individuals with their own purposes to be considered, but in this case the stress is not on the individuals but on the event as a whole. Examples of occasions could include a graduation party or a group of terrorists hijacking a plane. Occasions often severely proscribe possible behavior; they have what Barker calls a "standing behavior pattern" (as cited in Goffman 1963, p. 18), and what Scheflen calls a "behavioral program" (1964). Occasions generally have names, which is related to the fact that you can be invited to many of them, whereas if gatherings have names they are likely to be long descriptive ones, invented by the researcher.

The boundary line between gatherings and occasions can be extremely fluid. For example, if the passengers on the plane involved in a gathering were taken hostage by the terrorists who want to

---

[7] Frentz and Farrell (1976) present a parallel three-fold division, similar to that provided by Hymes (they use the labels context, episodes, and symbolic acts). Pearce and Cronen (1980) provide a more complex version, with six levels (content, speech acts, contracts, episodes, life-scripts, archetypes), but it seems a pretty close parallel to the one presented here so far.

establish an occasion, they will find themselves moving from a gathering (for which we really have no name, beyond "taking a flight from point x to point z") to an occasion ("a hijacking"), through no effort of their own.

In this case the different words for contexts can be visualized as dividing up the world horizontally, rather than vertically (see Figure 4.2).

Goffman also saw the need to study larger or smaller stretches of interaction and apply different analytic terms to each. He used the phrase *face engagements* to loosely parallel Hymes' *event,* but did not feel the need to draw finer distinctions than this. Despite the fact that they are not exactly parallel to either acts or events, they can be seen as interchangeable with either, as necessity requires. They fulfill the same role of being a name for a smaller piece of behavior. Face engagements can appear as part of either gatherings or occasions.

Rather than assume the different organizations of behavior suggested by different authors are mutually exclusive, it is help to try to combine them so as to benefit as much as possible from the insights of many authors. There is no reason why we cannot look at gatherings and see them as composed of events, for example, if that seems productive.

PUNCTUATED

The concept of *punctuation* is adapted from grammar, and means essentially the same thing when applied to behavior that it does

Figure 4.2. Hierarchies

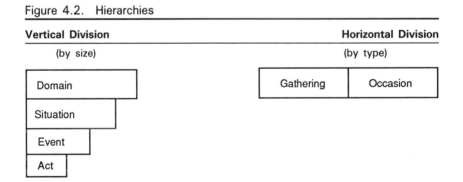

Vertical Division	Horizontal Division
(by size)	(by type)

when applied to conventions of writing. Just as a paragraph is not presented to us in the form of a continuous listing of letters without spaces or indications of sentences, so behavior is not presented to us in a single monolithic whole. It would be almost impossible to react to the world if that were the case. Instead, we divide behavior into chunks to better manage it. The ways in which we divide up the world are referred to as *punctuation.* In other words, punctuation is how the multichannel continuous stream is decomposed into *meaningful* pieces. I say that the pieces must be meaningful because it is not the case that just any division of behavior will be accepted. In English, the word *replay* is made up of the pieces *re* and *play,* not *re,* and *pl* and *ay.* An example of this is language learning, where the first problem in learning a second language is to learn how to divide the stream of talk into meaningful elements (words).

As Lawrence Frank pointed out more than 50 years ago, "each object or occurrence is a consequent or an antecedent in a sequence of events" (1926, p. 332). That is, every utterance and every action comes before others and can thus be viewed as an antecedent—"that which came before," a cause—some of the time. Yet every object and every action comes after some things and can thus be viewed as a consequent—"that which comes after," an effect—at other times. What is important to stress is that every object and every action is *both an antecedent and a consequent at the same time,* not just in one case, but in many. Dean Barnlund has phrased it differently, saying that "every act is both prologue and epilogue" (1981, p. 96), but his concept is essentially the same as Frank's.[8] We must not fail to take into account the simultaneous, multiple roles that every act or utterance plays, and we cannot assume others divide events into acts in the same way we divide them.

> In the South Milwaukee grade school, there were significant differences in the way transitions from one activity to another occurred between the third and fourth grade classrooms. In the third grade, students made their own transitions, within a specific set of guidelines set down by the teacher. They knew what the assignments for the day were, and knew that any work left unfinished at the end of the day was to be brought home as homework, and then turned in the next morning. Some activities included the entire class (movies, snack, trips to the bathroom), and the teacher made a verbal transition to ensure that everyone noticed the shift. Other activities included

---

[8] Hawes provides a slightly different wording (1973, pp. 14–15).

specific subsets of the class, such as reading groups or individual visits to the psychologist, and for these the students usually knew what time they were scheduled to be where, and took responsibility for leaving on time themselves. The class as a whole tended to know where any one child was at the moment, so that, if the teacher queried them, someone would generally be able to tell her where an absent child could be found. In between all of the class activities, students knew they had their own individual work to do, and they took responsibility for doing it. They then had projects which could be worked on if all else was finished, but, if they had not finished everything else, they were reminded by the teacher about there being an order to activities. All in all, there was little extended discussion about either the order of activities or the transitions from one to another in this room, although many of the transitions made by the group as a whole were marked by small rituals. (The example previously given of starting every day in the same way was typical of the sort of rituals meant.)

In the fourth grade class, the teacher was concerned that there be more flexibility in the schedule, with the result that a great deal of time and energy was spent on ensuring that the students knew what activity would occur when, and which particular subset of students should be participating at a given time. There often were calls for clarification by students. There was generally a list of the day's activities on the blackboard, but the teacher wanted to remain able to change it as that seemed appropriate, and therefore either verbal changes (not reflected in the written schedule) or written changes (not mentioned verbally) often occurred, and it was the students' task to keep abreast of the changes. One student was often engaged in an activity that others had completed, which was permitted, but if anyone had left the group activity unfinished and gone on to the next activity without explicit permission, comment was generally made. In this class there was much informal walking around, as students helped each other, or showed each other their art work, or simply gossiped about friends in common. The teacher made extensive comments made about the noise level, but rarely named a particular student, and little action was taken to lower the noise level.

We do have social rules which tell us how to punctuate the stream of behavior (McLaughlin, 1984, p. 25). But these rules are the least regular of them all. If we all divided up the world in the same way, and into the same size chunks, we would have few problems, but, unfortunately for world harmony, this is not the case. I see an event from my perspective, and you see it from yours. I don't know your past history very well, and you don't know mine, so it is not possible for me to interpret an event in exactly the same way you will. I see my action as primary, and yours as a response to it; you see your action as primary, and mine as a response to you.[9] Once we accept that meaning lies, not in a particular behavior, but in the context, and once we accept an extensive context for any event, we discover the difficulty involved in expecting two people to ever supply the same meaning to a behavior. But individual punctuations of behavior are not idiosyncratic.

We learn to punctuate the behavioral stream, as we learn other aspects of communication. This means that we learn to match current interaction with past, and punctuate the current behavior in accordance with what we have done previously. We have been at similar events in the past, and we assume the boundaries of this event will be similar to those previously experienced, whether in fact this turns out to be true or not. This helps lead different participants to punctuate the stream of behavior in different ways: their past experiences have been diverse, and they have learned to divide up behavior differently, and into different sized chunks.

In her work with Israeli schoolchildren, Tamar Katriel concludes that, as with pronominal reference in the verbal domain:

> the offering of a treat can both signal the existence of a particular social relationship and establish one. The latter is particularly so in uncertain or marginal cases when acquaintanceship has not been formally established either on an interpersonal or an institutional basis (e.g., shared membership in a larger group). (1987, p. 313)

In this way, a gray area of interaction can be clarified through the use of a communicative act.

Much humor seems to depend upon the fact that different people are likely to punctuate events in different ways. Whether it is a stand-up comedian's joke or a comic strip, we seem to find it funny that others to not divide up the world into precisely the same size and shape chunks that we use. Students view their behavior as unique—a professor views them as part of a long stream of students in the same course and compares performance over the years. Students cannot and do not wish to perceive reality so, and are

---

[9] See Watzlawick (1976, pp. 61–64) for a discussion of what appears to me as cause, appearing to you as effect.

insulted if they ever find out this is how they are viewed, not realizing that they, in turn, see any single professor as but one in a chain of many professors.

In sum, punctuation of an interaction simply refers to the fact that we divide up the communication stream into parts, and that the ways we do so are not necessarily the same as the ways someone else does so. Since there is no "real" beginning to interaction, it is easy for us to assign different behaviors the status of a beginning marker. Did our fight begin when you called me names, or when I ran my bicycle over your foot? Is the problem that you were rude and eavesdropped on my telephone conversation when I did not want you to, or that I spoke too loudly and attracted your attention to my words?[10] Punctuation adds order to interaction, but the placement of punctuation marks is often negotiable. The concept reminds us that even something so basic as the division of behavior into segments needs to be studied.

Much social effort is devoted to the task of aligning our punctuation with others as closely as possible. This is one interpretation of the elaborate beginning and ending markers we find necessary. In his study of greeting and farewell rituals, Firth suggests "it may not be important *what* forms are used, but it is essential for social relationships that *some* forms are used" (1973, p. 34; his emphasis). This is necessary because stretches of interaction do not come with precoded beginnings and endings (Halliday, 1978, p. 136). If they did, life would be much simpler, but far more boring.

---

[10] Watzlawick, Beavin Bavelas, and Jackson (1967, p. 59) provide further discussion and illustrations.

CHAPTER 5
Communication as Multichannel Behavior

It makes no sense to speak of 'verbal communication' and 'nonverbal communication.' There is only communication.
—Adam Kendon (1972, p. 443)

The older, more traditional view of communication, closely allied with the stimulus–response model, suggests everything that is significant in communication is verbal. Early models implied communication was to be seen as the sending of messages back and forth, messages in the form of words. Zabor labels this traditional approach to communication the *psychological* paradigm, and cites the view that "communication is the transmission of a sequence of words from one individual to another" as one of its main assumptions (1978, p. 136). That traditional view is now generally recognized as being an oversimplification. Zabor labels the newer approach the *social* paradigm and counters the initial assumption with the statement that "communication is multimodal." One of the points of this chapter is to expand her statement. Sari Thomas (1980) has described the shift as being a movement away from a *mechanical* model of communication and towards an *organic* model, and provides a good analysis of the shift in paradign which has occurred. She is using different labels, but describing the same two approaches as Zabor.[1] Carey (1975) uses the terms *transmission* view versus *ritual* view. McQuail (1975) uses *product* versus *process*. All of these authors, through various terms, are referring to the same basic dichotomy in communication research to date. Research dating from the Natural History of an Interview project in the 1950s has demonstrated beyond all question that the social (ritual, process, organic) view of communication is more elaborate (and therefore more dif-

[1] Sigman (1987) describes "social communication" in greater detail than either of these other two authors.

ficult to study), but, at the same time, since it recognizes communication as being made up of many types of behaviors all occurring simultaneously, it is the more appropriate (and therefore worth the trouble).[2]

It is common today to divide experience into parts for the sake of convenience, since the monolithic whole is too complex to study at one time and all of a piece. The most common division is into a set of what are called *channels.* A channel can be described as a bodily focused source of information. These channels are often separated into two *modes* of communication, maintaining the early duality of verbal and nonverbal. According to general practice, each is assigned part of the communication stream (see Figure 5.1).

In discussing communication as consisting of verbal and nonverbal modes, however, we leave ourselves open to the impression that the two are somehow distinct and should be studied separately. This is not at all the case, and there is now a current body of literature devoted to rejoining the two (Goodwin, 1981, 1987; Duncan & Fiske 1977, 1985; Heath, 1986, in press; Sanders, 1987; Pelose, 1987).

The problem with this common division of communication into a series of channels is that it is too easy. It tempts us to forget that any division is only a provisional measure, one practiced for the sake of study. Although much research has been organized in this way, and so it is absolutely necessary to recognize these terms and their meanings, it leads us to think (incorrectly) in terms of separate behaviors with little impact on one another. A more accurate view argues that all of the above channels are involved in communication

Figure 5.1. Modes of Communication

Verbal	Nonverbal
language	paralanguage (how things are said)
	kinesics (what we do with our bodies)
	proxemics (use of space)
	touch
	taste
	smell
	objects

NOTE: It is sometimes suggested that additional nonverbal aspects of communication be included in this list as well, such as time.

---

[2] See Leeds-Hurwitz (1987a) for a more extensive discussion of the Natural History of an Interview project.

at one and the same time; thus it is inappropriate to permit the division to become permanent. The exact boundary lines between the channels is insignificant; it is misleading to study any one channel to the exclusion of the others. The list works best as a basic remainder of what not to forget when studying communication, rather than as mutually exclusive categories. As Mary Douglas, among others, points out, although we assume nonverbal communication ought to be simple in comparison with speech, "It turns out to be highly complex" (1975, p. 216).

Social communication takes communicative events and the broad array of channels constituting them as a starting point, rather than accepting as adequate any single channel and the kind of information it alone is capable of displaying. Even so simple an event as conducting a casual conversation requires that the participants keep track of a large number of cues conveyed through a variety of channels (Condon & Ogston, 1967). We must study the complexity that is a conversation, rather than the simplicity of a written transcript of the words spoken. Transcripts are a valuable aid to analysis, but hardly a substitute for data (Craig & Tracy, 1983, p. 300).[3]

A facile division of the world into verbal and nonverbal behaviors implies words are "good" communication, and movements, or all nonverbal communication, are somehow "bad." This view originates in our traditional Western division of mind (verbal mode) from body (nonverbal mode). Historically, we have given more weight to that which we learn to control and can display at will (the mental aspect of interaction), and have devalued that over which we have only little control (the physical aspect of interaction). We therefore generally accept the idea that we are responsible for what we say, but not for how we move our bodies. We discount what we do in terms of nonverbal communication for this reason; if it is out of our control, it is not a legitimate focus for study.

When we view communication as only verbal, we exclude most of what happens when people are together. Once we recognize a broader range of behavior as communicative, and as a legitimate (or, at least, serious) focus for study, we risk implying that people should take responsibility for their actions as well as their words. This puts a heavy burden on us, one which most people are not

---

[3] After the early pioneering work of Soskin and John (1963), study of naturally occurring conversation has become a standard topic in a variety of fields. There has been much excellent research on discourse within communication recently, starting with Litton-Hawes (1977) and Nofsinger (1977). The research has now become so accepted that it is common to find entire articles devoted to a particular aspect of conversation, such as compliments (Knapp, Hopper, & Bell, 1984).

eager to accept. My intent here is to divide the basic proposition into two parts, and treat them separately. Yes, it is appropriate for us to study all of the behaviors which we now recognize as being a part of communication, if our studies are to be complete. No, just because we can study nonverbal out-of-awareness behaviors does not mean that we are suddenly responsible for them. They are still out-of-awareness, and are by definition those behaviors over which we have no conscious control. For all the reasons which cause the majority of communicative behaviors to be out-of-awareness in the first place, even if we were to try to control *all* our nonverbal behavior, we could not.

> In the South Milwaukee third grade classroom, the students are often quite literal. One day the teacher said, "Put your hands up like this when you've got it" (referring to a test they were working on). She happened to raise her hand with a bend in the elbow. When the students finished, they raised their hands just that way, even though usually they raised their hands with straight arms. This was presumably not something they did either consciously or deliberately, and it did not last beyond the one day.

There are a large number of textbooks which outline and describe the various channels, and my purpose here is not to duplicate that information.[4] But it does seem important to spend just enough time with each topic to insure knowledge of appropriate use of the terms. These channels should never be separated for any length of time, even for research purposes (see Figure 5.2).

Only when all of these separate aspects of communication are studied as a coherent whole do they take on any meaning. It is the combination of intonation and briefcase, color and cut of suit, posture and haircut, that result in the waiter's choice of a particular table for a particular customer, or the speed with which a receptionist passes a visitor through to the boss. The combination of art on the wall, music playing, style of furniture, other guests present, and type of greeting chosen by the hostess together carry a single meaning in the mind of the guest. The separation of the stream of behavior into small parts is only an analytic tool, and must not be confused with the way things are in the world.

---

[4] Among the best are Knapp (1978), Weitz (1979), Katz and Katz (1983).

Figure 5.2. Channels of Communication

Language: The words we say, which are then combined into utterances, and utterances into various forms of discourse. *Discourse* is the common term for any extended presentation of words, including everything from conversations to public speeches.

Paralanguage: Vocal behavior which is not verbal. This is, everything which is produced by the vocal tract except words. This includes four main aspects: voice quality (how your voice sounds: hoarse, raspy, etc.), vocal qualifiers (how you say things: stress, pitch, length, etc.), vocal characterizers (non-speech noises: laugh, cry, etc.), and vocal segregates (sounds which function like words: uh huh, shhh, etc.). Sometimes pauses and silences are studied as well; other times, these are studied as part of the use of language.

Kinesics: Everything we do with our bodies, from posture to facial expressions, to where we look with our eyes (sometimes studied separately as *eye gaze phenomena*). This is divided into three main aspects: prekinesics (physiological basis of movement), microkinesics (isolation of individual movements), and social kinesics (motion related to social performance). It is the level of social kinesics that is the most often studied.

Proxemics: Use of space. There are two main aspects. The first is use of space between people, that is, how close or far people stand from one another while interacting. The second is environmental influences: that is, the effects of such things as architecture and location of furniture on interaction.

Touch: This includes who touches who, where, for how long, in what way. There has only recently been much interest in the social use of touching.

Taste and Smell: Although these are rarely studied, it is generally agreed that they are an important part of many interactions.

Objects: Use of objects in communication is again often overlooked, but can be critical. This includes everything from clothing to type of furniture or presence of plants, from smoking cigarettes to carrying a briefcase.

There are a variety of connections between verbal and nonverbal communication. In some cases, there is an explicit connection. In the South Milwaukee third grade classroom, this was reflected on at least one occasion by the teacher explaining the ways in which she wanted the students to view the connection between movements and language.

Teacher: You're not thinking if your papers are rustling or if you're moving.

Ten minutes go by. One of the students is playing with crayons while the teacher reads a story out loud.

Teacher: Shadia, how can you listen if you're fooling around with something else?

For an adult to tell another that movement implies inattention would be ridiculous, but then adults have learned to regulate extreme amounts of movements that would be distracting. (One of the places where they have learned this is, presumably, from their grade school teachers.)

On another occasion, the first grade teacher made a similar connection, but less overtly. The teacher was working with a reading group consisting of two students. The story concerned a character named "Rackety Rabbit."

Teacher: "Rackety" means making a lot of noise.
Do we have any rackety rabbits in this room?

Students in several parts of the room had been fairly noisy; they quieted down.

Teacher: We have one.

She looks directly at Monserrate, who looks around the room to see who is making noise. No one is. Monserrate is standing up coloring a picture at the time, when the rest of the students are sitting. She sits down.

Here the student must make the connection between verbal noise and nonverbal noise that the teacher is implying by her statement in order to respond appropriately to the request for "quiet." The assumption that being "quiet" or "orderly" involves, not only minimal amounts of verbal noise, but of nonverbal noise as well, is not limited to this particular teacher.

Returning to the third grade classroom, the students are playing a spelling baseball game. The teacher asks the team captains to maintain order. One of them, Dawn, not only maintains quiet but also unobtrusively keeps her line in order. She taps students on the shoulder from behind, in such a way that the teacher cannot see what she's doing. It is very effective. The students in her group do stay in line, and do not call unwanted attention to themselves as being out of line.

There are three implications of communication as multichannel behavior which will be outlined below: first, the metaphor of communication as an orchestra will be presented; second, the concept of interaction rhythms will be outlined; and third, communication will be described as a continuous process.

ORCHESTRA METAPHOR

The traditional metaphor for communication was always that of a telegraph, and many models were designed using this notion. Reduced to their essence, all had a sender and a receiver and a message which flowed along something analogous to a telegraph wire from one to the other. They came in various degrees of elaboration, some quite complex.[5] Regardless of degree of complexity, none of the telegraph models is really the most useful way of studying communication. Even the most complex diagrams still clearly present communication as made up of a series of discrete, discontinuous behaviors.

The reason these sorts of models have been used so often is that they "feel right" to us. They fit with our general notion, derived from our membership in Western culture, of what communication is and how it works. In brief, we assume the following model as an appropriate distillation of conversation: I say something to you, you are decently quiet while I speak, then verbally respond when it is your turn. It makes sense to us that people communicate just as characters talk in the scripts of most plays: one at a time, with little overlap. Yet we should hesitate to accept the telegraph model if the only argument to recommend it is that it has been accepted as correct for a long time.

What is proposed as a substitute is the metaphor of an orchestra. This is not an original idea, since it has been suggested by others, but it has not yet been generally accepted, and therefore can use a little advertising. The basic model is a simple one. The main point is that, rather than viewing communication as transmitted through a single channel or a single behavior, we need to acknowledge the multiple channels and large number of behaviors which make up any interaction. Thus, each communicative act is viewed as a single note within a larger symphony; each channel as one instru-

---

[5] Berlo (1966) provides a typical example of the telegraph model; Birdwhistell (1970, pp. 67–69) provides further comments on the orchestra metaphor; Winkin (1981, pp. 13–26) provides a more detailed comparison of the two models.

ment among many. Meaning then resides, not in the single note taken out of context, but in the particular *combination* of notes present in the entire symphony. When we document and analyze communication, we are in effect writing down the score of the symphony for the first time. Unlike a real orchestra, we players in the symphony of social interaction are not given the notes to play (rules to follow) in concrete form before we go on stage. We have all played many concerts together before, however, so that our performance is not entirely improvised.

Perhaps the earliest use of the orchestra metaphor was Hall's (1959). He used it to illuminate, not the concept of communication, but that of culture, although his work stressed the link between the two. His emphasis in using the metaphor was on the image of creating a musical score (by analogy, description of a culture by an ethnographer), and he described his book as "the cultural analogue of a musical primer" (1959, p. 13; see also p. 167).

Using a comment by Claude Levi-Strauss on the similarities between myth and music as his starting point (1970, p. 17), Edmund Leach provides the most extensive discussion of orchestral performance as a metaphor. He uses a narrower definition than that suggested here, since he is only concerned with ritual sequences and not other aspects of communication, but his comments are relevant nonetheless. Of the points he makes, two are particularly useful here. The first is that "The meaning of the music is not to be found in the 'tunes' uttered by individual instruments but in the combination of such tunes, in their mutual relations, and in the way particular patterns of sound are transformed into different but related shapes" (1976, p. 45). In other words, we must not study a single channel (instrument) to the exclusion of the others, for it has little meaning alone; meaning is found when all channels (instruments) are combined into a whole. Both an orchestra and interaction are multimodal and consist of the combination of a variety of separable streams. This is one of the ways in which the metaphor can be usefully extended. Leach also shows how the orchestra metaphor is unsuccessful in its application to interaction. He points out that "The performers and the listeners are the same people" in interaction, unlike in a musical performance (1976, p. 45). We make the music (communication) by ourselves (as performers) and for ourselves (as audience). There is no separation between some who would be active in the social world, and others who are present only to observe; everyone is an integral part of what occurs, and contributes behavior to the whole. Since Leach is interested specifically in ritual, he finds the image of a conductor useful, since the majority of ritual events include a clear leader. But when we apply the metaphor to everyday interaction, we have to eliminate the conductor image, since only rarely is someone in charge, who controls the entire event, telling others what to do. For the same reason, we have to eliminate the composer's image, since no one person is responsible for the score we follow. If anything, we all are composers, just as we are the performers and the audience.

A large part of what we learn from any metaphor is taken from new insights gained from the extended comparison of aspects of the two systems. In keeping with this, there are other aspects of the orchestra metaphor that can be fruitfully extended, beyond those mentioned so far. Appropriate elaborations would include the division between competence and performance, for in either case it is possible to be competent and perform at a variety of levels. Not all musicians are equally good at their job, just as not all participants in an interaction are equally skilled or knowledgeable. In both cases, further practice aids in the production of a successful result.

Both an orchestra and interaction can be described as having emergent meaning; although this is not a common description of an orchestra, it is not incorrect. Meaning results from the entire piece as played by the orchestra, and one instrumental part does not convey anything like the total impact, just as meaning resides in the entire interactional event, rather than in a single sentence. We can gain something from analysis of one sentence, as we can gain something from listening to a solo, but that should not be confused with the impression given by the solo in the context of an entire symphony.

With either an orchestra or a group of people, coordination of the actors is essential to the final product. One of the hallmarks of an amateur orchestra is that the various members of the group are unsuccessful in their efforts to coordinate their playing with the playing of other musicians. In the same way, lack of ability to coordinate with other participants marks the inexperienced member of a social group, while ability to gracefully and successfully match rhythms and lines is essential to smooth interaction.

Despite these similarities, there are also ways in which the metaphor falls apart. One of these is that musicians in an orchestra expect their parts to be written down, but players in the interactional setting do not. In fact, if their parts are written down, we would assume we were watching a play, a piece of fiction devised ahead of time, rather than normal interaction. By their nature, we invent our interactions as we go along. Or do we? Perhaps we should view social rules as a sort of text prepared for us, a script or musical score to help us play our role.

The metaphor of an orchestra (or, by extension, of music) applied to interaction is not entirely unknown in the communication literature. For example, Robert Hopper suggests that "Talk seems coherent largely due to the activities of the silent partner. Interpretation performs the dance of coherence; speech hums the tune" (1983, p. 86). My argument here is that there remains more work to be done elaborating the metaphor; we have only begun to learn all we can from it.

INTERACTION RHYTHMS

The concept of *rhythm* in communication is taken from the image of communication as a dance we do together, for it can be said that we generally dance to the same musical rhythm as someone else when we interact with them. This metaphor is separate but related to that of the orchestra presented above. The two metaphors should not be seen as conflicting, but as complementary. In both cases, there is an attempt to recognize that we act in accordance with the actions of others; we are never entirely alone. We are in concert, *in synch* as the colloquial phrase puts it, with others most of the time. We coordinate our rhythms with the rhythms of the others performing the dance (or playing in the orchestra) with us.

As with any metaphor, it is possible to extend this one to see how well the details of a dance illuminate our understanding of interaction. One way of expanding the metaphor follows (see Figure 5.3). This is only one way of expanding the metaphor, of course, and does not preclude additions or substitutions. The chart should be read: "Dance is to Communication as . . ."

The concept of interaction rhythms can be divided into three separate ideas: self-synchrony, interactional synchrony, and asynchrony. *Self-synchrony* refers to being in rhythm with one's self. Technically, it has been defined as being "the organization of change of a speaker's body motion with thre articulated segmental organization of his or her speech" (Condon & Ogston, 1966). In simpler terms, we do not stop moving when we talk, and our movements and speech must stand in some relation to one another. When they are coordinated, as they generally are, we say that a person is self-synchronous. Our bodies dance in time to our speech; we speak in time to the music of our movements. The attempt is not to give one channel or mode of communication priority over

Figure 5.3.   Metaphor of Dance

Dance	:	Communication : :
Music	:	Culture
Dancers	:	Participants
Audience	:	Nonparticipants
Costumes	:	Clothing
Choreographers	:	Previous generations
Instruments	:	Channels of communication
Stage	:	Location
Scenery	:	Immediate surrounding
Score	:	Transcription of interaction
Dance instructor	:	Communication professor
Invitation to Dance	:	Greeting
Applause	:	Positive feedback (compliments, etc.)
Lack of applause	:	Negative feedback (insults, etc.)
Dress rehearsal	:	Preparation for a major event (wedding rehearsal)
Opening night	:	New experience (first day at school)
Solo dancer	:	Main speaker
Steps	:	Symbols
Slow dance	:	Love scene
Slam dance	:	Argument

NOTE: This chart owes much to class discussion by students in my course Communication in Everyday Life in Fall 1987.

the others, but to recognize that, since they all are ongoing most of the time, they are best understood as an integrated whole. The major breaks in our conversations are marked by shifts, not only of topic and, perhaps, style of speech, but also by changes of posture and small shifts in movements, such as what we do with our feet.

Interactional synchrony is a further result of the complexity of communication. It refers to the rhythm of movements and speech between two or more people.[6] Technically, it has been defined as a synchronous change of direction of movement on the part of the interactants (Condon & Ogston, 1966). Less technically, it has been described as "a way of physically celebrating a relation bathed in mutual attention, trust, and sensibility" (McDermott & Church, 1976, p. 127). In other words, not only do we move and speak in ways that mesh, we coordinate our movements and speech with the

---

[6] Much more research has been done on interactional synchrony than on either self-synchrony or asynchrony. See Davis (1982) for a good collection of essays, also Kendon (1977). Much research has been done on interactional synchrony in classrooms, for example, Sullivan (1986).

movements and speech of others as well, at least for the time that we are with them. In many situations, "the listener moves in synchrony with the speaker's speech almost as well as the speaker does" (Condon, 1976, p. 305). Listeners move their bodies even while they are not speaking, of course, and they normally do so in ways that are integrated with the speech of the person who is talking. This is only possible because we pay careful attention, albeit unconsciously, to the people with whom we interact.

One of those who is currently supplying new detailed analyses of the interrelations of speech and movement is Christian Heath (1986). He focuses on behavior in medical encounters specifically, but his conclusions are presumably applicable to all contexts. By careful analysis of videotapes of interactions, he demonstrates the astonishing extent to which we mesh our movements and our speech with the movements and speech of others.

One of the ways in which we utilize interactional synchrony is to coordinate turn-taking in conversation. It has been suggested that "the end of one interactant's speaking turn is defined partly in terms of his/her conversational partner's gestural or vocal behavior" (Pelose, 1987, p. 184). Since the initial work by Duncan (1972), turn-taking has been accepted as one of the standard tasks which must be managed if interaction is to occur.[7] Interactants need to insert their talk into the pauses or silences provided by each other, and they do this in part by matching speed with the person to whom they are speaking (Jaffe & Feldstein, 1970; Cappella, 1979).

The most extreme case of interactional synchrony, and thus the easiest example to notice, is when two or more people move into a "mirror image" of one another. For this to happen, they arrange their bodies into essentially the same positions but in reverse. When they are facing one another it looks like one is a figure and the other its reflection in a mirror; thus the term *mirror image*. This is easiest to see in a sketch of actual people (see Figure 5.4).[8]

Once this extreme example of paying attention to another person becomes noticeable, less blatant examples of interactional synchrony become easier to see. They include shifting position at the same time that the person you are speaking with shifts position, although not from, and not into the identical position; or developing

---

[7] See also Sacks, Schegloff, and Jefferson (1974) and Duncan and Niederehe (1974) for research on turn-taking.

[8] The drawings used here are an artist's rendering of photographs taken at a residential conference in France. The artist is Susan Schuder and the photographer is Régine Mahaux. See Leeds-Hurwitz and Winkin (n.d.) for further discussion of these and similar images and their uses for teaching and research.

Figure 5.4.

a sequence of actions such that, every time I play with my hair, you tug at your socks (Scheflen, 1965b).

Equally important, interactional synchrony is not limited to a single moment in time, but often occurs over an extended period. The following illustration shows four photographs taken over a period of a few minutes. The two people shown are sitting next to each other in the audience during a conference presentation. They know each other, but not well. Here they mimic each other's behavior, complete to placement of pen or movement of hand, over and over again. Once I alerted the photographer to such images, she was able to record them over and over again, demonstrating the frequency with which they occur (see Figure 5.5).

These examples might be taken to imply that interactional synchrony extends over only a few seconds, when in fact it extends over much greater periods of time. The following sequence of images took place over a period of 10 minutes. In them, two conference participants are depicted as they get coffee and sit together, effec-

Figure 5.5.

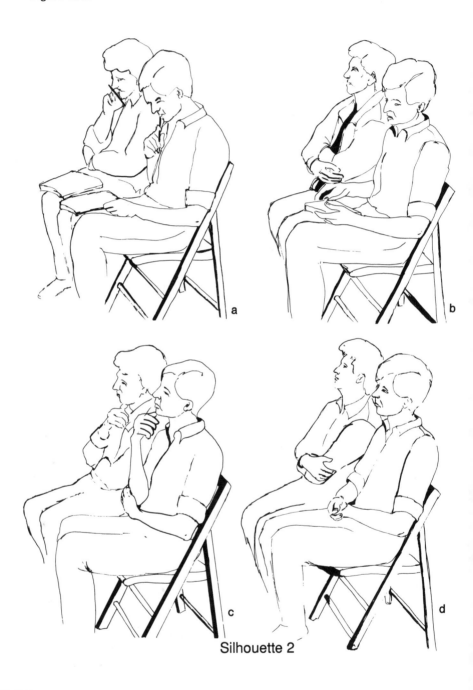

Silhouette 2

tively chase away a third conferee who attempts to join them, and gradually move into a series of more or less complete mirror images (see Figure 5.6).

Asynchrony (or, sometimes, dyssynchrony) is the word used to describe what happens when people move in ways that are *not* synchronous. It can refer to either self-asynchrony or interactional asynchrony. In extreme forms, both have been linked to various psychiatric diagnoses; it has been suggested that those who are diagnosed as schizophrenic or aphasic are likely to have various degrees of disruption of synchrony with self and others (Condon & Ogston, 1967), and autistic children display uneven behavior, where one side of the body does not move in accordance with the other (Condon, 1980, p. 59). Similar problems have been documented in dyslexic, retarded, or cerebral palsied children (Condon, 1976). There is also now some new research suggesting that assault victims display self-asynchrony, and in this way convey vulnerability to others (Grayson & Stein, 1981).

More importantly for those who study everyday interaction, it has been suggested that lesser forms of asynchrony occur when people of different cultural backgrounds interact. Since we learn to move appropriately to our culture, and since patterns of movements are not universal, our timing or rhythms may not match perfectly from one culture to the next. Erickson and Schultz (1982) have, for example, documented ethnic differences in interaction style in the context of counselor interviews that seem to be linked to differing amounts of information conveyed: the greater the synchrony, the more practical information conveyed from counselor to student; the greater the asynchrony, the less practical information conveyed. Synchrony was linked to similarities in either ethnic background or interests held in common; asynchrony was linked to differences in ethnic background or lack of interests held in common. Put very simply, when people know what to expect from each other, and feel comfortable with each other, it is easier for them to move in time with one another, for they will recognize the behavior they are observing. When they have little experience in interpreting the behavior they observe, they find it harder to move in rhythm with one another. By moving in time, they convey their affinity, and more useful conversation results.

What is being suggested here is not that, since it is easiest, it is therefore best to interact only with those most like us. Certainly it is easiest for us to interact with those who have similar assumptions, whether it be about ideas or movements, but this is hardly a reason for us to stop interacting with those who are unlike us. When we

Figure 5.6.

interact with those who are different in any significant way, however, we must learn to pay attention to details that we normally ignore, so that we can get past the differences in interactional style and reach the content. What is being suggested is less: Go where you know what to expect, as that is easy and therefore good, than: Go where you do not know what to expect, for that is where you will learn something, but go with your eyes open.

We do not normally notice interaction rhythms. What we notice instead as the interaction goes on is the impression we gain from the degree of synchrony. We "feel good" about an interaction when we have been in synchrony with someone, and "feel bad" when we have not. As Paul Byers has pointed out, "We have many words that refer to responses produced by temporal mismatches (irritating, rude, pushy) and we have a few (tender, loving, empathic, soothing, etc.) that describe the feelings we recognize when temporal relations (synchrony) are shared by both" (1977, p. 136).

Although we do not normally notice interaction rhythms, we can learn to become more aware of them. This is generally easiest with the aid of a camera, whether still or moving, for the camera permits us to slow down and view an interaction repeatedly. In this way we gain the time to notice far more than is possible when behavior goes by only once and at the usual speed. After becoming aware of the existence of synchrony most people begin to notice it everywhere.

One of the best-known studies to document interactional synchrony analyzed behavior in psychiatric interviews (a common situation for extended analysis, in part because of the extensive filming done for other purposes). The researcher, Albert Scheflen, was at first astonished and horrified by what looked like courtship behaviors between therapists and patients. (Courtship behaviors would be those between a couple, leading to their becoming a couple, and as such would be inappropriate in a psychiatric interview.) After further viewing, he analyzed the behaviors as being what he termed *quasi-courtship behaviors* instead (Scheflen, 1965a). They are like courtship behaviors, except for the presence of at least one behavior which indicates that they are not to be (mis)understood as courtship. There is no one behavior which serves as qualifier in all cases of quasi-courtship; instead, any behavior which is inappropriate for courtship will serve. Examples would include speaking in a too-loud voice, facing away, standing too far away, when the other behaviors indicate that the person would speak softly, face towards, and stand near.

What these examples of synchrony can serve to indicate is the great degree to which we not only monitor one another's behavior, but calibrate our behavior with one another, even though we do both out-of-awareness. Quasi-courtship is now generally understood as being a necessary part of what occurs when people are getting to know one another. A certain amount of careful attention to one another is one of the best ways to indicate clearly that we are interested in one another as people, and expect to continue the relationship beyond the present. But quasi-courtship, and other examples of interactional synchrony, should never be understood as conveying the same message as courtship, for they do not.

CONTINUOUS

Communication goes on and on and on. The phrase *stream of behavior* has often been applied to communication and, among other implications, we understand from this that communication never stops. There is no way to dam the flow of information, even for a short period of time, aside from retreating from others entirely. (But even our absence may convey meaning.) We know how to put a car into neutral, but we do not know how to put a person into neutral, and so information is continuously available to us when interacting with others. The result is that, even when we are not engaging in intentional, deliberate, conscious communication, we are still communicating.

> Behavior has no opposite. In other words, there is no such thing as nonbehavior, or to put it even more simply, one cannot *not* behave. Now, if it is accepted that all behavior in an interactional situation has message value, i.e., is communication, it follows that no matter how one may try, one cannot *not* communicate. (Watzlawick, Beavin Bavelas, & Jackson, 1967, pp. 48–49; their emphasis)

The absence of a message is yet another message (see Haley, 1959; p. 232; Mead & Byers, 1968, p. 105).

Tamar Katriel demonstrates this point well in her discussion of *brogez* among Israeli children, which, as she explains, "is defined in terms of behavioral avoidances: not playing together, not speaking to each other, not mentioning each other's name, and so on" (1985a, p. 469). The formalization of this state is not quite paralleled among American children, but the concept is certainly one we can understand. It is the opposite of friendship, and as such it occurs only among friends. Not speaking to a stranger is irrelevant; it is not noteworthy. Only not speaking to a friend is noticeable.

In a close-knit neighborhood, even those who move away return to visit. They learn that this is appropriate through observing others do it before them. In East Baltimore, I was told: "You'd be surprised how many people come back. People move out—move out to the country, but they always come back. They miss it—they miss the closeness, they miss the convenience of the stores, and movies, and their friends, their family." It may come as a surprise that even those who are no longer members of a group have some of their behavior constrained by group norms, but this is often the case. We learn what is appropriate within the group, but, once we leave the group that taught us, we have internalized the norms and so take them with us wherever we go (and, often, whether they are still appropriate or not). The behavior continues outside of the context we might have assumed limiting.

Nature is not divided up into clearly discernible events. Such division of the world is a human invention and has meaning only at a social level. We must learn to divide events at the same boundary points as others around us, in order to interact easily with them, but this does not come naturally to us. Imagine a child born with the knowledge of how to tell a wedding from a funeral, a practical joke from a final exam, or more subtly, when dinner is over and it is time for bed. We become so accustomed to the divisions we make, however, that it is difficult for us to remember that we have ourselves participated in creating them.

The notion that communication operated in fits and starts,—where I say something, and then there is a pause, and then you say something,—comes from the incorrect assumption that all communication is verbal and deliberate. Once we view communication as multichannel, we must accept the implication that some of it is not deliberate. Once we look at what must be included as communication, we reach the further implication that it is never-ending. There is always something going on.

A more adequate view of communication suggests that it is made up of "isolable discontinuous units," which, when put together, appear as a single continuous whole (Birdwhistell, 1970, p. 88). It is not the case that *any* one communicative behavior continues forever, but there are so many separate behaviors that when they are all put together they go on forever. No one channel is active all of the time (for example, there are a lot of times when participants in an event may not be touching one another), but we must recognize that their very lack of activity is in itself signalling something. Consider, for example, a couple on a first date. The lack of touch in itself contains information about the interaction, specifically, that they do not know one another particularly well, but since they have the potential for knowing one another better, and will use touch to signify establishing themselves as a couple, casual touch is often impossible for a period of time. In addition, other channels will be active while the one is not. While this couple is not touching, they are talking, or standing at particular distances from one another or laughing. When all of the channels are viewed together, it becomes apparent that there is a continuous stream of behavior. We are not only orchestra members participating in an elaborate symphony, but it is a nonstop symphony. Each musician may take a break and be silent for a time, but that does not mean the symphony comes to an end. There are plenty of other instruments available to carry the tune.

But it is not just a question of taking the various channels into account. We must also expand our view of how much of the past to consider in our understanding of the present. The answer is usually "more than we would have thought." Scheflen has pointed out that speakers respond not just to the immediate utterance, but "to what has been said hours or even months before, to something unsaid, to what might be said, and to matters unrelated to the immediate transaction" (1973, p. 6). In line with this, Sigman suggests that "speakers appear to direct their verbal contributions to the interaction as a totality, its goals, and their role requirements, and not only to the immediately preceding utterance(s)" (1983, p. 179). This notion can be expanded in two ways. One, we must examine the "continuities of information across episodes" if we are to correctly interpret communication (Sigman, 1987, p. 9). That is, we cannot look only to even a complete interaction to discover meaning, but must investigate other interactions between the same participants. And two, since " 'interpersonal' relations are never, except in appearance, *individual-to-individual* relationships," then "the truth of the interaction is never entirely contained in the interaction" (Bourdieu, 1982, p. 81). Thus, investigation does not stop with all of the interactions between particular individuals, for their interactions are strongly influenced by others who are not actually present.

The work of Susan Phillips adds to this the notion that there is a different approach to when a question needs to be answered depending upon what culture serves as the context. For the Warm

Springs Sahaptin Indians she studied, an answer supplied 15 minutes after the question was posed was normal, and hours later was within the realm of the possible (Philips, 1976, 1983). For mainstream Americans, this would be extremely unusual unless it was elaborately marked in some fashion.

> It is easy to think of a given school year as supplying adequate context for understanding what occurs within a given day, but after sitting in a third grade classroom with an authoritarian teacher who is quite rigid about schedules and activities, then in a fourth grade classroom in the same school, with a democratic teacher who considers flexibility in all things as the mark of the good teacher, it is difficult not to wonder about the effect on the students, who must make the transition from one to the other. There has to be carry-over, for the habits taught by the one are refuted by the other, the expectations encouraged by the one are never met by the other. And this is only a sequence of two classes; students normally experience a minimum of 12 such transitions.

It was Goffman who pointed out that "silence, coming from a person in a situation where participants are obliged to be busily engaged in tasks or talk, can itself be a noisy thing, loudly expressing that the individual is not properly involved and not attuned to the gathering" (1963, p. 214). Silence is only the absence of talk, not the absence of communication. Silence can be a positive phenomenon, even a deliberate performance (Dauenhauer, 1973, 1976; Tannen & Saville-Troike, 1985). This is a critical fact easily overlooked, since it goes against our "common sense" understanding of communication.

One of the important points to be made about silence is that not all cultures value it equally, or recommend it in reaction to the same events. In his early work on the Western Apache, Keith Basso conducted what has become a classic analysis of the use of silence within a culture which values it more positively than our own. He concluded that, "For a stranger entering an alien society, a knowledge of when *not* to speak may be as basic to the production of culturally acceptable behavior as a knowledge of what to say" (1972, p. 69; his emphasis).

Returning to mainstream American behavior, Thomas has pointed out that the use of silence can be significantly different depending upon the context. Silence in a classroom indicates attention and receptivity, thus being positively valued, while silence during a comedy routine would be more likely to indicate inattention and lack of appreciation for the routine, thus being negatively valued (1987, p. 227). A related point is made by Barry Brummett in article on the uses of silence as a political strategy: "Silence becomes strategic only when talk is expected" (1980, p. 289). Being silent when expected is only appropriate, and therefore not something we easily notice.

The fact that communication is continuous explains why much of it is out-of-awareness. *Out-of-awareness* is a phrase used to describe what happens when we *observe* something but do not really *see* it. That is, we do not consciously recognize what we have just observed, but we respond appropriately to it nonetheless. If we consciously recognized and categorized all the information which was made available to us, we would have a steady backlog of information which would require our attention. Even if we never slept, we would have no hope of adequately dealing with all of it. Bateson has pointed out that "no organism can afford to be conscious of matters with which it could deal at unconscious levels" (1972c, p. 143). One of the things we learn when we are socialized is which pieces of information we need to notice consciously and which can be dealt with unconsciously. Of course, the social rules regarding conscious attention are context-bound.

Contrary to popular opinion, the majority of communication is unconscious. As Bateson indicated, it has to be, if we are to survive. There are literally thousands of pieces of information which could be noticed at any given moment in an interaction, from the fact that someone is *not* wearing the tie we gave them, to the fact that they recently got a haircut, to the fact that they seem slightly slower of movement today than yesterday. We cannot busy ourselves noticing and responding to all of these behaviors, for there are simply too many of them. In sheer self-defense, we permit ourselves to notice only those things that reach a level of significance. I do not notice all of the other clothing you are *not* wearing today, just the tie I gave you. I never even consciously recognize your speed of movement, but only my interpretation of that behavior. Thus, I may ask if you feel a little depressed or tired today, without consciously recognizing what it is about your behavior that prompted my question.

Birdwhistell has supplied a wonderful example of different responses to illness in two communities he labels "Dry Ridge" and "Green Valley," both in Kentucky and only 15 miles apart. Briefly, he points out that, while in Dry Ridge, you are either healthy or critically ill (none of the in-between states being socially available for comment), in Green Valley mild illness is an appropriate and frequent topic for conversation. Description of mild illness in Dry Ridge would be viewed as evidence of malingering; lack of such discussion in Green Valley would be viewed with some puzzlement, and perhaps as evidence of unnecessary stoicism. He concludes with an understated comment on the implications the existence of these two systems has for intermarriage between the two groups (1970, pp. 209–211). Even in cases of intermarriage it is unlikely the participants will be able to verbalize the cause of their trouble, since patterns of response to illness are clearly learned behavior.

Understanding communication to be continuous suggests that it is inappropriate to assume that meaning is something which is intended by the speaker, and then either understood "correctly" or "incorrectly" by the listener. Instead, meaning is something which must be negotiated by all of the participants in an interaction, and it is subject to, not one, but many shifts during the course of even a single conversation.

One of the implications of communication being continuous is made clear in a discussion of ethnic and gender differences in conversational style by Deborah Tannen (1982). She suggests that problems which are due to stylistic differences are extremely difficult to resolve. Each speaker continues to use those strategies that caused the problem in the first place, and it is enormously difficult to step outside of the conflict long enough to resolve it. This work provides an elaboration of Bateson's conception of *schismogenesis* (which he never really defines, but which he paraphrases as "progressive differentiation," 1972c, p. 68). Schismogenesis comes in two varieties: *symmetrical differentiation* (in which we both compete along the same lines, causing parallel escalation), and *complementary differentiation* (in which we are move in opposite directions, but at a related pace).

Communication is not only continuous, it is also redundant. As generally used, the term *redundant* is often understood as meaning that the same information has been supplied more than once. Usually the use of the word redundant is given negative connotations. We say we don't like redundancy, and have as our goal the elimination of redundancy, and make jokes about "the department of redundancy department." In short, in its common usage, redundancy is generally assumed to be unnecessary, or even bad. As used in communication, however, the term loses its negative connotations and takes on merely descriptive implications. That is, we recognize that redundancy in actual communication events exists, and as students of communication we set out to describe it without making value judgments. Eventually we discover that far from being unnecessary, redundancy is essential to communication (Bateson, 1968). Redundancy can be said to occur when some information is both presented and confirmed in the same interaction. This can be done in two ways: it can be presented and reinforced through the same channel, as when we tell a child to "be quiet" and a moment later to "stop talking." Or, it can be presented through one channel, and confirmed through another, as when we tell a child to "be quiet" and our voice indicates annoyance. There is usually more than one confirmation of the initial behavior. In real life, we are likely to also frown, and put a hand on the child's shoulder, at the same time that we are trying to get him or her to be quiet.

The setting is a first grade classroom in South Milwaukee. The teacher has noticed that the room is getting very noisy. Rather than just announce the problem, and request a change, she also names those who are being quiet, moves to the children who are the noisiest, and puts her hand on their heads as she speaks.

Teacher: It's too noisy in the back—I want to see everybody busy like I see Debra busy, and Maria.
(said with her hands on Marcos' and Michael's heads, the two who are the noisiest at that point).

By doing both, she sends the same message twice, thus reinforcing it.

Redundancy in communication has a critical role to play: it reduces ambiguity. If there is no meaning in a single behavior, but only in the context, one part of the way meaning is developed is through this redundancy of behaviors through multiple channels. We learn something from each channel, but learn even more from the combination of them all. Clyde Kluckhohn has suggested that any culture is "a tissue of redundancies," seeing this not as a problem but merely a statement of fact (1963, p. 120).

One way to reinforce a particular style of teaching is through the use of objects. In the South Milwaukee school, there was a major difference between the authoritarian third grade teacher and the democratic fourth grade teacher. Their different beliefs about degrees of structure appropriate to the classroom were clearly demonstrated in their use of some of the props that classrooms traditionally provide.

Two such props will be described here: desks and blackboards. Both are standard classroom equipment, yet lend themselves to a variety of uses depending upon the teacher. The city provides students with desks, but their arrangement is up to the individual teacher. There are a variety of standard arrangements, from rows of individual desks to groupings of four or more desks. In this case, the third grade teacher started the students out in rows of desks for a month, but as soon as she thought they would be able to handle it, put the desks into permanent groups, keeping them that way for the remainder of the school year. Given the same desks, and approximately the same number of desks and same size classroom to work with, the fourth grade teacher put the desks in difference groupings for different activities, using the arrangement of individual desks in rows as the neutral arrangement at the start of every day. Often the specific location of a desk even in the neutral position was hard to determine (for example, the desk I sat in was at the back of the room, but some days the last seat was the sixth in the row, others it was the seventh). It was not important to her that each desk have a permanent "at ease" position, just that the desks be moved into a variety of groupings as they became appropriate to the activities of the hour or day.

The use of the blackboard, as well as desks, can help to reinforce teaching style. The third grade teacher had a few pieces of permanent information on the board (number of students in the room in a corner, for example), and a space for temporary use (working out the math problem from the homework assignment in the middle of the board) but primarily the board was reserved for semipermanent information. This took the form of categories of information that the students always knew would be on the board, such as reading assignments by reading group, math assignments by math group, with specific page numbers varying by day. This was information the teacher posted on the board in the morning before the students arrived, and then did not refer to again until a student demonstrated that he or she had forgotten to check the board (which only rarely happened by the time I was observing in February, since the students had been trained to check the board daily without further instruction when the school year started in September). An example of this would be when a student was told "What's the rule in this classroom? Ana, you're missing something. Anything on the board you have to do first?" Here it is clear that the student was not only required to check the board for the assignment she was to do individually, but also required to know the order in which various assignments were to be done.

In the fourth grade classroom, there was little permanent information on the blackboard (only the alphabet in cursive writing posted across the top of the board), and little semi-permanent (a weekly schedule of events could generally be found there, and a daily schedule of events as well, along with current art projects by either the students or the teacher). In this class the daily schedule of events was critical, for the students had no way of knowing what would happen at what time unless they read it on the board. The teacher did not use the same schedule each day, as the third grade teacher did, nor did she consistently read the schedule to the students in the morning, although this sometimes occurred. The majority of the board was devoted to temporary work, often a combination of vocabulary sentences for a particular reading group to write out, and math instruction for a small group at the front of the room.

Complete redundancy, 100% redundancy, would be the same information presented in the same way in the same context. It can never occur, for in reality the context is always changed, if by nothing else then simply by the same information having already been presented once. Gertrude Stein's "A rose is a rose is a rose" is a well-known example of how this operates. The opposite, 0% redundancy, is also impossible, for that would imply new behavior that has never occurred in any way before. If it did occur, we would have no way to interpret it. Science fiction stories sometimes suggest that communication between alien species will, if it occurs, have the problem that we will have so little in common we will be unable to understand one another at all. Luckily, this is not a problem so long as we stay on earth and attempt communication only within the same species.

Some degree of redundancy between 0% and 100% is necessary in order to make interaction flow smoothly. Redundancy functions to facilitate communication in spite of all the factors of uncertainty which act against it. Not the least of these is the fact that people do not really pay that much attention to one another. When was the last time you really listened to every word of the lecture from your mother? Presenting the same information in several forms helps to ensure that it will be noticed at least once.

Further, we use redundancy to tell us about the degree to which a particular piece of behavior is trustworthy. That is, if one act indicates something, and another action, conveyed through another channel, indicates something else, we know we have to pay attention and figure out what is going on. Someone who teases often uses one channel to get across the verbal message, which might be insulting if taken seriously, and uses another channel to get across the message that it is only a joke, and is not to be taken seriously. We do not react to the single behavior in a single channel, but instead to the overall pattern, or what psychologists term the *gestalt* of a situation.

Bateson's work on the double bind may be relevant here. His research into the etiology (development) of schizophrenia resulted in the *double bind theory*, now widely accepted. Basically, a double bind occurs when someone is required to do two things which are incompatible. Doing the one makes the other impossible, but in a double bind situation that is exactly what is required. The only other prerequisites for a double bind are that the person so trapped is not permitted to escape (or redefine the situation), and the same or similar double binds must be repeated often. Double binds often consist of a verbal message and a nonverbal message, although this is not a requirement (Bateson, 1972c, pp. 206–208). Double binds have two major results, they can lead to insanity, or to creativity. The only problem is that we do not yet know enough to ensure only the latter result (1972c, pp. 271–278).

The type and amount of redundancy in interaction which is viewed as appropriate and normal is one more aspect of communicative behavior that is different from group to group. Gumperz, Aulakh, and Kaltman have given a good example of this in their study how Indian English speakers, who use verbal repetition to mark significance, are likely to be interpreted by Western English speakers as indicating "mere" redundancy, or trivialization (1982). Thus the attempt, which would be successful with speakers of the same style of English, is ineffective with speakers of a different style.

In sum, although before giving the matter serious consideration we may initially assume that the majority of communication is linguistic, or that nonverbal communication is by nature simple, neither of these assumptions would be correct. We must investigate human behavior in all its complexity, whether that means increasing the context we take into account, or the number of channels we include in our analysis.

CHAPTER 6
Communication as Multifunctional Behavior

Communication is multifunctional: it not only composes the primary relations of interaction but maintains the rules for the regulation of these relationships.
—Ray Birdwhistell (1963, pp. 128–129)

People are complex. Their interactions are complex as well. We do not do one thing at a time when we interact, like a child who cannot yet pat his or her head with one hand and rub his or her stomach with the other; instead, we engage in a variety of activities, and in a variety of levels, at the same time. More importantly, what we do with each other has meaning at several levels and conveys different implications to different participants. To understand the complexity of interaction, we begin with the assumption that people usually do more than one thing at one time.

Part of the complexity has to do with the fact that, for every action we take, there are other actions we do not take, and at times an observer must pay at least as much attention to what is not occurring as to what is occurring. "We live in a world in which everything exists or happens as part of a sequence or space-time order; these sequences of things and events are not separate and distinct but are presented as simultaneous and coterminous; many things exist and happen in any one situation" (Frank, 1926, p. 332). In other words, everything that happens is some way connected to everything else that happens and has various ramifications and repercussions that must be understood.

One implication of this is that most events will have ramifications for a variety of contexts, not just one. Zabor puts this simply but well: "no communicative interaction can be reduced to a single message with a single meaning" (1978, p. 163). Part of the complexity is that each act has multiple interpretations, all of which are simultaneous, and all of which are correct. When I wear the sweater my mother gave me, I am not wearing the one my husband gave me; this says something about relationships. At the same time, I am not wearing a T-shirt, which says something about my ability to dress appropriately for the weather. At the same time, if I wear the sweater with pants of the exact same color, I make a statement about effort expended in matching clothes. Whether the sweater is dirty or clean, it makes an additional statement about my interest in keeping clothes clean.[1]

Saying that communication is multifunctional is not at all the same thing as saying that it is multichannel. Bateson saw it as a problem that we sometimes confuse the two. Specifically, he was concerned that the various levels of functions not be confused with the plurality of channels.[2] In other words, a function is not a channel, no one-to-one correlation between the two exists. We *need not* convey information regarding one function through one channel, and information regarding another function through another channel, although it certainly would be possible for this to occur.

One of the more explicit analyses of the multiple functions of a communicative event is that provided by Katriel (1987) for *bexibudim,* or ritualized sharing among Israeli children. She concludes that this event has four major functions:

1. it is related to the tension between self-gratification and social accommodation: sharing serves as invaluable practice for social living and therefore has an important socializing function;
2. it serves to mark the outer boundaries of the child's social world (since you share, not with all others, but with specific others);
3. it is one way of instituting the egalitarian values of the larger culture, and children easily assimilate these as part of their peer group culture;
4. it reasserts the very existence of children's peer group culture as such since the children share snacks on the way home from school, which is a transitional moment (temporally, spatially, and socially) between the two major domains of school and home.

One of the implications of communication as multifunctional is

---

[1] Because of the multifunctionality of communication, Hewes (1979) suggests that it makes sense to suspend mutually exclusive categories when doing functional coding of interaction.

[2] See Rawlins (1987, p. 71) for further discussion of this.

that a single behavior can function as a member of an obvious class, and a less apparent class, both at the same time.

In the South Milwaukee first grade classroom one day, the teacher was reading a story about Curious George to the class. When she first used the word ostrich, one of the students, Michael, repeated the word out loud. The teacher looked up from the book at him.

Michael: What's that noise?

The teacher looked puzzled, but did not answer. There was a lengthy pause, while everyone listened to see what the noise was.

Wendy: The men tearing up the roof.

The teacher made no response, but returned to the story. At one level, Michael has simply asked a reasonable question and received an answer. But at least one of the other things that happened here is that Michael first (legitimately) obtained the teacher's attention, but then asked a question having nothing to do with the book, or the immediate event (reading circle). It is important to realize that such unrelated questions were not normally permitted while reading a book. Only after re-reading my own fieldnotes did I decide that my response was probably inappropriate for this context. The teacher did not like the students to change the subject, that being a right she reserved for herself (on the grounds that it was impossible to run a class of first graders any other way) and by not responding to Michael, she indicated that he was asking an inappropriate question. By responding, I ratified the topic change.

Goffman provides extensive discussion of one component of how communication is multifunctional: frames. It actually was Gregory Bateson who first used the word *frame* in a nonliteral sense. He wanted to talk about social or psychological frames, and made use of two analogies in doing so. He was influenced by the physical analogy of the picture frame, and the more abstract analogy of the mathematical set (1972c, p. 186). Bateson attributed the following characteristics to social frames: (a) they are both exclusive and inclusive (since a frame marks a boundary, and when we put a boundary line around something we are both including everything inside the line in a single category, and at the same time excluding everything outside of that line as not part of the category); (b) they delimit the ground on which the figures are to be perceived (since one of the functions of a boundary line is to distinguish between figure and ground); and (c) they are metacommunicative (that is, they give the receiver instructions for interpreting the message in the frame) (1972c, pp. 187–188).

Goffman took Bateson's comments on frames and wrote a book on the topic, *Frame Analysis*. He never actually defines frames, but essentially views them as principles of organization used by people to structure social life (1974, pp. 10–11). The book makes the argument that several quite different activities are often successfully carried on at the same time, and that we all have the ability to maintain or change frames nearly as often as we like. Goffman calls the separate activities in which we engage *tracks*, and suggests that there are four major tracks to be considered. The first is the *dominant track*, and it is the main focus of attention. The second is the *disattend track*, which refers to our response to potentially disruptive events (or people): We are able to give them sufficient attention that we learn whether they are immediately threatening or not, and then can ignore them.[3] The third is the *overlay track*, which includes all events or people that have messages which must be heard or understood, but which do not constitute major interruptions. The fourth is the *concealment track* and includes all activity making my actions in the dominant track possible. An example will help to clarify the proper use of these terms. If my dominant track is typing a paper at a computer in a room where others are present, the fight two people are having at one end of the room could be relegated to the disattend track; the librarian who comes to tell everyone that the library will close in 30 minutes is understood but not permitted to interrupt my activity, and this is on the overlay track; and the discussion between librarians as to who would make the announcement about the closing (a discussion I did not hear) took place on the concealment track.

Framing is essentially a way of putting order where there was only disorder before (Smith, 1968, p. 2). In this, framing can be seen to function similarly to the act of classification. Both are ways of putting things, whether objects or ideas, or people, into categories

---

[3] Goffman points out the similarities between these directional signals and Bateson's concept of metacommunication. This idea will not be pursued here any further, since Bateson's metacommunication has not been introduced yet.

so we can better respond to them quickly. At the same time that frames are closely related to the act of classifying, in that both create categories, they also have much in common with the act of naming. Both in some sense are capable of creating what did not exist previously, which is what names do. This occurs because borders help to create representation. Before you have representation you must designate borders, but borders alone do not always result in representation (Uspensky, 1973, p. 140). Barbara Herrnstein Smith argues that we create something new in three ways: through labelling, through isolation, and through framing (1968, p. 259). *Labelling* is essentially a form of naming, which can be viewed as a kind of framing; *isolation* is clearly a form of framing (of drawing a boundary line around something); and so framing emerges as our main way of creating new things. Once we call attention to a thing, and cause others to notice it, it exists for people who had never noticed it before, and in this way can be said to exist for the first time.

Children must learn to recognize frames as they occur, and to mark their own frames so others can recognize them; adults we expect to have the knowledge.

David (4 years old) is playing with several orange crates in a Philadelphia day care center. I walk over to talk to him.

Wendy: Hello.
David: I am in the choo-choo train.

He gets out and walks away. A few moments later he returns.

David: I can go up the tractor.
Wendy: What do you do once you're up there?
David: I'm walking in the tractor. I can close the window and I can drive.

He gets out and again leaves. Steve comes over and begins talking to me. David returns.

David: No, you can't play.
Wendy: Why not?

David gets up on top of the orange crates.

David: This is a bed.

David lies down on the orange crates. Steve leaves.

What is happening here can be interpreted in many ways. I think the most reasonable assumption is that David is down-keying in-between each statement he makes. According to Goffman, *downkeying* is the name for what we do when we move out of one track or key and into the dominant track again. Here, every object David mentions is related only to the orange crates, and not to the objects appearing before or after it in his string of comments. He shifts between reality and play, between orange crates and imaginary objects that the crates become. Because he cannot yet create a structure consisting of several *laminations* (Goffman's word for series of tracks, all maintained at the same time), he must break frame every time he wants to shift from one imaginary object to another. Adults do not need to break frame so often: they can handle multiple laminations with ease, as Goffman's work demonstrates.

Because frames permits us to handle a variety of information in a variety of ways, and on a variety of levels, all at the same time, they are useful theoretical constructs in our efforts to understand communication as multifunctional. Goffman's discussion of frames does not directly address this, but I do not think he would object to this application of his work.

One of the implications of the discussion so far is the fact that what constitutes relevant background knowledge necessary to understanding interaction changes from moment to moment. It is never possible to once sit down and learn everything you will ever need to know about a family or the structure of an office, then ignore changes and interpret all new behavior based on that one-time learning. All past behavior is a part of how we interpret new behavior, whether past means 40 years ago or 10 minutes ago. We constantly reshuffle our interpretations of what occurs based on what else we are able to take into account. Since people have different experiences in life, it is likely that they also interpret the same behavior in different ways, and thus the same behavior can function in different ways for the various participants.

In the third grade South Milwaukee classroom one day, the teacher invented an eleventh and a twelfth commandment.

Teacher: Ana, the eleventh commandment is "Thou shalt mind thy own business," and the twelfth is "Thou shalt zip thy lip."

The day before an eleventh and twelfth commandment had similarly been mentioned, but they had been different. Then the eleventh was "Thou shalt zip thy lip" and the twelfth was "Thou shalt be quiet." I found it particularly interesting that none of the children tried to check which was the "real" set of commandments. Apparently they had correctly interpreted the teacher's desire to get them to change their behavior through appealing to their knowledge of the ten commandments, and no one thought these were traditional commandments their parents had somehow forgotten to mention, despite the teacher's use of traditional language (*thou* and *shalt*).

The various functions of communication are rarely described in detail; those who say it is multifunctional often assume their readers will know what is involved. In the following pages, therefore, several suggested lists of functions of communication will be outlined and compared, and then two of the functions, usually ignored but extremely important, will be described in further detail: metacommunication and phatic communication.

FUNCTIONS OF COMMUNICATION

One of the standard lists of functions in communication is that prepared by Roman Jakobson (1960). It initially was described as a list of the functions of language, but serves as an equally useful list of the functions of communication defined more generally, with only minimal changes required. Jakobson's list includes six functions: the referential, the emotive, the conative, the poetic, the phatic, and the metalingual. The *referential* function is that most generally acknowledged as important, though it has perhaps less significance than we generally grant it. It refers to fact that we need to pass on new information to others, and that we use language (communication) to do this. The focus here is the meaning of the message. Synonyms used by others for this function are denotative, cognitive, or new informational. The *emotive* function refers to the fact that we can convey information about the (emotional) state of the speaker at the same time as giving other new information to the listener. It is sometimes labelled the expressive function. The parallel to this is the *conative* function, which emphasizes the hearer. Jakobson suggests that the imperative is the purest expression of the conative. The conative is often less concerned with expressions of the listener's state than with getting the listener to do something. The *poetic* function (sometimes called the stylistic) describes a focus on the message itself—on the words in which it is put (or actions, for communication writ large). Here the interest is less in the new information generated by the message than the form in which it is presented. The *phatic* function is taken from Broislaw Malinowski, and stresses the maintenance of the relationship between the speaker and the hearer. Here the continuation of a state of interaction is the focus, rather than what is said or how it is said. And the last of the six, the *metalingual* function, refers to the ability to talk about talk, to refer to the code rather than just use it. By extension, what is usually termed the *metacommunicative* function, when we move to a discussion of not language but communication, refers to the ability to communicate about communication. Any comment on what has just been said or done and how it is to be understood, any question about the intent behind an action, is metacommunicative.

Although these are useful concepts, they are hardly the only version of what functions of communication should be taken into account.[4] Bateson has provided some useful comments on one particular aspect of the functions of communication: the fact that people do not limit themselves to a single function at a time, but are capable of demonstrating multiple functions concurrently. Bateson's work is extensive, and there is no one place to go for a precise view of this point, but Rawlins provides the following summary of his approach:

> Since the slightest human behavior exhibits multifunctional communicative potential, the embodiment or enactment of these functions is not necessarily conscious or intentional. Thus every person's communication with another human being continuously involves composites of the following functions, i.e. every communicative cue embodies sixfold message potential. (1987, p. 61).

He outlines the six functions presented by Bateson as being:

1. the *identity* function (the identity of the person emitting the cue is indicated; this would be roughly parallel to Jakobson's emotive function combined with the metacommunicative in an interesting way);
2. the *denotation* function (this connects the immediate communi-

---

[4] In addition to the Jakobson article mentioned, Halliday (1978) is one of the standard references, as is Hymes (1964). Leech (1974, pp. 10–27) provides a variation on the theme by his discussion of the seven types of meaning.

cation with some other event, and as such would comprise another part of the metacommunicative function);
3. the *codification* function (the larger culture is invoked; again, this comprises a part of the metacommunicative function);
4. the *command* function (this calls attention to other cues by the speaker or hearer; it is a combination of the conative plus the metacommunicative functions);
5. the *relationship* function (a combination of the phatic with the metacommunicative; it is a statement specifically of relationship, rather than of any other aspect of metacommunication); and
6. the *framing* function (this provides contextualization cues, and as such is one critical part of the metacommunicative function).

Since Bateson's main interest (in this connection) is in metacommunication, it should come as no surprise that the majority of the functions he discusses are in some way a part of that one function, or a combination of that plus others.

There are actually, then, not one but two meanings to the word *function*. The first refers to functions as they have been outlined by Jakobson and Bateson: A communicative act has a particular function when it serves a particular purpose. Yet the meaning of functions as described at the beginning of this chapter is important as well. Any communicative act has a particular role to play, a function, within at least one hierarchy of events; it does something, has some result, some influence over what else will occur. It has, in short, a place in the larger behavioral stream, which can be noted and studied.[5] In this sense we cannot create a short checklist of potential functions, although doing so would certainly make the researcher's job easier.

In observing children in the day care center in Philadelphia, I noticed many examples of how the same communicative act functioned in more than one capacity. When several children are playing together and one suddenly leaves the group, there is occasion for a variety of messages to appear concurrently. For example, at the end of one day, when a child's mother came to pick her up sooner than her friends' mothers, she left, and the play sequence was in danger of disintegrating while the other children stopped what they were doing in order to watch her leave. But then one of the children said, "This is a

---

[5] See Sigman (1987, pp. 61–65) for a related discussion of behavior functioning simultaneously in several hierarchies of meaning.

bed," pointing to an orange crate, and the play continued. This one statement can be said to have three functions. It establishes a play frame, it reaffirms a play frame when there was a danger that it would be broken, and it serves as an invitation to others to join in the play. In this way, one communicative act fulfills three functional slots.

We should probably spend more time paying attention to the various functions of behavior. It is difficult to do, for we all want to find the single meaning behind a behavior, and to have to handle multiple interpretations makes the analyst's job more difficult, but once we recognize that various functions can be fulfilled simultaneously, it is up to us to study how the process works.

METACOMMUNICATION

Literally, *metacommunication* means "communication about communication." Every act of communication has two parts: (a) content (or message), and (b) instructions on how to interpret the content (message about the communicative process or relationship). It is the instructions which are the metacommunicative component of the interaction (Ruesch & Bateson, 1951, p. 158; Watzlawick, Beavin Bavelas & Jackson, 1967, p. 54). The metacommunicative message "we are communicating," sent concurrently with all interaction, is probably the single most important message sent (Ruesch & Bateson, 1951, p. 213), and so, although it has rarely been studied in detail, it is important to describe it fully here.[6]

In addition to whatever else a communicative act does, "all communication defines, maintains, or changes the nature of the relationship between communicants" (Beavin Bavelas & Segal 1982, p. 105). This is an unqualified statement, for it is not just that some communication encompasses a metacommunicative function, *all* communication does. The point is taken from Bateson, but nowhere does he phrase it quite so bluntly. This is the reason we must study metacommunication: It is always present. Bochner and Krueger suggest that this understanding is "one of the most widely accepted doctrines in communication" (1979, p. 203). If this is more than

---

[6] Among the more interesting applications of the idea of metacommunication are Babcock-Abrahams (1977), Cazden (1974), Sanches (1975), Schiffrin (1980), McGuire (1980), and Clark (1978). In the communication literature, see Wilmot (1980).

wishful thinking on their part, it is strange that so little research has been devoted to the topic so far.

Metacommunication is to be understood as that part of communication which is at the abstract, rather than the concrete, level (Ruesch & Bateson, 1951, p. 223). Whatever its form, metacommunication is thus always to be thought of as a qualifier to behavior, rather than simply being more behavior. As such, metacommunication serves both to illuminate the patterns underlying daily interaction and to display the complexity of what happens when people interact with one another.

Raymond Firth suggests that rituals are metacommunicative, conveying information regarding control and regularization within a culture (1973, p. 301), and Katriel has taken this comment and demonstrated how it works in her study of a secular ritual, "griping," in adult Israeli discourse (1985b). The studies of a wide range of secular rituals by others provide additional supporting evidence (Moore & Myerhoff, 1977b).

In the study of conversation, Ragan has pointed out that metacommunicative talk is used "to frame messages for purposes of clarifying, interpreting, and managing conversational meaning and communicator roles" (1983, p. 159). These are important functions, and so it should be clear that metacommunicative messages do essential work in conversations, and also in other types of social interactions.

One implication is that not all metacommunication is verbal. Birdwhistell provides a superb example of what can occur when two metacommunicative messages (both nonverbal) conflict. He supplies illustrations (taken from a film) of a clinically diagnosed schizophrenic mother diapering her baby. She uses a push on the baby's arm to convey the metacommunicative message "move arm up," and a push against the baby's body to convey the metacommunicative message "move arm down." When, in the course of the film, the mother does both at one time, she causes a Batsonian double bind, in that the baby cannot possibly do both of the things she wants him to do. The result is that the baby's arm waves up and down (1970, pp. 18–23).

There are two types of metacommunicative messages. The first is overt or explicit, and involves the ability to openly discuss an interaction as it is occurring. In this case the interaction itself becomes the topic of discussion, and all other topics are temporarily put in abeyance. This implies that participants have the ability to stop the ongoing transaction at will for a brief period of time, in order to metaphorically step outside of it and comment upon it. In so doing, participants retain the ability to resume the interaction at the point where it was broken, when they have finished discussing it. In this way, the varying assumptions and interpretations of the participants can be verbalized and brought into the discussions before any conclusion is reached. Such comments as "did you really mean what you said?" or "you don't seem to understand what I'm talking about" are examples of explicit metacommunication. These are essentially a time-out from the interaction proper.

The following transcript involves three participants in the Philadelphia day care center: Malaika, who is 5 years old; Amy, who is 4; and myself.

Malaika: You want to hear ano—
a very short story?

Wendy: ⌈ Okay.
Amy: ⌊ No.

Malaika:⌈ Yes. Once upon a time—
Amy: ⌊ No.

Wendy: Yes. Tell a very very short story.

Malaika:⌈ Once upon a time—
Amy: ⌊ I wanna—
I wanna make two stories.

Wendy: Okay.

Amy: And the last one will be short.

Malaika: Once upon a time
No
The one that
The second story has to be a very very short one
like mine's gonna be.
Once upon a time there was a little girl
and she had a little kitty cat
the end.

Amy: ⌈ (laugh)
Wendy: ⌊ (laugh)

Wendy: That *is* a short story.

Malaika: You wanna hear a very very very very short story?
This is only a little joke.

Wendy: Okay.

Malaika: Once upon a time
the end.

Malaika: ⎡(laugh)
Wendy: ⎢(laugh)
Amy: ⎣(laugh)

Then Amy tells a long story about a little boy and a giant. When she appears to have run out of inspiration, Malaika prompts her.

Malaika: And that's the end?
Amy: Yeah.
Now let me tell you this very very short story.
Once upon a time there was a boy and then the end.
Malaika: Now tell a joke.
Amy: Once upon a time the end.

This is a transcript of two children learning to distinguish between two common genres of verbal interaction, stories and jokes.[7] There are several things which are important to notice about this text. One has to do with the influence that the presence of an adult may have upon the behavior of children. This story was produced in response to my request for a story, as part of a longer research project which resulted in my presence at the day care center 20 hours a week for 5 months. By asking for stories, I most likely encouraged the children to think about the definition of what exactly fit that request. That is, I initiated this and other storytelling sessions, in which a small group of children (between one and five) would sit or stand near me at one side of the room and tell stories of various sorts to me and my tape recorder. They frequently passed judgement on one another, in order to decide whether or not the narratives they produced for me were appropriate examples of *stories*. Children who were too young to be able to produce a coherent narrative were tolerated only by me,

---

[7] Barbara Herrnstein Smith (1968, p. 101) supplies an example of a similar story:

I'll tell you a story
About Jack a Nory,
And now my story's begun;
I'll tell you another
About Jack and his brother,
And now my story is done.

not by their peers. They were generally shuffled aside once they had demonstrated their inability to tell "good" stories, and were told in no uncertain terms that they were not yet big enough to participate. In this specific example, I laughed at the "joke" Malaika created. This served to reinforce her new understanding of the proper boundary between joke and story, for the children exhibited awareness of the fact that jokes result in a response of laughter, while stories normally do not.

Notice also that the "teacher" in this situation is not an adult, but a 5-year-old, who learns what she teaches the "student" (at other times her peer) only moments before she passes on her knowledge. As with adults who fill the role of teacher, Malaika checked Amy's newly acquired knowledge by requiring her to produce a joke after she completed both a story and then a "very very short story." The interaction between them is helpful to both: Malaika reinforces her definition of the boundary between story and joke by teaching it someone else immediately upon having worked it out for herself, and Amy learns it sooner than she probably would have under other circumstances.

Both children exhibit knowledge of the appropriate beginning and end markers of stories, by using the phrases *once upon a time* and *the end*. These are the earliest parts of the general concept *story* that young children acquire, passively (thus demonstrating competence, when they recognize them as story components) if not actively (which would require performance, that they be able to accurately produce them)[8] When some of the younger children told stories, they knew how to begin and how to end; the trouble came in the middle, when they told long, rambling sequences of events that others refused to recognize as appropriate, or certainly as good, stories. I have not transcribed the complete story that Amy begins to tell, for just this reason. To someone other than the storyteller, it is not obviously coherent.

This example permits us to actually watch as two children learn to label their behavior as belonging to particular categories and, by gradually narrowing down the field, to determine the exact borderline between them. In this case, it is a matter of learning names for and learning to distinguish between two

---

[8] See Heath (1983, pp. 294–295) for a related example of metacommunication in children's talk, where the topic under explicit discussion is the difference between "story" as used at home, and "story" as used at school.

frequently used categories of speech: story and joke. Bateson has suggested that the most important thing children need to learn about the world is that as adults we categorize everything, in order to divide up a complex world into manageable pieces. Learning any specific category is not nearly as important as learning that categories exist (1956, p. 148). This example demonstrates one part of exactly how children go about learning to distinguish between related and similar categories, and suggests that they have the ability to do so at a conscious, verbal level. Through the use of metacommunication, Malaika and Amy were able to step outside of the interaction in order to discuss it, and in so doing increased and confirmed their understanding of exactly what they had learned.

The second type of metacommunication is quite different in that it involves the ability to implicitly, or tacitly, give instructions on how to interpret an interaction. This implies not a single level of interaction, but a dual level: saying or doing something while at the same time sending a second message which explains how to interpret what is being said or done. In this case the primary transaction is not stopped in order for metacommunicative messages to be exchanged, but rather a secondary transaction is begun, and continued concurrently with the first. Despite the fact that Goffman is known best for his work on frames, it is Bateson who has devoted the most effort to analyzing our use of implicit metacommunicative messages (1956).

The activity known as *free play* in a school (in this case, the Philadelphia day care center with 40 children playing together) is difficult to observe.[9] It serves well as a test case for the concept of communication as patterned behavior, for, if this has pattern, surely all interaction must. It is hard to believe that what looks like nothing less than absolute chaos has any organizing principles. But even out of this apparent chaos, it is possible to observe a minimum of five metacommunicative messages. They are more or less chronological, meaning that, if all five were to occur in a single instance of play, they would occur in a particular order. Each of the messages fills a functional slot, which may be filled by a given behavior, rather than being specific behaviors in and of themselves. Upon occasion one specific behavior may be said to

[9] A previous discussion of these data was presented as Leeds-Hurwitz (1979).

serve two functions, or fill two slots. On other occasions, a slot will remain empty, which leads to the conclusion that some messages are optional rather than required.

The first message is the *invitation,* which might be phrased as "shall we play?" Every time one child walks up to another and says "Will you play with me?" or "Let's play," or hands another child a toy, he or she is making use of this signal. This message is optional rather than required, since presenting an invitation is not a prerequisite for the establishment of a play sequence. An example which demonstrates this is the following: a boy picked up a box and carried it over to his friend. He put it down, saying, "This is my suitcase and I'm coming to visit you." There was no separately voiced invitation to play, but rather an attempt to immediately establish the play frame.

Chronologically the second message is one identified by Bateson (1956), which he phrased as "this is play." It is clearly the most important marker, for it signals how the interaction as a whole is to be interpreted, not only by the participants but often by observers as well. Bateson suggests that "this is play" can stand as an invitation to play, and I would have to agree. Nevertheless, I make the argument for separating out an invitation which is distinct because there are occasions on which both communications of intent and of frame are clearly present. An example of the two messages occurring in the same sequence was provided by a girl walking over to two friends and saying, "Let's play house. You be the daddy, and you be the baby, and I'll be the mommy." Her first sentence is an invitation to play, while the second establishes the play frame.

This second possible message, "this is play," is the only one which is both necessary and sufficient in order for a given situation to be defined as play. The definition or *establishment of the play frame* must always occur at some point in play. If no participant supplies it, then the activity in which they are engaged cannot be considered to be play. A clear example of a verbal "this is play" signal occurred when a 5-year-old boy said to his 4-year-old friend, "Let's go fight in there," and the friend replied, "Okay. I won't even cry because we're just playing and it won't hurt."[10] Some additional nonverbal "this

---

[10] In the discussion of Bateson's presentation "The Message 'This is Play'" at the Macy Conference, one of the participants, John Spiegel, suggested that the functional

is play" signals which I have observed on numerous occasions include exaggeration of actions, extended repetition, and laughter.

It is possible for the establishment of a play frame to be in doubt, or not accepted by all participants. Bateson briefly refers to the message "is this play?" discussing it in terms of the teasing that occasionally occurs, when the question at hand is whether the interaction is intended to be playful or serious (1956, p. 173; see also 1972b, p. 182). He suggests that this should be considered to be metaplay, because it is on a different level than play, since it questions the entire interaction (1956, p. 207). I would argue that, since all of the metacommunicative messages are metaplay rather than play itself, this message should simply be considered an alternative form of the basic message, "this is play." The only difference is that, while establishment of the play frame is essential, questioning it is not, and, in fact, only occasionally occurs.

The third metacommunicative message, "this is still play," is a *maintenance* signal. This is again an optional message, for it often seems to be omitted. One of the reasons this is possible is that, as before, a "this is play" message can serve double duty and be interpreted, not only as establishing the play frame but as a maintenance marker as well. In fact, it is possible to argue that every "this is play" marker which occurs after the first (which only establishes the play sequence, since there is as yet nothing to be maintained) serves this dual function. As with the invitation, the argument for including a separate maintenance slot is that there are some messages which do not seem to be anything except a "this is still play" signal. An example occurred when three boys were taking turns building with blocks. After the first two had taken their turns, the third said, "It's my turn now." By saying this, he can be understood to make the statement that there has been play, and to attempt to insure that there will be further play. But this is not really a "this is play" signal.

Many of the "this is still play" messages appear when there is a chance that the play frame will be broken. For example, every day at 12:00 the director of the day care center would

---

slot of "this is play" might be filled by the absence of expected signals such as yelping (in Bateson, 1956, p. 189). They were discussing animals rather than children; with children, the absence of crying might be the parallel. The fact that a metacommunicative message can be the *absence* of behavior which might otherwise be expected to occur is an important point.

say, "It's time for lunch; put away your toys and stop playing now." As a result there was often some doubt on the part of the children as to the precise moment they would stop playing (they rarely stopped immediately; there was some room for negotiation). At this point there often occurred an exchange of signals between the children, and any "this is play" signal offered reaffirmed that the play frame would be maintained, thus serving double duty, and being interpreted as a "this is still play" signal as well.

The fourth metacommunicative message is the one which *breaks the frame:* it says "this is no longer play." This is clearly not an optional signal, since children are not always in a play frame. The signal "this is no longer play" serves either to terminate the play of the group or to mark one child's exit from the group. An example of the latter occurred when a 4-year-old boy said, "I'm not the bad guy anymore, so stop chasing me," and left the room.

It is quite possible that presentation of a "this is no longer play" message can be viewed as requiring a "this is still play" message in response by some of the participants, if the play is to continue. For example, when one child said, of an orange crate, "This is my car," and his friend answered, "No, it isn't, it's an orange crate," the first child said loudly, "But we're playing it's my car."

There are cases in which the "this is no longer play" message is imposed by someone or something outside of the group of participants in the play sequence. Sometimes it may be sufficient to break the play frame, as in the above example of the director telling the children to stop playing, for many of them do stop. In this case, the children do not themselves provide an additional "this is no longer play" signal.

These four signals would seem to complete the entire sequence: there is an invitation to play, establishment of the play frame, maintenance of that frame, and breaking of it. However, in some instances there is another added on to the previous ones. This comes in two varieties: "that was play" and "that was not play." The function both of these messages serves is to renegotiate the frame of an activity after it has ended. At least one of them frequently occurs when there is some doubt or dispute as to the type of play just completed, or they may simply occur as a reaffirmation of type of frame. A very common "that was play" marker is laughter immediately following disintegration of the play frame. An example of the "that was not play" marker occurred when what was intended as play had all too real results. When, after a pretend fight, one child ran over to me and said, "He hit me," and started to cry, he was saying that the pretend fight had had real consequences. Thus he was reinterpreting the sequence of events after the fact as having been real rather than play, since the consequences had been real.

Although these two markers would appear to be mutually exclusive, they often occur one after the other. This happens when children disagree about whether what has just occurred was play or not. In the example given above, I asked the child who had been accused of hitting his friend what had happened, and he responded, "But I didn't mean to hurt him. We were only playing."

In some cases, when there is disagreement among participants over whether what has occurred was play or not, an entire play sequence will be reenacted once, or even several times, until a consensus has been reached. I have watched three children play with blocks, and a fourth come over and knock them down. A discussion ensued regarding whether his doing so had been an appropriate part of their play or whether it had been done on purpose to stop them from playing. After they agreed that his knocking over the blocks was acceptable as play, they reenacted the entire sequence.

The difference between these renegotiation messages and the message mentioned earlier, "is this play?" is really only one of timing: "is this play?" occurs during the event, asking what sort of interaction is occurring; "that was (not) play" asks the same sort of question after the event is over.

It has been suggested that there are five different metacommunicative messages which occur in children's free play, and that they are related chronologically. They are not all required, since only the establishment of frame and breaking of frame are necessary; the others are optional. The five are summarized in Figure 6.1.

Figure 6.1.   Metacommunicative Messages Occurring in Free Play

(invitation)	"shall we play?"
establishment of play frame	"this is play" / "is this play?"
(maintenance of play frame)	"this is still play"
breaking of play frame	"this is no longer play"
(renegotiation of play frame)	"that was play" / "was not play"

( ) = optional

This example demonstrates that even an activity such as free play, which appears random to the observer, is actually highly rule-governed. The metacommunicative messages provide a structure for the event and inform the participants' interpretations of it. The children rarely overtly discussed the interaction, yet they were busy learning the rules despite this. My suggestion here is that these messages, and others that could be described, need to be viewed, not as behaviors, but as functional slots which are filled by specific behaviors. This permits a single behavior to fill more than one slot at a time.

As with other aspects of communication, use of at least overt metacommunication has been demonstrated to vary with cultural background. Gumperz, Aulakh, and Kaltman found that Indian English makes little use of explicit markers warning listeners of what is to come; Western English politeness norms require extensive use of such markers. Their example concerns a speaker stating that a request is about to be made (1982, p. 55). This becomes a problem when, instead of interpreting a lack of explicit metacommunicative statements as different norms of interaction, Western English listeners interpret the lack as rudeness.

Metacommunicative messages tell participants in an interaction what to expect from one another in the future, and how to interpret what has already happened in the past. Beinstein (1975) suggests that an entire community can exhibit metacommunicative messages, intended at the same time both for members and for outsiders. One of the interesting implications of her research is that we should perhaps expect fewer public conversations in troubled neighborhoods, and more in cohesive ones. Obviously, metacommunicative messages are closely tied to how meaning is negotiated through interaction, and are therefore very important to study.

PHATIC COMMUNICATION

Once we agree that communication is continuous, and there is a constant stream of behaviors which must be taken into account, the question might be asked, "How is it possible that we can handle all of this input?" One part of the answer has already been provided: We learn to let our unconscious sort the stream of behavior, and only pay conscious attention to a small percentage of what occurs.

The rest of the answer is that a majority of communication can be described as having a *phatic* function. The term was invented by an anthropologist, Bronislaw Malinowski (1956, p. 315), and refers to all interaction by which we assure one another that we are still interacting. Obviously this includes the majority of our behavior. We do not really need to pay close attention to what a friend says in the course of a 2-hour telephone call, for the main function of the call is not so much to transmit particular pieces of new information as to reaffirm that we are close enough friends to spend two hours talking together. In the evening, parents traditionally ask their children what happened in school that day, and ask each other what happened at work. Again, the main function of the interaction is not to transmit information about the events in question, but to reassure one another that, as members of the same family, they are sufficiently interested in one another's lives to ask the question, and to take the time to listen to an extended answer. Does it really matter whether your husband knows what your boss said to you this morning? Of course not, but it does matter that he wants to pay enough attention to you to listen while you tell him. The argument here is not that we do not transmit new information to one another, or that it is never important, but that we be wary of considering the transmission of new information to be the primary function of communication. It rarely is.

A good deal of communication concerns social identity and social relationship messages. Among other things, every time we manage an interaction successfully, we reaffirm the fact that we, as participants, belong to the same culture, and follow the same norms for interaction. We mutually define ourselves as appropriate members of the group; we do things our mothers would have called "polite," but that we merely call practical. We do not take a time out from the content of the interaction in order to establish our identities, or our relationship, instead we do it at the same time that we convey the content of our messages. Both are important, but, if one has to be chosen as more important, I would probably suggest, contrary to what common sense would argue, that the phatic function far outweighs the new informational function. There is time for only so much new information during a day; but reaffirming our social identities and reestablishing our relationships with others can never be done often enough.

Since the publication of *The Presentation of Self in Everyday Life* in 1959, much of Goffman's work has been explicitly concerned with the social construction of identity, and he tells us that "self, then, is not an entity half-concealed behind events, but a changeable formula for managing oneself during them" (1974, p. 573).[11] Saville-

---

[11] See Bourdieu (1987), Erickson and Schultz (1982, p. 69), McCall (1976), and

Troike points out the value specifically of language in establishing identity, calling it an identification badge (1982, p. 188). That is true, but we should not assume that language is the only ID badge we wear by which others more readily identify us.

Phatic communication operates between strangers as well as within a family. When we glance at another person on the street as we pass, we are telling them that we recognize their existence. By following the rules of public order so well documented by Goffman, we acknowledge that others are there, and that they deserve to be treated properly, just as we hope they will treat us. As a consequence, "many so-called empty gestures seem to serve primarily as signs that the sender is 'responsible' and can be counted on to play the social game of maintaining a surface agreement with and acceptance of the others" (Goffman, 1953, p. 40). In breaking social rules of interaction between strangers, we imply that others are not quite human, not quite deserving of the respect we normally pay to everyone we pass.

> In a neighborhood, there are a large number of strangers who fall into the category of "recognizable," yet we may never learn their names or hear their stories. In East Baltimore one of the long-time residents expressed this well when she explained to me that "There was a little old lady that I recognized from walking around the neighborhood, and we always exchanged hi and all that."

The majority of what we communicate has a phatic function. And most of the phatic messages we "send" are not "addressed" to anyone in particular, but rather to anyone who notices them. Lawrence Frank has quoted Norbert Wiener as suggesting that "the world is a myriad of To Whom it May Concern Messages" (1966, p. 1). Put this way, it is clear that we act in such a manner as to convey to any interested observers who we are, what we are like, and how we can be expected to act in the future.

In sum, phatic communication is concerned with the relationship between participants in an encounter, rather than with the exchange of information in the usual sense. The mere fact that two people are interacting is probably the most important thing to know about their interaction. The words they choose and the topics they discuss are secondary to the primary fact of interaction.

McDermott and Church (1976) for further good insights on identity as a social construction.

CHAPTER 7
Conclusion

Each of us is as much embedded in communication as communication
is embodied in all of us.
                              —Anthony Wilden (1981, p. 1)

The social world is by definition one created by the people who
live in it. And what we have created is a world of symbols. This
world has a pattern to it, it is not at all haphazard, but makes
sense to those who understand it. Since it has pattern, we, as
analysts, can study that pattern. New members of the group, whether
they are children joining adults for their first experience of symbols,
or members of one culture joining another, must learn the symbols
particular to that group. Since participants can learn it, we, as
analysts, can learn it as well. Our conception of communication as
patterned and learned must influence the techniques we use to
study interaction.

No behavior has meaning out of its proper context, and most of
the meaning we learn is taken from the context rather than the
behavior itself. This has implications for our research. Most importantly, it means that we must study interaction in its natural setting,
must have a natural history of human behavior. Part of the argument
that communication is bound to context is that it is multichannel.
We cannot utter words by themselves without intonation, and the
meaning comes as much from the inonation as from the vocabulary,
as much from our facial expression when we speak as from the
clothes we wear, as much from our movements as from the amount
of space between us when we speak. Therefore, we must study all
the channels of communication simultaneously, not one at a time.
We must look for the interplay between them which we know is
there, not ignore it or leave it for someone else to study. And, if
we understand communication to be multifunctional, we must take
into account much more than we are accustomed to taking into
account. We can no longer assume that each action has but one

151

purpose and meaning; we must look for the several functions that it can serve simultaneously, and look to see which functions are in play for which participants.

Understanding communication to be patterned, learned, context-bound, multichannel, and multifunctional complicates our lives terribly. But if it is a more accurate representation of communication, we must accept the complexity and learn to cope with it. We must match our research methods to our theoretical understandings; must apply what we know to be the case, rather than separate our methods from theory. Geertz (1980) suggests that interpretive theories *in and of themselves* imply an end to the rigid separation of theory and data, and I would have to agree.

The five concepts outlined in this book are those which I think central to an understanding of social communication theory. So far, they have been presented as distinct, but there is considerable overlap between them. Taken together, they form a shorthand guide to what is important in social interaction. That these concepts were discussed separately is not to imply that they are not in fact closely intertwined. But, although it may be accurate, it is difficult to discuss five things at once.

Each concept was described separately, as if the whole were a child's tower, easily disassembled into separate blocks. In fact, these various ideas are closely interrelated and were only separated so they might be described more easily. The purpose of this approach is to take the object of study (communication) apart in order to look at the composite parts more closely, and then put it back together again and observe the structure of the whole in all its complexity more clearly. The problem with this technique is that it can become difficult to ever really see the whole again without considering the separate parts; they tend to take on a life of their own. Despite the fact that I felt it necessary to destroy the total structure of communicative behavior briefly in order to look at it, much as a frog is destroyed when dissected by biology students, unlike the frog, who will never jump again, it is possible to reassemble the parts of behavior into a functioning, coherent whole again. The ultimate aim is not to permanently separate the characteristics of communication and point to precise boundary lines between them, but to reassemble the object of study at the end.

Let me return, then, to my five concepts, in order to stress a few of the major implications for method and research.

Communication as behavior with pattern

If communication has pattern, it is not random, but highly structured. What we observe in one interaction will help us learn how to interpret the next. The advantage is that we do not have to be exposed to all possible situations before we know how to react properly in them. The disadvantage is that the pattern is terribly complex, and we can never know how much we have left to learn in a new culture.

So, how does this translate into research methods? If communication has pattern, we have reason to study what are sometimes called the rules of interaction. We do not look for the rules so either we or others can conform to them. In fact, it is quite important to look at the ways in which it can be appropriate to break rules, for, with a little creativity, it is possible to break virtually any rule. At the same time, behavior is, and must be, to a large extent predictable if groups are to function at all. There is not enough time in the world to begin every interaction with a tabula rasa. We must be able to assume that a majority of what occurs will serve the purpose of maintaining a joint, coherent view of the world, of co-constructing a social reality we can all continue to support.

Communication as behavior we learn

We are not born knowing how to communicate properly for the culture in which we find ourselves, but learn how to interact as we grow up. Thus every culture can and does have different styles of interaction. The advantage is that even a newcomer to the society can learn to communicate appropriately. The disadvantage is that it means we must temporarily assume the role of a child, or of one who does not know how to interact appropriately, until we learn what will be taken for granted by others.

If people learn to communicate, we need to take the time to study them doing so. This suggests two major research thrusts. The first is that we must focus on children, and how they learn to communicate in a variety of settings; the second is that we should not leave questions of intercultural communication to a small subgroup of researchers. More of us need to make the attempt to compare behavior, if not from one country to another, then from one subgroup within a country to another, in order to discover more about how new members of a group learn to communicate appropriately.

Communication as behavior in context

No behavior has meaning in and of itself, outside the situation in which it occurs. The same gesture which "meant" resignation in one context can "mean" humor in another. The advantage is that, once we have been in a particular context, we will have learned something which can be transferred to all similar contexts. The disadvantage is that, when faced with an entirely new context, we may have little of the knowledge necessary to react properly.

Accepting that communication is context-bound carries with it the implication that we *must* study communication in its natural setting, thus leading to the approach known as the ethnography of communication. This is not a particularly easy way to do research, requiring both extensive training and a great deal of time, but it does result in a more complete understanding of interaction than is possible using many other methods.

Communication as multichannel behavior

More than language is involved in interaction. Language is just one of what are labelled *channels* of communication; the others are all nonverbal. This may seem obvious, but is something we tend to forget, or ignore. The most commonly mentioned channels are language, paralanguage (how we say what we say), kinesics (body movements), proxemics (use of space), touch, and use of objects. The advantage is that we communicate complex messages through the use of several channels at once. The disadvantage is that it is difficult to properly study even one nonverbal channel at a time, and attempting to study several simultaneously can be intimidating.

The prime methodological implication here is that we need to put the study of language (or discourse analysis, or conversation analysis) and various channels of nonverbal communication back together into the same research projects. If we divide ourselves into those who know how to study language and others who know how to study nonverbal behaviors, we are left with no one to put the pieces of the puzzle back together again.

Communication as multifunctional behavior

In our research we cannot look for "the" function of behavior, as if there were only one, nor can we afford any longer to ignore those functions we have traditionally ignored: phatic and metacommunicative. We must be willing to look to multiple interpretations of behavior rather than single ones, for people are complex. This is not necessarily easy to study, but, if it is shown to be the way people construct the world, we must be willing to study what is present rather than what we wish were present.

Each of these concepts builds upon the others. Taken together, they are a summary, a distillation, of much of what researchers into social communication have discovered and by now assume as obvious. Taken together, they demonstrate that communication is terribly complex. It takes a great deal of effort and skill to unravel seemingly obvious or superficial behaviors so the underlying structure is revealed. But the time spent in study is repaid when we discover precision where we saw before only random action, continuity where we saw only unrelated acts. Communication is a dance, a long, elaborate, difficult dance, and the most amazing thing about it is that so many of us learn to dance so well and with so little apparent effort. If we wish to study this dance, we cannot simplify the complexity merely in order to make it convenient for the researcher, but must come to terms with interaction as it exists in the real world.

What I would like to do by way of conclusion to this book, in addition to the traditional theoretical summary, is to provide a single extended example of how one might analyze the sort of data that would be acquired if the assumptions outlined in this book were in fact followed to their logical conclusion. This example is about ambiguity, and about what can happen when all the variables do not fit neatly into the prescribed categories. The participants in the interaction are able to handle the ambiguity constructively, and so it is the analyst's problem to understand what they are doing in all its complexity.[1] At the same time, this example has been chosen to demonstrate all five characteristics of communication, one in relation to the others. It shows how a small piece of behavior (use of names) is part of a larger pattern, how it demonstrates the learning the participants must have to utilize it properly, the important role of context to our understanding what is occurring, as well as the role played by other behaviors in other channels, and the many functions this one small behavior fulfills.

In offices, as in the majority of contexts for social interaction, people refer to one another by names.[2] The forms of address

---

[1] We rarely analyze ambiguity within communication, and so there is not an extensive list of references to mention. A rare article that considers ambiguity in organizational communication is Eisenberg (1984). There is a long tradition of studying the ambiguous within anthropology, however, and the work of Mary Douglas on pollution (such as 1966) and of Victor Turner on liminality (such as 1977) may be consulted to good effect.

[2] A version of the analysis presented below was previously published as Leeds-Hurwitz (1980).

they choose are easy to study, since they are particularly short and discrete items of communicative behavior. They also are important to study, for we attach great significance to the names we have for things, and even more to the names we have for the people we know.[3] There are few other symbolic behaviors, in fact, which are so useful to the analyst in terms of being both extremely important and extremely easy to study. The result is that there is a large literature on the study of naming behavior, but most of it occurs within the field of linguistics, particularly within sociolinguistics, rather than in the field of communication.

The choice of an address form is determined primarily by the relationship between the speaker and the person addressed (Brown & Ford, 1961, p. 375; Slobin, Miller, & Porter, 1968, p. 289). This statement should not, however, be taken to imply that, for any given situation, there is only a single appropriate form of address; it is more often the case that any one of several would be acceptable. As a result, the choice of a specific one from among the possibilities can be seen as a way of conveying subtle shades of meaning. As Fielding and Fraser have said of the more general use of language: "role relationships do not completely determine the selection of particular conversational behaviors. Indeed, it is the existence of choice which allows the individual to express particular meanings by selecting a 'marked' form rather then the expected socially prescribed form" (1978, p. 218). In each situation there are many factors involved in the choice of a particular form of address, from such obvious facts as the relative age, status, and sex of participants, to those usually of less significance, such as whether the exchange is a greeting or not. Some of these factors have a more direct influence on the choice of address form than others, but there is rarely only one acceptable form. Rather, of the possible forms, one is chosen which stresses something about the participants or their relationship which another would not have shown as well.[4]

In some studies the assumption seems to be made that there is a limited number of address forms. But often it is only a matter of recognizing that new forms can be created, or that

---

[3] "Names provide convenient clues to the degree of knowledge and involvement each person has with the other" (Denzin, 1970, p. 263).

[4] For further discussion of this notion, see Goffman's explanation of a "medley of voices" (1967, p. 61) and Berreman's description of "segments of social selves" (1972, p. 574).

infrequently used ones can be used in new ways. As Wittermans has documented, in a period of rapid social change,
forms of address are among those linguistic forms which most
clearly and immediately reflect that change (1967, p. 48). It
will be suggested in these pages that other causes also contribute to change in address forms, and that, whatever the
cause, new forms are deserving of careful study.

It follows from this that a priori assumptions regarding which
forms of address will prove to be significant in a given situation
are self-defeating; a researcher with such assumptions is likely
to miss anything new or unusual. The use of questionnaires
and other techniques designed to gather data quickly from the
largest possible sample can only increase the chance that any
new developments will either be missed or discounted as insignificant. For certain uses, there is no doubt that questionnaires are the best choice. As Bates and Benigni point out,
"the questionnaire responses do reflect what the informants
believe to be the ideal system of address" (1975, p. 286). When
the ideal system is understood already, however, as it is for
American English, they are of little help.

In her study of address forms in India, Bean clearly states
the argument against any form of quantification: "No attempt
was made to quantify the data: quantification is not an appropriate technique for the elucidation of semantic structures
where the rare usage may be as illuminating as common ones"
(1978, pp. xv-xvi). Once it is recognized that uncommon address
forms are significant, and further, that they are not likely to
be revealed in the study of ideal behavior, different methods
of research are clearly called for. Certainly the most useful of
these is the direct observation of actual behavior. Only when
the researcher is able to become an accepted part of the
situation can the development of an unusual address form be
studied from its inception through its acceptance (or rejection)
within a specific group of people.

In the following pages the development and use of two
uncommon forms of address in an office setting will be presented and analyzed.[5] In order to place these in context, the

---

[5] In recent years there has been much literature on organizational symbols of a
variety of sorts. See Dandridge, Mitroff, and Joyce (1980); Putnam and Pacanowsky
(1983); and Carbaugh (1986). One section of Pondy, Frost, Morgan, and Dandridge
(1983) stresses the role language plays in shaping organizational behavior, attitudes,
images, and values. This chapter was not conceived as a contribution to that literature,
but it certainly is parallel in its emphasis on the need to pay attention to the language

people, the situation, and the other address forms in use will be described in some detail. As Hymes has suggested, "appropriateness is a *relation* between sentences and contexts, requiring analysis of both" (1974, p. 156; his emphasis). Without an understanding of the context, the need for a new address form would not be apparent; with it, generalizations can be made and later tested in other situations.

Before continuing, a brief note on what this analysis does not include. It is a discussion of forms of *address* (terms used in speaking directly to someone), but not of forms of *reference* (terms used in speaking about someone). They are held by this author to be distinct categories, each worthy of separate consideration. And it is a discussion of personal names as forms of address almost exclusively. The other possible types of address usually studied are kinterms, pronouns, and status markers. Of these, kinterms were not applicable to the situation, pronouns in English do not convey information on status or intimacy, and status markers simply were not found in this situation, although they certainly would have been one possible option.

Context

The setting is a large business organization. Of primary concern is the office of the director, made up of the director, ten associate directors, supporting staff members, and secretaries. The director has two staff members (each with their own secretary), an administrative assistant (a clerical position just above that of secretary), and a secretary. Each associate director has at least one secretary; the majority also have one or more staff members.

The administrative assistant to one of the associate directors, Sue, will be the focus of this paper due to her use of unusual forms of address. She has worked for the same associate director for 9 years, starting as his secretary. She is a woman in her late thirties, extremely well-organized and efficient. When a vacancy as manager of the Committee Control (CC) office occurred, she applied for, and was given, the job.

The job she accepted has an ambiguous position in the

---

used in organizational settings. As Putnam summarizes the point: "Stories, myths, rituals, and language use are not simply reflections of organizational meanings; they are the ongoing processes that constitute organizational life" (1983, p. 40).

organizational hierarchy. There are ways in which Sue is now in a position parallel to that of the associate directors; however, there are just as many ways in which her position is unequal to theirs. The most important way in which Sue's position is equal to that of the associate directors is that she is now, as they are, accountable only to the director or a member of his immediate staff. An abbreviated version of the organizational chart is given in Figure 7.1.[6] Just as the director's own supporting staff members are in a sense outside of the main flow of information and responsibility in the organization, so is the CC manager.

The reason the manager of CC has such a high place in the organization hierarchy is that she has direct contact with the public. Nearly all of the work in the office is repetitive, mundane, and often simple to the point of being boring. But on occasion a situation will occur which poses a potential problem. If the wrong decision is made, the result will be adverse publicity for the organization as a whole. And so the primary qualifications for this job are the ability to efficiently organize and process a large amount of routine work, in conjunction with the ability to recognize immediately and correctly

Figure 7.1. Organizational Chart (Director's Office)
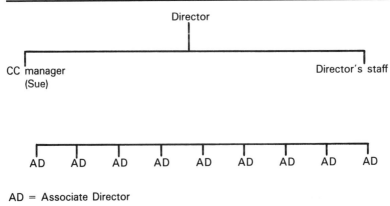

[6] Linda Putnam points out that: "functionalists typically treat organizational charts as fixed, concrete structures that determine authority and task relationships. Interpretivists, in turn, view hierarchical structure as an outgrowth of sets of relationships that have real consequences on everyday interaction. Both the chart and the behaviors that create it are in states of change. . . . Therefore, the chart is symbolic in that it represents previous and potential relationships, but it is also structural in that the use of or reference to it impacts on daily actions among members" (1983, p. 35).

resolve the few potential problems. So that these potential problems might be immediately brought to the attention of the director, the CC office is placed under his direct control.

That Sue's new job has status similar to that of the associate directors' in reality, and not just on paper, can be demonstrated in several ways. First, within a year of taking the job she succeeded in nearly doubling the physical size of the office by moving it across the hall. Second, in the same time period, she increased the size of her staff from three people to five. In an organization where additional space and employees are in constant demand, CC was granted both.

It must be recognized that, by requesting additional people and space, Sue put herself in direct, although certainly passive, competition with the associate directors. There is only a limited amount of space available in the present building, and, since there are no plans to move to another building in the near future, only as many people can be hired as fit into the available space. The result is that the director could agree to grant increased space and additional employees to CC only if he at the same time denied them to one of the associate directors (they being the only others with the authority to ask for either space or additional staff).

Furthermore, by gaining space and employees, Sue not only demonstrated her status, she actually increased it. First, she proved herself willing to enter into competition with the associate directors, and able to win. Second, by becoming responsible for a larger space and more people, she increased the prestige of both CC and its manager, for, in an environment of limited resources, the larger an office, and the more numerous its staff, the more important it is considered to be.

In contrast to the ways in which Sue has a position equaling that of the associate directors, there are many ways in which she is clearly not their equal. Some of these are intrinsic to the job, and others are due to the characteristics of the particular person holding that job. Of the former, the most significant can be called the *area of responsibility*. That is to say, decisions made in CC have virtually no impact on either the policy decisions or the day-to-day management of the institution (these being the primary concerns of everyone else in the building).

This fact leads to several results, the most important of which is that Sue has no legitimate, business-oriented reason for daily contact with anyone else in the building, neither the associate directors, nor their staff members and secretaries, nor the director. In some ways equal to the associate directors, she is in fact separated from them by a lack of common interests. She has never gotten to know many of the staff members, and has no reason to now. Formerly on familiar terms with all the secretaries, she is no longer one of their number. And, although contact with her boss, the director, is both present and legitimate, the amount of such contact is severely limited. This is not to say that Sue has no contact with anyone in the building outside of her own staff; the point is that she has virtually no *legitimate, work-oriented* contact. For all practical purposes, CC functions independently of the rest of the building, and could easily be located outside of it.

Of lesser importance, but still significant, are problems with the location of the office, and the type of staff working for Sue. It has been noted that she was able to increase both physical space and staff, but, impressive as this is, quantity of space and people is not the only important consideration. Looking first at the question of space, CC is located on the third floor of the building. There is nothing intrinsically wrong with the location, but the director is located on the first floor, and the space closest to him is viewed as being the most desirable, and that furthest away least so. Therefore, in a building made up of three floors, to be on the third floor has unfavorable connotations. (Only one of the associate directors is on the third floor; the others are either on the first or second floors.)

An additional problem with the particular space assigned to Sue is that she has no private office to call her own. She originally had one, but was able to gain additional staff members only at the expense of having to share her office with them. It should be noted that all of the associate directors have private offices, as do many of their staff members.

Looking next at the present staff of CC, differences again appear when they are compared with the staff of the associate directors. Each of the associate directors has responsibility for at least one staff member (usually male, usually well educated, usually well paid) who is hired to help the associate director with his many responsibilities, and at least one secretary. But the CC staff members can all be best described as clerks: they do simple, routine work which Sue, as the manager, oversees. Furthermore, in contrast to the associate directors' staff members, they are all female, all have only a minimal education (no one has more than a B.A., in a building where Ph.D.s and

M.D.s abound), and all are paid correspondingly lower salaries. In addition, Sue has no secretary; she either does her own typing and secretarial duties, or lets whoever has a free moment take over.

Looking now at the characteristics of the person presently holding the job of manager of CC, there are several important factors. One of these factors is Sue's age, for she is younger than all of the associate directors by at least 10 years. Another is her education, for she never went to college, and all of the associate directors have either an M.D. or a Ph.D., or both. A third is her sex, for all of the associate directors are men.[7] In addition to these, there is the factor of her prior history of employment with the organization. She has been a secretary and administrative assistant within the director's building, rather than coming from a position of authority in another part of the organization, as the associate directors have.

If the associate directors consider Sue's present job as nothing more than an upgraded clerical position, they do have some justification. The woman who had the job before Sue took it was originally administrative assistant to one of the associate directors and left the job as manager of CC to become administrative assistant to the director himself. Precedent thus suggests that the position as manager of CC should be considered to be a step above administrative assistant to an associate director, and a step below administrative assistant to the director.

To summarize briefly: Sue has similar status to the associate directors by virtue of her place in the organizational hierarchy, and her ability to engage in competition with them and win (demonstrated by her having obtained additional space and staff members); but her status is less than theirs in the areas of responsibility, location of her office, type of staff under her, amount of private space, her age, sex, education, and prior and future career path. The result of the combination of these factors is that her position in the organization can best be described as ambiguous. Due to this, choice of which address forms to use is unusually complicated.

When Sue was appointed manager of CC, it consisted of

---

[7] It is recognized that gender is clearly a factor in this situation, but as it is only one of many it is not discussed in great detail. For further readings on the role of gender as a variable in the use of address forms, see Key (1975), Kramer (1975), and Thorne and Henley (1975).

three people, and two crowded rooms connected by a narrow passageway. Not only did the manager not have a private office, she had no more space allotted to her than to anyone else. Within 6 months Sue had petitioned for and been granted a larger set of offices across the hall. The initial distribution of space provided one room as the manager's office, and the other as a shared office for the rest of the staff (Fanny, Marj, and Albertha). Within another 6 months Sue had increased her staff by two (Betty and Wendy) and reorganized the office, giving the two new staff members desks in what had previously been her private office.

Sue is the appointed manager of the office, but Fanny is the acknowledged second in command. She has worked in CC longer than anyone else, remaining through several changes in personnel (mainly changes in those over rather than under her). Marjorie and Albertha have both been in the office longer than Sue and are accustomed to taking their orders from Fanny. The two rooms are thus in many ways separate from each other, with Fanny occupying the position of greatest authority in her room.

Of the two new employees, Betty was secretary to one of the director's own staff members, but he left the organization, and the newly-appointed man brought his own secretary with him. Her acceptance of a job in CC was one of the few ways in which she could stay in the building. I had previously worked with Sue under the same associate director for 3 months, and when she changed jobs she asked if I would make the move with her; I spent 4 weeks with her in the first office, and nearly a year of part-time work in the second.

The relative status of the six people in CC can best be described as a simplified hierarchy, and can be diagrammed as indicated in Figure 7.2. Relative status within CC depended upon age, as well as on current and former areas of reson-sibility.

Figure 7.2.   Organizational Chart (Immediate office)

Naming Behavior

It is by now an established fact that "the principal option of address in American English is the choice between use of the first name (hereafter abbreviated to FN) and the use of a title with the last name (TLN)" (Brown & Ford, 1961, p. 375). As a result, much of the research on naming behavior has concentrated on the use of these two forms, and the meaning of each in relation to the other. There are three possible patterns of use in a dyad, and these have been analyzed in detail in Brown and Ford (1961, p. 380) and in Slobin, Miller, and Porter (1968, pp. 291–292). Briefly, they are:

1. Mutual exchange of FN, which has been related to intimacy, informality, and equal status;
2. Mutual exchange of TLN, which has been related to distance and formality; and
3. Nonreciprocal exchange of FN and TLN, where the FN is used to the person of lower status, and the TLN is used to the person of higher status.

Looking at these options, the address system used in American English would seem to be exceedingly simple, being composed of any two people and only three possible patterns of address. As a description of the ideal system, it is no doubt correct, but it is nonetheless misleading, for the actual system used in American English is not nearly so simple. The principal forms of address are not the only ones used, nor do people limit themselves to the convenient dyads postulated by the majority of researchers. Once all of the occurring forms of address are considered, and all of the people in a given environment are included, the system outlined above can no longer be viewed as sufficient and complete.

Obviously, the research described in this paper makes no false claim to being a description of the complete repertoire of address forms for all speakers of American English. The claim cannot even be made that all of the address forms used by all of the people within a single building are described. The only thing being attempted is the description of the address forms used by a single person in her relations to others in the building. The point is not to gather all of the existing data, but to describe two unusual pieces of behavior in their context, so that their use may be better understood, in the hopes that this will lead to a further comprehension of how address systems function in everyday life.

There are really two separate parts of the business organization under study to be considered, each in its relation to Sue: the immediate context (the CC office) and the larger context (the building as a whole). The patterns of address in each level of context will be described separately.

Within CC everyone uses FN as their primary form of address to each other and to their manager. It is not used to the exclusion of other forms, however, for no-naming (ø) (avoiding the use of a name entirely) and TLN also appear, though infrequently. The use of these forms is rare, and seems to depend primarily on the immediate context in which they are found. For example, TLN might occur in a conversation which included a stranger, someone who did not know the staff of CC and would not immediately recognize the use of FN. And in an extended conversation, repeated usage of FN itself becomes marked, and ø is likely to occur, once the person being addressed has already been named. (This is clearly a different usage of ø than when it occurs without the addressee having been named at all.) The point is that people rarely find a single address form appropriate for every occasion.

It would appear that Sue can use either of the two principal options, FN or TLN. The problem is that her staff members use FN when referring to her, and, so, for her to use TLN for them would be in contradiction of the status relationship existing between them. Yet for her to accept the use of mutual FN would result in her giving up a certain amount of the status she has so recently earned. And so she has chosen instead to adopt a form common to some situations, but uncommon in business: nicknames (NN). She uses NN for three of the five people under her (a possible explanation for the two exceptions will be given shortly).

Sue has created nicknames for three of her staff: Betty she calls "Betty B" (the first letter of her last name); Wendy she calls "Wendy-Loo" (L being the first letter of her last name) or occasionally "Lendy-Woo" (a simple reversal); and Fanny she calls "Fanny Mae" or "Fanny Maybell" (neither of which have anything to do with her last name). Marjorie is normally called Marj, and rarely referred to by her full name, but it is impossible to say that either should be considered a NN. Albertha is never called anything else.

The use of nicknames is very complicated. They occur in

many forms, on many different occasions, for many reasons. Too few NN appeared in the situation described here for a detailed analysis of them to be presented. Therefore, although it would clearly be desirable to have a classification of the different types, and an analysis of the use and meaning of each, nothing of the sort can be attempted. Until further research can be conducted, all the nicknames found will have to be considered essentially equivalent. And what follows must be accepted as only a tentative analysis, subject to later verification.

The use of a single NN is closely related to the use of multiple names (MN). Brown and Ford describe MN as "the case in which two or more versions of the proper name are used in free variation with one another" (1961, p. 378). They have suggested that the use of MN represents a greater degree of intimacy than the use of FN. Assuming that the creation and subsequent use of a NN for a person also represents an increased intimacy, it is possible to interpret Sue's use of NN as an attempt to create a nonreciprocal use of address forms with her staff. This can be expressed in the form of the relationship:

$$TLN : FN :: FN : NN$$

To explain: if it is assumed that asymmetric usage of forms of address is related to a difference of rank or status; and if the person with a higher degree of status uses FN to a person of lower status, receiving TLN in return; then it is possible to see the use of FN by someone of lower status to someone of higher status as permitting, or at times even requiring, the use of NN in return, thus assuring that the asymmetric relationship be maintained. At the same time, remembering that the use of NN implies an intimacy between the namer and the one named, the asymmetric relationship of FN : NN is restricted to use between people on intimate terms but of unequal status.

The above is only a hypothesis, but it does make sense in explaining the given situation. It is important that this hypothesis not be considered a necessary cause and effect relationship, such that every time an ambiguous situation of the sort described so far arises the only or even the best solution will be the one that Sue has found. Rather, since this form of address is used in an unusual manner and accepted, the problem is to discover some of the causes of its usage and acceptance.

Sue's symmetrical usage of FN with two members of her staff (Marj and Albertha) can now be explained as indicative of the fact that she is not on intimate personal terms with them, as is indeed the case. This leads to the suggestion that intimacy is a more important consideration in choice of address forms than is status. Support for this suggestion is provided by the two following examples of NN usage outside of CC.

The first example involves the staff member to the associate director for whom Sue worked previously. He began to use a NN ("Fru-Fru") instead of FN as his principle form of address for Sue. Utilizing the rules previously suggested, it would seem that he indicates two things by this choice. One is that he has more status than Sue, which he certainly did at the time she worked in that office. The other is that they are on close personal terms, which they certainly were not, and to the best of my knowledge never had been. Thus, he is breaking the unstated rules and reversing the order of priority in which they should be used. For this reason Sue's reaction of intense dislike is readily explained. If he were merely reiterating his position of status as being above hers, she could not object. But since he is implying a personal relationship which does not exist, she has justification for objecting. (The result of her negative reaction is that he has decreased usage of the NN, although, even when she left the office, he did not completely discontinue it.)

The second example involves another staff member, working for a different associate director. He has greater status than Sue, but they are friends, and she has created a NN for him. His name is Dr. Charles McElroy, and she calls him "Moctor Darly." Possibly because of the specific attributes of this NN (it has a double exchange of letters, it has a pleasing sound, and it cannot be confused with any specific English words), it has not only been accepted by the person named but is occasionally used by several others in the building as well.[8]

It is time now to look at the larger context, the building as a whole. The primary form of address used for Sue by virtually everyone is FN. For some this is the reciprocal FN of equal status; for others it is the nonreciprocal FN of unequal status.

---

[8] It would be interesting to follow this up, but unfortunately at the time I did not pay sufficient attention to the spread of this NN, and so cannot document it here.

As with the staff of CC, other address forms occur occasionally in certain situations, but this serves only as proof that, no matter what the ideal system, in reality it is rare to find a single address form appropriate 100% of the time. (This holds true for all the cases discussed below as well, of course.)

The director is Sue's immediate boss, and in accordance with his clearly higher status and the lack of intimacy between them, Sue uses TLN as her form of address for him. This is clearly the expected form, and as such its use is unmarked. For the secretaries, who are Sue's friends, and with whom she has used the FN of equal status for so long, she continues to use a reciprocal FN. Again, this is the expected, unmarked form. For the staff members, her choice depends on the status and degree of intimacy with each as an individual. Depending on the balance of these variables, she uses FN, TLN, NN, or ø as her primary forms of address. Since she has so little contact with the staff members, form of address does not pose a very serious problem: when contact does occur, it is usually brief, and for these occasions ø is always available.

It is only when speaking with the associate directors that Sue has a real problem in the choice of address. As their equal, in all the ways previously mentioned, she would legitimately call the associate directors by their FN, as they call each other. But choice of FN would be likely to antagonize, since there are so many ways in which she is not their equal, it would be thought presumptive. As a person of lesser status in all those ways previously mentioned, she should use TLN. But this choice is no better; since there are some ways in which Sue is their equal, she is justified in using something more intimate. Choice of either form would indicate what Sue views her status to be, and how she wishes others to view her.

The option of NN, which Sue has used successfully within CC, cannot be used with the associate directors, for she does not know them well enough individually to overcome the status difference. The most common choice in a situation of ambiguity is ø, as Ervin-Tripp has suggested (1972, p. 221). Use of this form by graduate students to their professors, as a means of transition, after they stop using TLN and before they being using FN, has been analyzed by McIntire (1972). Certainly, this form was frequently used by Sue, but, if ø is used to the complete exclusion of other direct forms of address, it can become awkward and stilted after a short time.

Since there was really no other standard alternative available, Sue invented her own. More exactly, as with her use of NN, she adopted a form available for occasional use in a different situation. In this case, she took first name and last name (FN + LN) as her standard form of address with the associate directors. This form is rarely used as a direct address form in American English, although it does occasionally appear as a means of emphasis. This use is favored by parents 'manding' their children, as in the example, "Mary Beth Goodman, you come inside right this minute!" (see Brown & Ford, 1961, p. 182). Key has suggested that it may also be used as a salutation in a letter, if the relationship between addressee and addressor is ambiguous (1975, p. 48). More often FN + LN appears as a form of reference, although its use is not consistent, as pointed out by Adler (1978, p. 184).

It should be mentioned that, when FN + LN is used, whether by Sue in this situation or by others in different situations, the FN is usually the full name. That is, if a person's name is Charles, but he is usually called Charlie or Chuck, when FN + LN is used he will be called Charles + LN. This serves as a means of emphasis and increases the oddity of the form, at least with men, since, as Brown and Ford have suggested, "male first names in American English very seldom occur in full form" (1961, p. 376). The same is probably true for female first names as well.

The form FN + LN is so uncommon that its usage is highly marked. Ervin-Tripp has pointed out that: "When there is agreement about the normal, unmarked address form to alters of unspecified status, then any shift is a message" (1961, p. 61). It would seem that, even in a situation where alters have unspecified status and there is only agreement about what the normal, unmarked address forms are, a shift is no less significant a message. Further, it is apparent from the present situation that amount of usage by a single person does not change the fact that a given form is marked. Thus, no matter how often Sue calls the associate directors by FN + LN, it still remains a marked form of address. This is demonstrated by the fact that Sue's usage of the form seems to be accompanied by paralinguistic features which clearly separate it from the rest of the sentence in which it occurs.[9]

---

[9] Unfortunately I was not able to analyze this at the time, so cannot provide further details.

This markedness may be one reason why Sue can continue to use this form of address. Every time she uses the form, she calls attention to her ambiguous status position and forces the person she addresses to recognize it. This legitimizes her use of an unusual form of address, since it serves a specific function for her which no other form would serve as well. Everyone in the building knows that her position of status is ambiguous, so, rather than try to ignore the fact, she calls attention to it. She is breaking the established unspoken rules for address, but in such a way that everyone can continue to permit her to do it.

It is possible to analyze the reaons why everyone continues to permit Sue to use this alternative even more closely. She has previously shown that she knows what the rules for proper forms of address are, so that her usage of an unusual form does not indicate merely a mistake which should be corrected. Only someone who has proven knowledge of the rules would be permitted to break them so blatantly. More important, *only one who was well aware of what the rules were could break then with such proficiency.* If she did not know the rules, she would break them at times when it would not serve a useful purpose, as does the man who continues to call her by NN. Further, it is possible that only in a situation where there is a paradox which calls for an unusual solution, such as Sue's apparent versus her actual status, would she be permitted to break the rules. By her solution she has found a way to minimize any negative reactions she might otherwise cause (such as if she used either FN before it was acceptable or TLN when it was too formal). The associate directors are perceptive men and are fully aware of Sue's problem. That they accept her solution probably plays an important part in her continued usage of FN + LN. If they refused to accept it, she could no longer use it, for it would then serve a negative rather than a positive function.

Brown and Ford have suggested that "in the progression towards intimacy of unequals the superior is always the pace-setter initiating new moves in that direction" (1961, p. 389). It is important to recognize as well that, once the superior uses FN, it is then up to the person of lower status to interpret whether reciprocal FN or nonreciprocal TLN is expected in return. Due to this, the progression towards intimacy must be considered a *mutual* decision rather than unilaterally the responsibility of the person with the greatest status. In this case,

Sue initiated the progression, by her use of any address form other than TLN, but the associate directors agreed to the change by accepting her use of the new form. It is apparent that Sue felt uncomfortable using the reciprocal FN, and so created a new form as an intermediary step between FN and TLN.

One consideration in her choice of the new form may have been that it had no implications already attached, as would the use of either FN or TLN. That is, FN and TLN are clearly linked to additional meanings of status and intimacy, whereas the use of a new form could not be. As a result, the participants in the situation had to agree upon the new implications to be assigned the new form. These were suggested by Sue (ambiguous status, lack of intimacy) and accepted by the others. That this at no time had to be verbalized is a tribute to the influence of context over linguistic form.

Conclusion

Perhaps it is because forms of address seem to be discrete entities that they have so often been treated as separable from the context in which they occur. Whatever the reason, the assumption of this study has been that, in order to understand any but the most common behavior, forms of address, like so many other subjects, are best studied in context.

It has been shown that one cause of the use of unusual forms of address may be an ambiguous status position in an organization. In this particular situation, the result was the use of NN to those of ambiguous (somewhat lower) status but high intimacy, and the use of FN + LN to those of ambiguous (somewhat higher) status but low intimacy. Two transitional steps, to be used in making finer distinctions between levels of status and intimacy, were thus added to the available options of address in American English.

References

Abrahams, R.D. (1983). *The man-of-words in the West Indies: Performance and the emergence of Creole culture.* Baltimore, MD: Johns Hopkins Press.

Adler, M.K. (1978). *Naming and addressing: A sociolinguistic study.* Hamburg, Germany: Helmut Buske Verlag.

Agar, M. (1985). *Speaking of ethnography.* Beverly Hills, CA: Sage.

Ardrey, R. (1969). *African genesis.* New York: Delta.

Babcock, B.A. (1978). Too many, too few: Ritual modes of signification. *Semiotica, 23,* 291–302.

Babcock-Abrahams, B.A. (1977). The story in the story: Metanarration in folk narrative. In R. Bauman (Ed.), *Verbal art as performance* (pp. 61–79). Rowley, MA: Newbury House.

Barnlund, D.C. (1981). Toward an ecology of communication. In C. Wilder-Mott & J. Weakland (Eds.), *Rigor and imagination* (pp. 87–126). New York: Praeger.

Basso, K.H. (1972). "To give up on words": Silence in Western Apache culture. In P.P. Giglioli (Ed.), *Language and social context* (pp. 67–86). Baltimore, MD: Penguin Books.

Bates, E., & Benigni, L. (1975). Rules of address in Italy: A sociological survey. *Language in Society, 4,* 271–288.

Bateson, G. (1956). The message "This is play." In B. Schaffner (Ed.), *Group processes: Transactions of the Second Conference, 1955* (pp. 144–242). New York: Josiah Macy, Jr. Foundation.

Bateson, G. (1968). Redundancy and coding. In T. Sebeok (Ed.), *Animal communication* (pp. 614–626). Indianapolis, IN: Indiana University Press.

Bateson, G. (1971). communication. In N.A. McQuown (Ed.), *The Natural History of an Interview* (pp. 1–40). Microfilm Collection of Manuscripts on Cultural Anthropology, Fifteenth Series. Chicago, IL: University of Chicago, Joseph Regenstein Library, Department of Photoduplication.

Bateson, G. (1972a). Social planning and the concept of deutero-learning. In *Steps to an ecology of mind* (pp. 159–176). New York: Chandler. (Original work published 1942).

Bateson, G. (1972b). A Theory of Play and Fantasy. In *Steps to an ecology of mind* (pp. 177–193). New York: Chandler. (Original work published 1956).

Bateson, G. (1972c). *Steps to an ecology of mind.* New York: Chandler.

Bateson, G. (1975a). Orders of change. In R. Fields (Ed.), *Loka II: A journal from Naropa Institute* (pp. 59–63). New York: Anchor Books.

Bateson, G. (1975b). Some components of socialization for trance. *Ethos, 3,* 143–135.

Bateson, G. (1978, Summer). The pattern which connects. *The CoEvolution Quarterly,* 4–15.

Bateson, G. (1979). *Mind and nature: A necessary unity.* New York: Dutton.

Bateson, G., & Mead, M. (1942). *Balinese character: A photographic analysis.* New York: New York Academy of Sciences.

Bauman, R. (1977). Verbal art as performance. In *Verbal art as performance* (pp. 3–58). Prospect Heights, IL: Waveland Press.

Bauman, R. (1983). *Let your words be few: Symbolism of speaking and silence among seventeenth-century Quakers.* Cambridge, England: Cambridge University Press.

Bauman, R., Irvine, J.T., & Philips, S.U. (1987). Performance, speech community, and genre. *Working papers and proceedings of the Center for Psychosocial Studies* (No. 11).

Bauman, R., & Sherzer, J. (Eds.). (1974). *Explorations in the ethnography of speaking.* Cambridge, England: Cambridge University Press.

Bauman, R., & Sherzer, J. (1975). The ethnography of speaking. *Annual Review of Anthropology, 4,* 95–119.

Bean, S.S. (1978). *Symbolic and pragmatic semantics: A Kannada system of address.* Chicago, IL: University of Chicago Press.

Beattie, G. (1983). *Talk: An analysis of speech and non-verbal behaviour in conversation.* Milton Keynes, England: Open University Press.

Beavin Bavelas, J., & Segal, L. (1982). Family systems theory: Background and implications. *Journal of Communication, 32,* 99–107.

Beinstein, J. (1975). Small talk as social gesture. *Journal of Communication, 25,* 147–154.

Benedict, R. (1959). *Patterns of culture.* Boston, MA: Houghton Mifflin. (Original work published 1934)

Berger, A. A. (1984). *Signs in contemporary culture.* New York: Longman.

Berger, J. (1973). *Ways of seeing.* New York: Viking Press.

Berger, P.L., & Luckmann, T. (1967). *The social construction of reality.* New York: Doubleday Anchor.

Berlo, D.K. (1966). *The process of communication: An introduction to theory and practice.* New York: Holt, Rinehart and Winston.

Bernstein, B. (1961). Social structure, language, and learning. *Educational Research, 3,* 163–176.

Bernstein, B. (Ed.). (1971). *Class codes and control* (vol. 1 and 2). London: Routledge and Kegan Paul.

Berreman, G.D. (1972). Social categories and social interaction in urban India. *American Anthropologist, 74,* 567–86.

Birdwhistell, R.L. (1959). Contribution of linguistic-kinesic studies to the understanding of schizophrenia. In A. Auerback (Ed.), *Schizophrenia* (pp. 99–123). New York: Ronald Press.

Birdwhistell, R.L. (1963). The kinesic level in the investigation of the emotions. In P.H. Knapp (Ed.), *Expressions of the emotions in man* (pp. 123–139). New York: International Universities Press.

Birdwhistell, R.L. (1968a). Communication. *International Encyclopedia of the Social Sciences, 3,* 24–29.

Birdwhistell, R.L. (1968b). Certain considerations in the concepts of culture and communication. In C.E. Larson & F.E.X. Dance (Eds.), *Perspectives on communication: Colloquium proceedings* (pp. 144–165). Milwaukee, WI: Speech Communication Center, University of Wisconsin-Milwaukee.

Birdwhistell, R.L. (1970). *Kinesics and context: Essays on body motion communication.* Philadelphia, PA: University of Pennsylvania Press.

Birdwhistell, R.L. (1977). Some discussion of ethnography, theory and method. In J. Brockman (Ed.), *About Bateson* (pp. 103–141). New York: Dutton.

Birenbaum, A., & Sagarin, E. (1973). Understanding the Familiar. In *People and places: The sociology of the familiar* (pp. 3–11). New York: Praeger.

Blom, J.P., & Gumperz, J.J. (1972). Social meaning in linguistic structures: Code-switching in Norway. In J.J. Gumperz & D. Hymes (Eds.), *Directions in sociolinguistics: The ethnography of communication* (pp. 407–434). New York: Holt, Rinehart and Winston.

Bloomfield, L. (1926). A set of postulates for the science of language. *Language, 2,* 153–164.

Blumer, H. (1969). *Symbolic interactionism: Perspective and Method.* Englewood Cliffs, NJ: Prentice-Hall.

Bochner, A.P. (1981). Forming warm ideas. In C. Wilder-Mott & J.H. Weakland (Eds.), *Rigor and imagination* (pp. 65–81). New York: Praeger.

Bochner, A.P., & Krueger, D.L. (1979). Interpersonal communication theory and research: An overview of inscrutable epistemologies and muddled concepts. In D. Nimmo (Ed.), *Communication Yearbook* (vol. 3, pp. 197–211). New Brunswick, NJ: Transaction Books.

Bourdieu, P. (1973). Cultural reproduction and social reproduction. In R. Brown (Ed.), *Knowledge, education, and cultural change: Papers in the sociology of education* (pp. 71–112). London: Tavistock.

Bourdieu, P. (1982). *Outline of a theory of practice.* Cambridge, England: Cambridge University Press. (Original work published 1977)

Bourdieu, P. (1987). The biographical illusion (Y. Winkin & W. Leeds-Hurwitz, Trans.). *Working papers and proceedings of the Center for Psychosocial Studies,* No. 14.

Brown, M.H., & Ragan, S.L. (1987). Variations on a theme: An ethnographic case study of family blessings. *Research on Language and Social Interaction, 21,* 115–141.

Brown, R., & Ford, M. (1961). Address in American English. *Journal of Abnormal and Social Psychology, 62* (2), 375–85.

Brummett, B. (1980). Towards a theory of silence as a political strategy. *Quarterly Journal of Speech, 66,* 289–303.

Bruneau, T.J. (1979). The time dimension in intercultural communication. In D. Nimmo, (Ed.), *Communication Yearbook 3.* New Brunswick, NJ: Transaction Books.

Burke, K. (1968). Definition of Man. In K. Burke (Ed.), *Language as symbolic action* (pp. 3–24). Berkeley, CA: University of California Press.

Byers, P. (1966). Cameras don't take pictures. *Columbia University Forum, 9,* 27–31.

Byers, P. (1977). A personal view of nonverbal communication. *Theory into Practice, 16,* 134–140.

Cappella, J.N. (1979). Talk-silence sequences in informal conversations I. *Human Communication Research, 6,* 130–145.

Carbaugh, D. (1986). Some thoughts on organizing as cultural communication. In L. Thayer (Ed.), *Organization—communication: Emerging perspectives I* (pp. 85–101). Norwood, NJ: Ablex Publishing Corp.

Carey, J. (1975). A cultural approach to communication. *Communication, 2,* 1–22.

Carey, J. (1983). The origins of the radical discourse on cultural studies in the United States. *Journal of Communication, 33,* 311–313.

Cavan, S. (1973). Bar sociability. In A. Birenbaum & E. Sagarin (Eds.), *People in places* (pp. 143–154). New York: Praeger.

Cazden, C.B. (1974). Play and metalinguistic awareness: One dimension of language experience. *The Urban Review, 7,* 28–39.

Cicourel, A.V. (1970). The acquisition of social structure. In J.D. Douglas (Ed.), *Understanding everyday life* (pp. 136–168). Chicago, IL: Aldine.

Cicourel, A.V. (1978). Language and society: Cognitive, cultural, and linguistic aspects of language use. In W. Dressler & W. Meid (Eds.), *Proceedings of the Twelfth International Congress of Linguists* (pp. 32–47). Innsbruck, Austria: Innsbrucker Beitrage zur Sprachwissenschaft.

Cicourel, A.V. (1981). Language and medicine. In C. Ferguson & S.B. Heath (Eds.), *Language in the USA* (pp. 407–429). Cambridge, England: Cambridge University Press.

Clark, E.V. (1978). Awareness of language: Some evidence from what children say and do. In A. Sinclair, R.J. Jarvella, & W.J.M. Levelt (Eds.), *The child's conception of language* (pp. 17–43). New York: Springer Verlag.

Combs, J.E., & Mansfield, M.W. (Eds.). (1976). *Drama in life: The uses of communication in society.* New York: Hastings House.

Condon, W.S. (1976). An analysis of behavioral organization. *Sign Language Studies, 13,* 285–318.

Condon, W.S. (1980). The relation of interactional synchrony to cognitive and emotional processes. In M.R. Key (Ed.), *The relationship of verbal and nonverbal communication* (pp. 49–65). The Hague: Mouton.

Condon, W.S., & Ogston, W.D. (1966). Sound film analysis of normal and pathological behavior patterns. *Journal of Nervous and Mental Disease, 143,* 338–347.

Condon, W.S., & Ogston, W.D. (1967). A segmentation of behavior. *Journal of Psychiatric Research, 5,* 221–235.

Conklin, H. (1968). Ethnography. *International Encyclopedia of the Social Sciences, 5,* 172–178.

Cook-Gumperz, J., & Corsaro, W.A. (1976). Social-ecological constraints on children's communicative strategies. In J. Cook-Gumperz (Ed.), *Papers on Language and Context* (pp. 1–47).

Working Paper #46, Berkeley, CA: Language Behavior Research Laboratory, University of California.

Corsaro, W.A. (1985). *Friendship and peer culture in the early years.* Norwood, NJ: Ablex Publishing Corp.

Cowell, C.R. (1972). Group process as metaphor. *Journal of Communication, 22,* 113–123.

Craig, R.T., & Tracy, K. (Eds.). (1983). *Conversational coherence: Form, structure, and strategy.* Beverly Hills, CA: Sage.

Cronen, V.E., Pearce, W.B., & Harris, L.M. (1982). The coordinated management of meaning: A theory of communication. In F.E.X. Dance (Ed.), *Human communication theory* (pp. 61–89). New York: Harper and Row.

Cronkhite, G. (1986). On the focus, scope, and coherence of the study of human symbolic activity. *Quarterly Journal of Speech, 72,* 231–246.

Cushman, D., & Sanders, R.E. (1982). Rules theories of human communication processes: The structural and functional perspectives. *Progress in Communication Sciences, 3,* 49–83.

Cushman, D., & Whiting, G. (1972). An approach to communication theory: Towards consensus on rules. *Journal of Communication, 22,* 217–38.

Dandridge, T.C., Mitroff, I., & Joyce, W.F. (1980). Organizational symbolism: A topic to expand organizational analysis. *Academy of Management Review, 5,* 77–82.

Dauenhauer, B.P. (1973). On silence. *Research in Phenomenology, 3,* 9–27.

Dauenhauer, B.P. (1976). Silence: an intentional analysis. *Research in Phenomenology, 6,* 63–83.

Davis, F. (1985). Foreword. In R.S. Perinbanayagam (Ed.), *Signifying acts: Structure and meaning in everyday life.* Carbondale, IL: Southern Illinois University Press.

Davis, M. (Ed.). (1982). *Interaction rhythms.* New York: Human Sciences Press.

Denzin, N.K. (1970). Symbolic interactionism and ethnomethodology. In J.D. Douglas (Ed.), *Understanding everyday life* (pp. 261–286). Chicago, IL: Aldine.

Diez, M.E. (1984). Communicative competence: An interactive approach. In R.N. Bostrom (Ed.), *Communication Yearbook 8* (pp. 56–79). Beverly Hills, CA: Sage.

Dingwall, R. (1980). Ethics and ethnography. *Sociological Review, 28,* 871–891.

Donahue, W.A., Cushman, D.P., & Nofsinger, R.E., Jr. (1980). Creating and confronting social order: A comparison of rules perspectives. *The Western Journal of Speech Communication, 44,* 5-19.

Douglas, J.D. (1970a). *Understanding everyday life.* Chicago, IL: Aldine.

Douglas, J.D. (1970b). Understanding everyday life. In J.D. Douglas (Ed.), *Understanding everyday life* (pp. 3-44). Chicago, IL: Aldine.

Douglas, J.D. (1971). *American social order.* New York: Free Press.

Douglas, M. (1966). *Purity and danger.* London: Routledge and Kegan Paul.

Douglas, M. (1975). *Implicit meanings: Essays in anthropology.* London: Routledge and Kegan Paul.

Duncan, H.D. (1962). *Communication and social order.* New York: Bedminster Press.

Duncan, S.D., Jr. (1972). Some signals and rules for taking speaking turns in conversations. *Journal of Personality and Social Psychology, 23,* 283-292.

Duncan, S.D., Jr., & Fiske, D.W. (1977). *Face-to-face interaction: Research, methods, and theory.* Hillsdale, NJ: Erlbaum Press.

Duncan, S., Jr., & Fiske, D. (1985). *Interaction structure and strategy.* Cambridge, England: Cambridge University Press.

Duncan, S.D., Jr., & Niederehe, G. (1974). On signalling that it's your turn to speak. *Journal of Experimental Social Psychology, 10,* 234-247.

Eco, U. (1973). Social life as a sign system. In D. Robey (Ed.), *Structuralism: An introduction* (pp. 57-72). Oxford, England: Clarendon Press.

Edgerton, R. (1979). *Alone together: Social order on an urban beach.* Berkeley, CA: University of California Press.

Efron, D. (1941). *Gesture and environment.* New York: King's Crown.

Eisenberg, E.M. (1984). Ambiguity as strategy in organizational communication. *Communication Monographs, 51,* 228-242.

Ekman, P., & Friesen, W.V. (1972). Hand movements. *Journal of Communication, 22,* 353-374.

Elliot, H.C. (1974). Similarities and differences between science and common sense. In R. Turner (Ed.), *Ethnomethodology* (pp. 21-26). Baltimore, MD: Penguin.

Erickson, F., & Schultz, J. (1977). When is a context? Some issues and methods in the analysis of social competence. *Quarterly Newsletter of the Institute for Comparative Human Development, 1,* 5-10.

Erickson, F., & Schultz, J. (1982). *The counselor as gatekeeper: Social and cultural organization of communication in counseling interviews.* New York: Academic Press.

Ervin-Tripp, S.M. (1961). Sociolinguistics. In J.A. Fishman (Ed.), *Advances in the sociology of language* (vol. 1). The Hague: Mouton.

Ervin-Tripp, S.M. (1972). On sociolinguistic rules: Alternation and co-occurrence. In J.J. Gumperz & D. Hymes (Eds.), *Directions in socialinguistics: The ethnography of communication* (pp. 213–250). New York: Holt, Rinehart and Winston.

Fairchild, H.P. (1944). *Dictionary of sociology.* New York: Philosophical Library.

Fast, J. (1971). *Body language.* New York: Pocket Books.

Ferguson, C.A. (1964). Baby talk in six languages. In J.J. Gumperz & D. Humes (Eds.), *Special Issue: The Ethnography of Communication. American Anthropologist, 66* (6, part 2), 103–114.

Fernandez, J.W. (1986). *Persuasions and performances: The play of tropes in culture.* Bloomington, IN: Indiana University Press.

Fielding, G., & Fraser, C. (1978). Language and Interpersonal Relations. In I. Markova (Ed.), *The social context of language* (pp. 217–232). Chichester, NY: John Wiley and Sons.

Firth, R. (1973). Verbal and bodily rituals of greeting and parting. In J.S. La Fontaine (Ed.), *The interpretation of ritual* (pp. 1–38). London: Tavistock.

Fisher, B.A. (1981). Implications of the "interactional view" for communication theory. In C. Wilder-Mott & J.H. Weakland (Eds.), *Rigor and imagination* (pp. 195–209). New York: Praeger.

Ford, F.R. (1983). Rules: The invisible family. *Family Process, 22* (3), 135–45.

Frank, L.K. (1926). The problem of learning. *Psychological Review, 33,* 329–351.

Frank, L.K. (1966). The world as a communication network. In G. Kepes (Ed.), *Sign image symbol* (pp. 1–14). New York: George Braziller.

Frentz, T.S., & Farrell, T.B. (1976). Language-action: A paradigm for communication. *Quarterly Journal of Speech, 62,* 333–349.

Frow, J. (1980). Discourse genres. *Journal of Literary Semantics, 9,* 73–81.

Fuller, L.L. (1981). Means and ends. In K.I. Winston (Ed.), *The principles of social order: Selected essays of Lon L. Fuller* (pp. 47–64). Durham, NC: Duke University Press.

Garfinkel, H. (1964). Studies of the routine grounds of everyday life. *Social Problems, 11,* 225–250.

Garfinkel, H. (1967). *Studies in ethnomethodology.* Englewood Cliffs, NJ: Prentice-Hall.

Geertz, C. (1966). *Person, time, and conduct in Bali: An essay in cultural analysis.* Cultural Report Series Number 14. New Haven, CT: Yale University, Southeast Asia Studies.

Geertz, C. (1973). *The interpretation of cultures.* New York: Basic Books.

Geertz, C. (1980). Blurred genres: The refiguration of social thought. *American Scholar, 49,* 165–179.

Geertz, C. (1983). Common sense as a cultural system. In *Local knowledge* (pp. 73–93). New York: Basic Books.

Gerbner, G. (1974). Teacher image in mass culture: Symbolic functions of the "hidden curriculum." In D.R. Olson (Ed.), *Media and symbols: The forms of expression, communication, and education* (pp. 470–497). Chicago, IL: University of Chicago Press.

Giddens, A. (1976). *New rules of sociological method: A positive critique of interpretive sociologies.* New York: Basic Books.

Giddens, A. (1979). *Central problems in social theory.* Berkeley, CA: University of California Press.

Giddens, A. (1984). *The constitution of society: Outline of the theory of structuration.* Berkeley, CA: University of California Press.

Goffman, E. (1953). *Communication conduct in an island community.* Unpublished Ph.D. Dissertation, Department of Sociology, University of Chicago.

Goffman, E. (1959). *The presentation of self in everyday life.* New York: Doubleday Anchor.

Goffman, E. (1961). *Encounters: Two studies in the sociology of interaction.* Indianapolis, IN: Bobbs-Merrill.

Goffman, E. (1963). *Behavior in public places: Notes on the social organization of gatherings.* New York: Free Press.

Goffman, E. (1967). *Interaction rituals: Essays on face-to-face behavior.* Garden City, NY: Anchor Books.

Goffman, E. (1971). *Relations in public: Microstudies of the public order.* New York: Harper and Row.

Goffman, E. (1974). *Frame analysis.* New York: Harper.

Goffman, E. (1977). The arrangement between the sexes. *Theory and Society, 4,* 301–331.

Goffman, E. (1983). The interaction order. *American Sociological Review, 48,* 1–17.

Goldschmidt, W. (1972). An ethnography of encounters: A methodology for the enquiry into the relation between the individual and society. *Current Anthropology, 13,* 59–78.

Goodwin, C. (1981). *Conversational organization: Interaction between speakers and hearers.* New York: Academic Press.

Goodwin, C. (1987). Forgetfulness as an interactive resource. *Social Psychology Quarterly, 50,* 115–131.

Goodwin, M.H., & Goodwin, C. (1987). Children's Arguing. In S.U. Philips, S. Steele, & C. Tanz (Eds.), *Language, gender and sex in comparative perspective* (pp. 200–248). Cambridge, England: Cambridge University Press.

Grayson, B., & Stein, M.I. (1981). Attracting assault: Victims' nonverbal cues. *Journal of Communication, 31,* 68–75.

Green, J., & Wallat, C. (Eds.). (1981). *Ethnography and language in educational settings.* Norwood, NJ: Ablex Publishing Corp.

Grimshaw, A.D. (1980). Mishearings, misunderstandings, and other nonsuccesses in talk: A plea for redress of speaker-oriented bias. *Sociological Inquiry, 50,* 31–74.

Gumperz, J.J. (1968). The speech community. In D. Sills (Ed.), *International encyclopedia of the social sciences* (Vol 9, pp. 381–386). New York: Macmillan.

Gumperz, J.J. (1982a). *Discourse strategies.* Cambridge, England: Cambridge University Press.

Gumperz, J.J. (Ed.). (1982b). *Language and social identity.* New York: Cambridge University Press.

Gumperz, J.J., Aulakh, G., & Kaltman, H. (1982). Thematic structure and progression in discourse. In J.J. Gumperz (Ed.), *Language and social identity* (pp. 22–56). New York: Cambridge University Press.

Gumperz, J.J., & Cook-Gumperz, J. (1982). Introduction: Language and the communication of social identity. In J.J. Gumperz (Ed.), *Language and social identity* (pp. 1–21). New York: Cambridge University Press.

Gumperz, J.J., & Hymes, D. (Eds.). (1972). *Directions in sociolinguistics: The ethnography of communication.* New York: Holt, Rinehart and Winston.

Haley, J. (1959). An interactional description of schizophrenia. *Psychiatry, 22,* 321–332.

Hall, E.T. (1959). *The hidden dimension.* New York: Fawcett.

Hall, E.T. (1984). *The dance of life: The other dimension of time.* New York: Anchor.

Halliday, M.A.K. (1978). *Language as social semiotic: The social interpretation of language and meaning.* London: Edward Arnold.

Harris, L. (1979). *Communication competence: Empirical tests of a systemic mode.* Ph.D. dissertation, University of Massachusetts.

Haslett, B. (1987). *Communication: Strategic action in context.* Hillsdale, NJ: Erlbaum.

Hawes, L. (1973). Elements of a model for communication processes. *Quarterly Journal of Speech, 59,* 11–21.

Hawes, L.C. (1977). Toward a hermeneutic phenomenology of communication. *Communication Quarterly, 25,* 63–68.

Heath, C.C. (1986). *Body movement and speech in medical interaction.* Cambridge, England: Cambridge University Press.

Heath, C.C. (in press). Embarrassment and interactional organization: Behaviour in the medical examination. In P. Drew & Wooton, T. (Eds.), *Erving Goffman: An interdisciplinary appreciation.* Cambridge, England: Polity Press.

Heath, S.B. (1983). *Ways with words.* Cambridge, England: Cambridge University Press.

Heller, M.S. (1982). Negotiations of language choice in Montreal. In J.J. Gumperz (Ed.), *Language and social identity* (pp. 108–118). New York: Cambridge University Press.

Heritage, J.C., & Atkinson, J.M. (Eds.). (1984). Introduction. In *Structures of social action: Studies in conversation analysis* (pp. 1–15). Cambridge, England: Cambridge University Press.

Heritage, J.C., & Watson, D.R. (1980). Aspects of the properties of formulations in natural conversations: Some instances analysed. *Semiotica, 30,* 245–262.

Hewes, D.E. (1979). The sequential analysis of social interaction. *Quarterly Journal of Speech, 65,* 56–73.

Hopper, R. (1983). Interpretation as coherence production. In R.T. Craig & K. Tracy (Eds.), *Conversational coherence: Form, structure, and strategy* (pp. 81–98). Beverly Hills, CA: Sage.

Hopper, R., Koch, S., & Mandelbaum, J. (1986). Conversation analysis methods. In D. Ellis & W. Donahue (Eds.), *Contemporary issues and discourse processes* (pp. 169–186). Hillsdale, NJ: Erlbaum.

Hymes, D. (1962). The ethnography of speaking. In T. Gladwin & W.C. Sturtevant (Eds.), *Anthropology and human behavior* (pp. 13–53). Washington, DC: Anthropology Society of Washington.

Hymes, D. (1964). Introduction. In J.J. Gumperz & D. Hymes (Eds.), *Special issue: The Ethnography of Communication. American Anthropologist, 66* (6), 1–34.

Hymes, D. (1967). The anthropology of communication. In F.E.X. Dance (Ed.), *Human communication theory: Original essays* (pp. 1–39). New York: Holt, Rinehart and Winston.

Hymes, D. (1971). Competence and performance in linguistic theory. In R. Huxley & E. Inghram (Eds.), *Language acquisition: Models and methods.* New York: Academic Press.

Hymes, D. (1972). Models of the interaction of language and social life. In J. Gumperz & D. Hymes (Eds.), *Directions in sociolinguistics: The ethnography of communication* (pp. 35–71). New York: Holt, Rinehart and Winston.

Hymes, D. (1974). Linguistic theory and functions in speech. In *Foundations in sociolinguistics: An ethnographic approach* (pp. 145–178). Philadelphia, PA: University of Pennsylvania Press.

Hymes, D. (1976). Towards linguistic competence. *Sociologische Gids, 76,* 217–239.

Hymes, D. (1977). The state of the art in linguistic anthropology. In A.F.C. Wallace (Ed.), *Perspectives on anthropology* (pp. 48–68). Washington, DC: American Anthropological Association.

Hymes, D. (1980). What is ethnography? In *Language in education: Ethnolinguistic essays* (pp. 88–103). Washington, DC: Center for Applied Linguistics.

Irvine, J.T. (1987). Domains of description in the ethnography of speaking: A retrospective on the "speech community." *Working Papers and Proceedings of the Center for Psychological Studies, 11,* 13–24.

Jaffee, J., & Feldstein, S. (1970). *Rhythms of dialogue.* New York: Academic Press.

Jakobson, R. (1960). Closing statement: Linguistics and poetics. In T.A. Sebeok (Ed.), *Style in language* (pp. 350–377). Cambridge, MA: Massachusetts Institute of Technology Press.

Katriel, T. (1985a). *Brogez:* Ritual and strategy in Israeli children's conflicts. *Language in Society, 14,* 467–490.

Katriel, T. (1985b). "Griping" as a verbal ritual in some Israeli discourse. In M. Dascal (Ed.), *Dialogue—An interdisciplinary approach* (pp. 367–381). Amsterdam, Netherlands: John Benjamins.

Katriel, T. (1986). *Talking straight: Dugri speech in Israeli Sabra culture.* Cambridge, England: Cambridge University Press.

Katriel, T. (1987). *"Bexibudim!":* Ritualized sharing among Israeli children. *Language in Society, 16,* 305–320.

Katriel, T., & Nesher, P. (1986). *Gibush:* The rhetoric of cohesion in Israeli school culture. *Comparative Education Review, 30,* 216–231.

Katriel, T., & Philipsen, G. (1981). "What we need is communication": "Communication" as a cultural category in some American speech. *Communication Monographs, 48,* 302–317.

Katz, A.M., & Katz, V.T. (Eds.). (1983). *Foundations of nonverbal communication: Readings, exercises, and commentary.* Carbondale, IL: Southern Illinois University Press.

Kendon, A. (1972). Review of *Kinesics and context* by Ray Bird-whistell. *The American Journal of Psychology, 85,* 441–455.

Kendon, A. (1977). *Studies in the behavior of social interaction.* Bloomington, IN: Indiana University Press.

Kersten, A. (1986). A critical–interpretive approach to the study of organizational communication: Bringing communication back into the field. In L. Thayer (Ed.), *Organization—Communication: emerging perspectives* (pp. 133–150). Norwood, NJ: Ablex Publishing Corp.

Key, M.R. (1975). *Male/female language: With a comprehensive bibliography.* Metuchen, NJ: Scarecrow Press.

Kluckhohn, C. (1959). Common humanity and diverse cultures. In D. Lerner (Ed.), *The human meaning of the social sciences* (pp. 245–284). New York: Meridian Books.

Kluckhohn, C. (1963). Parts and wholes in cultural analysis. In D. Lerner (Ed.), *Parts and wholes* (pp. 111–133). New York: Free Press.

Knapp, M.L. (1978). *Nonverbal communication in human interaction.* New York: Holt, Rinehart and Winston.

Knapp, M.L., Hopper, R., & Bell, R.A. (1984). Compliments: A descriptive taxonomy. *Journal of Communication, 34,* 12–31.

Kochman, T. (1981). *Black and white styles in conflict.* Chicago, IL: University of Chicago Press.

Kosinski, J. (1975). *Cockpit.* New York: Bantam Books.

Kramer, C. (1975). Sex-related Differences in address systems. *Anthropological Linguistics, 17,* 198–210.

La Barre, W. (1980). *Culture in context: Selected writings of Weston La Barre.* Durham, NC: Duke University Press.

Leach, E. (1976). *Culture and communication: The logic by which symbols are connected.* Cambridge, England: Cambridge University Press.

Leech, G. (1974). *Semantics.* New York: Penguin.

Leeds-Hurwitz, W. (1979, May). *Metacommunication and children's play.* Paper presented to the International Communication Association.

Leeds-Hurwitz, W. (1980). The use and analysis of uncommon forms of address: A business example. *Working Papers in Sociolinguistics* (No. 80).

Leeds-Hurwitz, W. (1984). On the relationship of the "ethnography of speaking" to the "ethnography of communication." *Papers in Linguistics, 17,* 7–32.

Leeds-Hurwitz, W. (1986, July 8–11). *Erving Goffman and the concept of social order*. Erving Goffman: An Interdisciplinary Appreciation, York, England.

Leeds-Hurwitz, W. (1987a). The social history of the *Natural History of an Interview:* A multidisciplinary investigation of social communication. *Research on Language and Social Interaction, 20*, 1–51.

Leeds-Hurwitz, W. (1987b, June 17–24). *Le travail de la société: L'ordre social et l'ordre de l'interaction dans l'oeuvre de Goffman*. Lectures de Goffman en France, Cerisy-la-Salle.

Leeds-Hurwitz, W., & Winkin, Y. (n.d.) *Learning to see the ordinary: The use of silhouettes in teaching interpersonal communication*. Unpublished manuscript.

Levi-Strauss, C. (1970). *The raw and the cooked* (J. Weightman & D. Weightman, Trans.). London: Jonathan Cape.

Lincoln, Y.S., & Guba, E.G. (1985). *Naturalistic inquiry*. Beverly Hills, CA: Sage.

Linde, C. (1981). The organization of discourse. In T. Shopen & J. Williams (Eds.), *Style and variables in English* (pp. 84–114). Cambridge, MA: Winthrop.

Litton-Hawes, E.M. (1977). A foundation for the study of everyday talk. *Communication Quarterly, 25*, 2–11.

Lofland, J. (1971). *Analyzing social settings*. Belmont, CA: Wadsworth.

Malinowski, B. (1956). The problem of meaning in primitive languages. In C.K. Ogden & I.A. Richards (Eds.), *The meaning of meaning* (pp. 296–336). New York: Harcourt, Brace and Company. (Original work published 1923)

McCall, G.J. (1976). Communication and negotiated identity. *Communication, 2*, 173–184.

McDermott, R.P., & Church, J. (1976). Making sense and feeling good: The ethnography of communication and identity work. *Communication, 2*, 121–142.

McGuire, M.T. (1980). Metakinesic behavior—Some theoretical considerations. In W. von Raffler-Engel (Ed.), *Aspects of nonverbal communication* (pp. 125–131). Lisse, The Netherlands: Swets and Zeitlinger.

McIntire, M.L. (1972). Terms of address in an academic setting. *Anthropological Linguistics, 14*, 286–291.

McLaughlin, M.L. (1984). *Conversation: How talk is organized*. Beverly Hills, CA: Sage.

McQuail, D. (1975). *Communication*. New York: Longman.

McQuown, N.A. (1971). *The natural history of an interview*. (Microfilm Collection of Manuscripts on Cultural Anthropology, Fifteenth

Series.) Chicago, IL: University of Chicago, Joseph Regenstein Library, Department of Photoduplication.

Mead, G.H. (1974). *Mind, self and society* (C.W. Morris, Ed.) Chicago, IL: University of Chicago Press. (Original work published 1934)

Mead, M. (1951). Appendix 1: Practical and theoretical steps involved in this research. In M. Mead & F.C. Macgregor (Eds.), *Growth and culture: A photographic study of Balinese childhood* (pp. 189–208). New York: G.P. Putnam's Sons.

Mead, M., & Byers, P. (1968). *The small conference: An innovation in communication.* The Hague, The Netherlands: Mouton.

Mehan, H. (1979). *Learning lessons: Social organization in the classroom.* Cambridge, MA: Harvard University Press.

Mehan, H., & Wood, H. (1975). *The reality of ethnomethodology.* New York: John Wiley and Sons.

Mennel, S. (1974). *Sociological theory: Uses and unities.* New York: Praeger.

Montgomery, M. (1986). *An introduction to language and society.* New York: Methuen.

Moore, S.F., & Myerhoff, B. (1977a). Introduction: Secular ritual: Forms and meanings. In S.F. Moore & B. Meyerhoff (Eds.), *Secular ritual* (pp. 3–24). Assen, The Netherlands: Van Gorcum.

Moore, S.F., & Myerhoff, B. (Eds.). (1977b). *Secular ritual.* Assen, The Netherlands: Van Gorcum.

Morris, G.H., & Hopper, R. (1987). Symbolic action as alignment: A synthesis of rules approaches. *Research on Language and Social Interaction, 21,* 1–29.

Murray, S.O. (1983). *Group formation in social science.* Edmonton, Canada: Linguistic Research, Inc.

Nelson, G. (1977). *How to see: Visual adventures in a world God never made.* Boston, MA: Little, Brown.

Nierenberg, G.I., & Calero, H.H. (1971). *How to read a person like a book.* New York: Simon and Schuster.

Nofsinger, R.E., Jr. (1977). A peek at conversational analysis. *Communication Quarterly, 25,* 12–20.

Ochs, E. (1979). Transcription as theory. In E. Ochs & B. Schieffelin (Eds.), *Developmental pragmatics* (pp. 43–72). New York: Academic Press.

Parsons, T. (1951). *The social system.* Glencoe, IL: The Free Press.

Pearce, W.B., & Cronen, V.E. (1980). *Communication, action, and meaning: The creation of social realities.* New York: Praeger.

Pearce, W.B., & Foss, K.A. (1987). The future of interpersonal communication. *ACA Bulletin, 61,* 93–105.

Pearce, W.B., Stanback, M.H., & Kang, K.W. (1982) Some cross-cultural studies of the reciprocal causal relation between communication and culture. In S. Thomas (Ed.), *Studies in communication* (vol. 2, pp. 3–10). Norwood, NJ: Ablex Publishing Corp.

Pelose, G.C. (1987). The functions of behavioral synchrony and speech rhythm in conversation. *Research on Language and Social Interaction, 20,* 171–220.

Perinbanayagam, R.S. (1985). *Signifying acts: Structure and meaning in everyday life.* Carbondale, IL: Southern Illinois University Press.

Philips, S.U. (1976). Some sources of cultural variability in the regulation of talk. *Language in Society, 5,* 81–95.

Philips, S.U. (1983). *The invisible culture: Communication in classroom and community on the Warm Springs Indian Reservation.* New York: Longman.

Philipsen, G. (1977). Linearity of research design in ethnographic studies of speaking. *Communication Quarterly, 25,* 3, 42–50.

Philipsen, G., & Carbaugh, D. (1986). A bibliography of fieldwork in the ethnography of communication. *Language in Society, 15,* 387–397.

Pondy, L.R., Frost, P.J., Morgan, G., & Dandridge, T.C. (Eds.). (1983). *Organizational symbolism.* Greenwich, CT: JAI Press.

Powers, R. (1985). *Three farmers on their way to a Dance.* New York: McGraw Hill.

Putnam, L.L. (1983). The interpretive perspective: An alternative to functionalism. In L.L. Putnam & M.E. Pacanowsky (Eds.), *Communication and organization: An interpretive approach* (pp. 31–54). Beverly Hills, CA: Sage.

Putnam, L.L., & Pacanowsky, M.E. (Eds.). (1983). *Communication and organization: An interpretive approach.* Beverly Hills, CA: Sage.

Ragan, S.L. (1983). Alignment and conversational coherence. In R.T. Craig & K. Tracy (Eds.), *Conversational coherence: Form, structure, and strategy* (pp. 157–171). Beverly Hills, CA: Sage.

Rappaport, R.A. (1979). The obvious aspects of ritual. In R.A. Rappaport (Ed.), *Ecology, meaning, and religion* (pp. 173–221). Richmond, CA: North Atlantic Books.

Rawlins, W.K. (1987). Gregory Bateson and the composition of human communication. *Research on Language and Social Interaction, 20,* 53–77.

Ray, G.B. (1987). An ethnography of nonverbal communication in an Appalachian community. *Research on Language and Social Interaction, 21,* 171–188.

Rieff, P. (1964). Introduction. In C.H. Cooley (Ed.), *Human nature and the social order* (pp. ix–xx). New York: Schocken Books.

Rommetveit, R. (1981). On meanings of situations and social control of such meaning in human communication. In D. Magnusson (Ed.), *Toward a psychology of situations: An interactional perspective* (pp. 151–168). Hillsdale, NJ: Erlbaum.

Rosaldo, M.Z. (1980). *Knowledge and passion: Ilongot notions of self and social life.* Cambridge, England: Cambridge University Press.

Rosengren, K.E. (1983). Communication research: One paradigm, or four? *Journal of Communication, 33,* 185–207.

Ruesch, J. (1974). An outline of social communication. *Communication, 1,* 67–81.

Ruesch, J., & Bateson, G. (1951). *Communication: The social matrix of psychiatry.* New York: W. W. Norton.

Ruesch, J., & Kees, W. (1972). *Nonverbal communication: Notes on the visual perception of human relations.* Berkeley, CA: University of California Press. (Original work published 1956)

Sacks, H. (1972). Notes on Police assessment of moral character. In D. Sudnow (Ed.), *Studies in social interaction* (pp. 280–293). New York: Free Press.

Sacks, H. (1984). Notes on methodology. In J. Heritage & J.M. Atkinson (Eds.), *Structures of social action: Studies in conversation analysis* (pp. 21–27). Cambridge, England: Cambridge University Press.

Sacks, H., Schegloff, E.A., & Jefferson, G. (1974). A simplest systematics for the organization of turn-taking for conversation. *Language, 50,* 696–735.

Sanches, M. (1975). Introduction to Part 2: Metacommunicative acts and events. In M. Sanches & B. Blount (Eds.), *Sociocultural dimensions of language use* (pp. 163–176). New York: Academic Press.

Sanders, R.E. (1983). Tools for cohering discourse and their strategic utilization: Markers of structural connections and meaning relations. In R.T. Craig & K. Tracy (Eds.), *Conversational coherence: Form, structure, and strategy* (pp. 67–80). Beverly Hills, CA: Sage.

Sanders, R.E. (1984). Style, meaning and message effects. *Communication Monographs, 51,* 154–167.

Sanders, R.E. (1987). The interconnection of utterances and nonverbal displays. *Research on Language and Social Interaction, 20,* 141–170.

Sapir, E. (1949). Language. In D. Mandelbaum (Ed.), *Selected writ-*

ings of Edward Sapir (pp. 7–32). Berkeley, CA: University of California Press. (Original work published 1933)

Saville-Troike, M. (1982). *The ethnography of communication: An introduction.* Baltimore, MD: University Park Press.

Scheflen, A.E. (1964). The significance of posture in communication systems. *Psychiatry, 27,* 316–331.

Scheflen, A.E. (1965a). Quasi-courtship behavior in psychotherapy. *Psychiatry, 27,* 245–257.

Scheflen, A.E. (1965b). *Stream and structure of communicational behavior: Context analysis of a psychotherapy session.* Philadelphia, PA: Eastern Pennsylvania Psychiatric Institute.

Scheflen, A.E. (1967). On the Structuring of Human Communication. *American Behavioral Scientist, 10,* 8–12.

Scheflen, A.E. (1973). *Communicational structure: Analysis of a psychotherapy transaction.* Bloomington, IN: Indiana University Press.

Scheflen, A.E. (1980). Systems in human communication. In W. von Raffler-Engel (Ed.), *Aspects of nonverbal communication* (pp. 7–28). Lisse, The Netherlands: Swets and Zeitlinger.

Schegloff, E.A. (1968). Sequencing in conversational openings. *American Anthropologist, 70,* 1075–1095.

Schegloff, E.A. (1979). Identification and recognition in telephone conversation openings. In G. Psathas (Ed.), *Everyday language* (pp. 23–78). New York: Irvington.

Schegloff, E.A., & Sacks, H. (1973). Opening up closings. *Semiotica, 8,* 289–325.

Schiffrin, D. (1980). Meta-talk: Organizational and evaluative brackets in discourse. *Sociological Inquiry, 50,* 199–236.

Schutz, A., & Luckmann, T. (1973). *The structures of the life world* [R.M. Zaner & A.T. Engelhardt, Jr., Trans.]. Evanston, IL: Northwestern University.

Sherzer, J. (1983). *Kuna ways of speaking: An ethnographic perspective.* Austin, TX: University of Texas Press.

Shimanoff, S. (1980). *Communication rules: Theory and research.* Beverly Hills, CA: Sage.

Sigman, S. (1980). On communication rules from a social perspective. *Human Communication Research, 7,* 37–51.

Sigman, S. (1983). Some multiple constraints placed on conversational topics. In R.T. Craig & K. Tracy (Eds.), *Conversational coherence: Form, structure, and strategy* (pp. 174–195). Beverly Hills, CA: Sage.

Sigman, S.J. (1987). *A perspective on social communication.* Lexington, MA: Lexington Books.

Sigman, S.J., Sullivan, S.J., & Wendell, M. (1988). Conversation: Data acquisition and analysis. In C.H. Tardy (Ed.), *A handbook for the study of human communication* (pp. 163–192). Norwood, NJ: Ablex Publishing Corp.

Simons, H.W. (1978). In praise of muddleheaded anecdotalism. *Western Journal of Speech Communication, 42,* 21–28.

Slobin, D.I., Miller, S.A., & Porter, L.W. (1968). Forms of address and social relations in a business organization. *Journal of Personality and Social Psychology, 8,* 289–293.

Smith, B.H. (1968). *Poetic closure: A study of how poems end.* Chicago, IL: University of Chicago Press.

Snyder, A. (1971). Rules of language. *Mind, 318,* 161–178.

Soskin, W.F., & John, V.P. (1963). The study of spontaneous talk. In R. Barker (Ed.), *The stream of behavior* (pp. 228–281). New York: Appleton-Century-Crofts.

Speier, M. (1973). *How to observe face-to-face communication: A sociological introduction.* Pacific Palisades, CA: Goodyear Publishing Company.

Spradley, J.P. (1980). *Participant observation.* New York: Holt, Rinehart and Winston.

Steier, F., Stanley, M.D., & Todd, T.C. (1982). Patterns of turn-taking and alliance formation in family communication. *Journal of Communication, 32,* 148–160.

Stewart, J. (1986). Speech and human being: A complement to semiotics. *Quarterly Journal of Speech, 72,* 55–73.

Stewart, J., & Philipsen, G. (1984). Communication as situated accomplishment: The cases of hermeneutics and ethnography. In B. Dervin & M.J. Voigt (Eds.), *Progress in communication sciences* (vol. 5, pp. 177–217). Norwood, NJ: Ablex Publishing Corp.

Sullivan, S.J. (1986, October). *Interactional synchrony in the classroom.* Paper presented to the Temple Conference on Culture and Communication.

Tannen, D. (1980). Toward a theory of conversational style: The machine-gun question. *Working Papers in Sociolinguistics, 73,* 1–16.

Tannen, D. (1982). Ethnic style in male-female conversation. In J.J. Gumperz (Ed.), *Language and social identity* (pp. 217–231). New York: Cambridge University Press.

Tannen, D., & Saville-Troike, M. (Eds.). (1985). *Perspectives on silence.* Norwood, NJ: Ablex Publishing Corp.

Tedlock, D. (1972). On the translation of style in oral narrative. In A. Paredes & R. Bauman (Eds.), *Towards new perspectives in folklore* (pp. 114–133). Austin, TX: University of Texas Press for the American Folklore Society.

Thayer, L. (1982). Introduction to the series. In D.J. Crowley (Ed.), *Understanding communication: The signifying web* (pp. ix–xii). New York: Gordon and Breach.

Thomas, S. (1980). Some problems of the paradigm in communication theory. *Philosophy of the Social Sciences, 10,* 427–444.

Thomas, S. (1982). Introduction. In S. Thomas (Ed.), *Studies in communication* (vol. 2, pp. ix–xi). Norwood, NJ: Ablex Publishing Corp.

Thomas, S. (1987). Non-lexical soundmaking in audience contexts. *Research on Language and Social Interaction, 21,* 189–228.

Thorne, B., & Henley, N. (Eds.). (1975). *Language and sex: Difference and dominance.* Rowley, MA: Newbury House.

Treichler, P.A., & Kramarae, C. (1983). Women's talk in the ivory tower. *Communication Quarterly, 31,* 118–132.

Turner, V. (1967). *The forest of symbols.* Ithaca, NY: Cornell University Press.

Turner, V. (1969). *The ritual process.* Chicago, IL: Aldine.

Uspensky, B. (1973). *A poetics of composition: The structure of the artistic text and typology of a compositional form* (V. Zavarin & S. Wittig, Trans.) Berkeley, CA: University of California Press.

Van Hoeven, S.A. (1985). What we know about the development of communication competence. *Central States Speech Journal, 36,* 33–38.

Warner, W.L. (1962). *American life: Dream and reality.* Chicago, IL: University of Chicago Press. (Original work published 1953)

Watzlawick, P. (1976). *How real is real? Confusion, disinformation, communication.* New York: Random House.

Watzlawick, P., Beavin Bavelas, J., & Jackson, D. (1967). *Pragmatics of human communication.* New York: Norton.

Weinstein, E. (1969). The development of interpersonal competence. In D.A. Goslin (Ed.), *Handbook of socialization theory and research.* Chicago, IL: Rand McNally.

Weitz, S. (1979). *Nonverbal communication: Readings with commentary.* New York: Oxford University Press.

Wentworth, W.M. (1980). *Context and understanding: An inquiry into socialization theory.* New York: Elsevier.

West, C., & Zimmerman, D.H. (1982). Conversation analysis. In K. Scherer & P. Ekman (Eds.), *Handbook of methods in nonverbal behavior research* (pp. 506–541). Cambridge, England: Cambridge University Press.

White, R.A. (1983). Mass communication and culture: Transition to a new paradigm. *Journal of Communication, 33,* 279–301.

Wiemann, J.M., & Knapp, M.L. (1975). Turn-taking in Conversations. *Journal of Communication, 25,* 75–92.

Wilden, T. (1981). Semiotics as praxis: Strategy and tactics. *Recherches Semiotiques/Semiotic Inquiry, 1,* 1–34.

Williams, J.M. (1981). The English language as use-governed behavior. In T. Shopen & J.M. Williams (Eds.), *Style and variables in English* (pp. 27–60). Cambridge, MA: Winthrop Publishers.

Wilmot, W.W. (1980). Metacommunication: A re-evaluation and extension. In D. Nimmo (Ed.), *Communication yearbook 4* (pp. 61–69). New Brunswick, NJ: Transaction Books.

Wilson, J. (1986, November). *The sociolinguistic paradox: Data as a methodological product.* Paper presented to the Speech Communication Association.

Winkin, Y. (Ed.). (1981). *La nouvelle communication.* Paris: Éditions du Seuil.

Wittermans, E.P. (1967). Indonesian terms of address in a situation of rapid social change. *Social Forces, 46,* 48–51.

Zabor, M.R. (1978). *Essaying metacommunication: A survey and contextualization of communication research.* Unpublished doctoral dissertation, Indiana University.

Zerubavel, E. (1981). *Hidden rhythms: Schedules and calendars in social life.* Chicago, IL: University of Chicago Press.

Zimmerman, D.H. (1978). Ethnomethodology. *American Sociologist, 13,* 6–15.

Zimmerman, D.H., & Power, M. (1970). The everyday world as a phenomenon. In J.D. Douglas (Ed.), *Understanding everyday life* (pp. 80–104). Chicago, IL: Aldine.

Author Index

195

Subject Index

199